Gender and the Academic Experience

Berkeley Women Sociologists

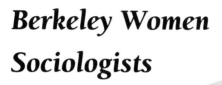

Edited by KATHRYN P. MEADOW ORLANS and RUTH A. WALLACE

Gender and the Academic Experience

University of
Nebraska Press
Lincoln &
London

42390

The paper in this book meets the minimum requirements of
American National Standard for Information Sciences—Perma-
nence of Paper for Printed Library Materials, ANSI Z39.48–1984.

Library of Congress Cataloging-in-Publication Data
Gender and the academic experience : Berkeley women soci-
ologists / edited by Kathryn P. Meadow Orlans and Ruth A.
Wallace.

    p. cm.

  Includes bibliographical references.

  ISBN 0-8032-3558-5 (cloth : alk. paper). —

  ISBN 0-8032-8606-6 (pbk. : alk. paper)

  1. Women sociologists—United States—Biography.
2. University of California, Berkeley. Dept. of Sociology—
Graduate students—Biography.   3. Sex discrimination in
education—California—Berkeley.   I. Meadow Orlans,
Kathryn P.   II. Wallace, Ruth A.
HM22.U62G46   1994
301'.092'273—dc20
[B]   93-27763
                                   CIP

Dedicated to young women entering the halls of academe.
May their lives be satisfying and creative, blending
personal with professional achievement, meaningful work
with friendship and love.

Contents

Acknowledgments

This book had a lengthy gestation followed by a relatively painless delivery. Almost twenty-five years ago, Kathryn Meadow talked with other women graduate students in the Berkeley sociology department about contributing to a volume modeled on *Sociologists at Work*.[1] Each agreed to write a chapter describing the theory, method, and results of her dissertation research, but other projects always took precedence and "Berkeley Women" continued to be postponed. Years later, both of us moved to Washington, D.C., where we reestablished our graduate school friendship. We agreed to collaborate on the Berkeley project, expanding the number of contributors and the scope of requested memoirs.

The Berkeley sociology department, established only in 1948, awarded 126 Ph.D.s between 1952 and 1972, 32 to women. We decided to include the first twenty, later adding three to replace those who declined or could not be located.

Our guidelines asked for an account of the contributor's experience as a female student in a male-dominated department and profession, the choice of sociology and Berkeley, the graduate student years (major professors, friendship groups, stipends, dissertation), how conflicts between family responsibilities and school were managed, the career influence provided by Berkeley, and major work completed after the Ph.D. Almost everyone responded with enthusiasm. A typical reply was: "What an honor to be invited to participate in what could be a very interesting volume, but even more exciting to be *encouraged* to examine my life in thirty pages. . . . I'd love to!" Eighteen months later, most chapters had been edited at least twice; the eight-pound manuscript was delivered for review.

Completion of the project reflects the efforts of many people. Our first debt of gratitude is to our contributors. Their enthusiasm, promptness in meeting deadlines, and willingness to make revisions have made our work a pleasure, an exercise in nostalgia, friendship, and sociology.

Harold Orlans's belief in the significance and interest of the book was very important. His knowledge of the issues and the literature of higher education and his superb editorial skills improved the final product considerably. We also thank Jim Coriden and Neil Smelser for their encouragement throughout the development of this book.

Kathryn P. Meadow Orlans
Ruth A. Wallace

Note

1. Phillip E. Hammond, ed., *Sociologists at Work: Essays on the Craft of Social Research* (New York: Basic Books, 1964; Anchor, 1967).

Gender and the Academic Experience

Chapter 1

Introduction

KATHRYN P. MEADOW ORLANS
and RUTH A. WALLACE

The years launching the latest women's movement are captured in these memoirs by sixteen women sociologists who received doctorates from the University of California, Berkeley, between 1952 and 1972. These two decades encompass that department's golden years: founded in 1948, it was ranked first in the nation by 1964.[1]

The authors came to Berkeley from the slums of New York City, an affluent suburb of Toronto, small towns in Missouri and Nebraska; from the London School of Economics, the University of Denver, San Jose State, and Radcliffe. One was a nun in full habit, another born in Jakarta to Chinese parents. They tell how they came to sociology and Berkeley, their trials and successes as graduate students, the course of subsequent careers. They recount difficulties that were then regarded as normal; a view of life before affirmative action and sexual harassment became part of the general vocabulary. Despite the changes in campus climate and attitude, many of their concerns are similar to those of young women today.

These women did not conform to the idealized version of femininity prevalent in the late forties and fifties.[2] By preparing for an academic career, they became marginal in their urban and suburban neighborhoods. Compared with male graduate students, they were peripheral because of home responsibilities. Burdened by traditional expectations for wives and mothers, they managed the care of young children, contributed to the family budget, prepared meals before writing term papers. Their stories are very diverse, but together they provide a view of those times. This book is unique in that discipline and department are controlled; the women's experiences vary within that academic environment.

Our authors followed women who blazed more difficult and lonely trails to academia early in the century[3] and those who followed in the 1920s.[4] These

Berkeley pioneers were admitted more readily to graduate school; the opposition to their ambitions was more subtle. Women received little or no financial aid and were warned not to expect academic positions.[5] A smaller proportion of women than men completed their degrees. From 1952 to 1972, one-third of Berkeley sociology graduate students were women. Only one-quarter received doctorates, compared with one-third of the men.[6]

Reshaping traditional roles, our authors were part of the trickle that soon became a torrent of women pouring into the academy and the professions.[7] They describe what it was like during two distinctive decades before the latest women's movement changed the ways women thought about themselves, their families, their careers.

These memoirs reflect family histories: grandparents who traveled in steerage from Europe or by covered wagon to Indian territory. Their parents, as well as some of the authors themselves, were children of the Great Depression.[8] They grew up in the forties and fifties, during the hot and the cold wars. In the sixties, they saw the civil rights struggle and student protests against the Vietnam War. Their stories document those times.

Personal documents have an honored place in sociology. W. I. Thomas used immigrants' diaries and letters for *The Polish Peasant,* an important work of the early Chicago School. Nevertheless, "autobiography is usually regarded as risky. . . . We are taught to flee from the first person singular."[9] Autobiographical sociology has been characterized as "retrospective participant observation requiring the recollection, reconstruction and interpretation of past events and processes."[10] Theorist Robert Merton saw autobiography as "a personal exercise . . . in the sociology of scientific knowledge . . . [illustrating] the interplay between the active agent and the social structure."[11]

Barbara Laslett suggests that biography should be viewed as a case study, making it possible to "address the subjective meaning of life events."[12] Two long-admired women sociologists, Jessie Bernard and Alice Rossi, have exemplified that approach.[13] The sixteen views of one department presented here reflect the richness of objectively similar but subjectively disparate perceptions of reality.

Our framework draws on the theoretical traditions of Mills and Mead. C. Wright Mills wrote that "the sociological imagination enables us to grasp history and biography and the relations between the two within society."[14] George Herbert Mead explains the connection between the individual and society as the self develops from the reflected appraisals of significant others.[15] One of Mead's heirs, Erving Goffman, reminds us that the successful presentation of self[16] requires that the "back-stage region" remain hidden. Autobiographical writing demands a self-examination that may uncover forgotten masks and unveil some backstage props.

How much of their true selves do our authors disclose? Self-revelation involves the revelation of others, since no life is self-contained. Each touches family members, friends, professors, fellow students, professional colleagues. How much of a relationship is it necessary or fair to expose? A memoir should reveal enough but not too much, be candid but tactful. One contributor likened this writing to "tiptoeing through a minefield."

This "tiptoeing" may explain why so many of the memoirs are gentle, positive, nostalgic. Perhaps time has dulled the edges of pain. In the foreword to his autobiography, John Updike observed, "Merciful forgetfulness has no doubt hidden many other echoes from me, as well as eroded the raw material of autobiography into shapes scarcely less imaginary, though less final, than those of fiction";[17] and he adds, "a life-view by the living can only be provisional. Perspectives are altered by the fact of being drawn."[18] Jill Ker Conway suggests that, because we crave coherence, a well-written memoir seems to flow in a straight line that frees us "momentarily, from ambiguity."[19]

Women's lives are understood through their childhood experiences, adolescent dreams, and adult dilemmas; "family relationships, intimacy, emotion, sexuality are central."[20] This must also be true for men. But past and present, personal and professional are more closely entwined for women, more compartmentalized for men. Earlier synthesizers of academic or professional women's autobiographies have noted that the encouragement of a particular person or set of people is crucial for women of achievement: "father, mother, teacher, friend, or professional colleague; the continuous influence of husbands receives significant emphasis. . . . Only self-reliant women can respond effectively to such kinds of encouragement and support."[21] Arlie Hochschild observed that, like members of racial or ethnic minorities, successful women often deny the difficulties they have surmounted. They become part of another marginal group, situated between, but outside, both male and female cultures.[22]

Lives are influenced by their context: global, national, and local events. In 1952, when the first woman received a Berkeley sociology Ph.D., the Korean War was winding down; the first hydrogen bomb was tested in the Pacific. In 1954, the Supreme Court banned segregated public schools; Senator Joseph McCarthy's hearings into "Communist influence" in the Army were televised. (Margaret Hodgen, from the faculty of the old Berkeley Department of Social Institutions, was dismissed for refusing to sign a loyalty oath [see chapter 2, this volume].) In 1955, Rosa Parks's refusal to move to the back of a Birmingham bus ignited the civil rights movement; by September 1961, more than 70,000 students had participated in sit-ins throughout the South. (One of our contributors spent the summer of 1963 with a Quaker student project in a Memphis, Tennessee, ghetto [see chapter 16].)

Several authors, then Berkeley students, vividly recall the day in 1963 when President John F. Kennedy was assassinated. From 1965 to 1972, national attention focused on civil rights and the Vietnam War; the 1966 Watts riot; the 1968 assassinations of Martin Luther King, Jr., and Robert Kennedy; protests at school busing. More than 500,000 American troops were stationed in Vietnam; when troops entered Cambodia in 1970, four Kent State students were killed in a protest. Throughout this period, Berkeley students demonstrated against the war in Southeast Asia and for civil rights at home. (One author went to jail after a sit-in protesting U.S. recruitment for the Cambodian action.)

In the late sixties, groups like the National Organization for Women and the Women's Equity Action League campaigned for equal access to jobs, equal pay, flexibility of working hours, and adequate day care for children of working mothers. (Two contributors, among the founders of Sociologists for Women in Society, describe their early involvement in women's groups.)

The Berkeley campus has an international scientific and scholarly reputation. Like other state universities, it offers high-quality, low-tuition education to many who cannot afford expensive private institutions. At the time most of our contributors matriculated, tuition for California residents was about three hundred dollars a year.

In September 1964, the Free Speech Movement (FSM) erupted to protest an administrative ruling barring campus political activity aimed at the larger community. Some 750 students occupying administrative offices were arrested; graduate teaching assistants went on strike; students boycotted classes; faculty committees and the Academic Senate drafted bitter proposals and counterproposals. On January 2, 1965, Chancellor Edward Strong was replaced by Acting Chancellor Martin Meyerson, who issued more permissive regulations, and the free speech controversy subsided.[23]

The FSM had a strong impact on the ten contributors who were students at the time. Many of them participated in the demonstrations, although two in the United States on student visas were fearful of deportation. The FSM conflicts led six tenured department members to resign; others departed after Ronald Reagan's victory in the 1966 gubernatorial election.[24]

The Department of Sociology was an outgrowth of one called Sociology and Social Institutions, which emerged from the Department of Social Institutions, established in 1919. It was "both the creation and the empire of Frederick Teggart, a renowned scholar who contributed . . . to the study of evolution and historical change."[25] He scoffed at sociology as a discipline, but in 1946, five years after he retired, the Department of Sociology and Social Institutions was formed, headed by philosopher Edward Strong.

When Herbert Blumer came from Chicago to replace Strong in 1952, the "golden age of growth" began. In 1951, the department had nine faculty members; by 1964, thirty-six. Blumer, a towering intellectual force and physical presence who insisted on both "quality and catholicity,"[26] is mentioned frequently in these memoirs. A proponent of the micro theory emanating from George Herbert Mead at the University of Chicago, Blumer named the theory "symbolic interactionism." Successive cohorts of Berkeley students heard his ardent lectures on the importance of "taking the role of the other" to explain the individual's behavior in groups.

Tamotsu Shibutani and Erving Goffman, both trained at Chicago, also represented that orientation. Goffman, an unusual and colorful figure, alternately charmed and infuriated graduate students who clamored to join his small, select coterie.[27] Other social psychologists were Bernard Cohen (small groups) and John Clausen (socialization and mental health). Clausen's National Institute of Mental Health training grant in personality and social structure provided support for about ten trainees each year; many were women.

European classical theory was represented by Weberian scholar Reinhard Bendix, Leo Lowenthal from the Frankfurt School of Critical Theory, and Wolfram Eberhard in comparative sociology. Neil Smelser was recruited from Harvard to translate and interpret functionalism, a macro social system theory rooted in the work of Emile Durkheim, expanded and made famous by Smelser's mentor and colleague, Talcott Parsons. Columbia-trained professors included Survey Research Center director Charles Glock (religion), Nathan Glazer (race relations and urban problems), Seymour Martin Lipset (political sociology), Hanan Selvin (survey methods), Philip Selznick (organizations), and Martin

Kathryn P.
Meadow
Orlans and
Ruth A.
Wallace

———

5

Trow (education). Students were trained in demography by Kingsley Davis, William Petersen, and Nathan Keyfitz (plus Judith Blake, in the School of Public Health).

Middle-range theorists of institutions and organizations included William Kornhauser and Harold Wilensky from the University of Chicago. David Matza, Princeton, was a specialist in deviant behavior, particularly juvenile delinquency. Two Berkeley-trained men specializing in race relations were hired in the sixties: Bob Blauner and Troy Duster.

From 1948 through 1970, the department hired no woman in a tenure-track position. Dorothy Smith had a two-year appointment as lecturer in the sixties; Gertrude Jaeger Selznick and Arlie Hochschild shared one appointment in the early seventies. The absence of women faculty members was noted by most women students as a fact of life; their anger came later.

Our sixteen contributors are surprisingly diverse. One retired almost before her career began, devoting herself to her husband and four children. Six attended graduate school while caring for young children, two as divorced single mothers. One managed a commuting marriage in her later career. (Readers will note the emphasis on family situations here and by contributors themselves. Autobiographies of male sociologists differ radically in this respect.) [28]

Three women work in Canada, one in Indonesia, three on the East Coast, two in the Midwest, six in California. One Californian resigned her professorship in midcareer to write and consult on international women's issues. Some are dedicated to qualitative research methods; some use quantitative data extensively; others are methodologically eclectic.

Several contributors helped to form early women's movement organizations; many are ardent and active feminists; most have specialized in research on women's issues. Other specialties include demography, religion, education, deviance. Two are credited with major theoretical contributions, one in the sociology of emotions, one in feminist theory. Two have combined academic careers with advocacy. Four have been presidents of national professional organizations. Most have published widely, some for a broad public as well as a professional audience.

Despite this diversity, common themes emerge. Most had no clear plan, no goal that initially included a doctorate, research or teaching, an academic career. Many express surprise at finding themselves in responsible positions. The member of a religious order, obeying her Mother Superior's instruction to study for a Ph.D., was only slightly less "in charge" of her destiny than those who enrolled at a husband's urging.

One who thought it might be "fun" had no better plan than another who had wearied of volunteer work.

Likewise, sociology was often an accidental choice. One shifted from a physical education major after she broke her neck in a diving accident. One aimed for law school until a sociology professor suggested that her term paper could be published. Another describes the prefeminist click of recognition that sent her back to school for a Ph.D. when a job counselor referred her to secretarial positions after she had earned a master's. Several saw sociology as a path to social change.

Kathryn P. Meadow Orlans and Ruth A. Wallace

7

Many expected to fail, were reluctant to speak in class, to articulate ideas, to question or challenge professors or compete with male students, even though they were older and more mature. Only three matriculated immediately after college at age twenty-one or twenty-two—another basic distinction between these women and male peers. The orientation week warning ("Look to your left, look to your right. By this time next year, one of you three students will no longer be here") made a chilling and lasting impression on several. One kept her bags packed until the first-semester grades were filed. The "impostor syndrome" dogged some during their postdoctoral years. Few women students protested sexist speech or behavior. One author who had a professorial lover notes that the erotic aspect of student-professor relationships is viewed differently by a current feminist than it was by a young woman in the 1960s.

Many who returned to graduate school after some years as full-time mothers had found that homemaking and child care alone were not sufficient challenges. In the fifties, a return to graduate school for a Ph.D. made these women marginal both on campus and in their suburban neighborhoods. Some professors regarded them as "bored housewives."

On the whole, professors receive high marks from their former students, although some contributors are plainly being tactful or ambiguous and a few are quite candid about negative experiences. One professor who had a sexist reputation was most helpful to his women students. Another, described as unfailingly supportive in one chapter, is termed dismissive and hurtful in a subsequent piece. Most contributors admired their professors, appreciated their intellectual and practical help, and continue to express gratitude today.

In the mid-fifties, the median age for first-time motherhood was twenty-one. One author matched that national trend, and eight others were close; all nine postponed graduate study until their children were at least of preschool age, facing the problems of managing households and child care while in graduate school. Five women credit supportive husbands for helping to balance their juggling acts. Two report difficult races against time and wonder if their young children suffered in the process. One benefited from university day care provided during earlier graduate study in North Carolina, but not at Berkeley. One woman made endless lists of household chores and wrote her dissertation from 9:00 P.M. to midnight over many lonely months; another slept in her car between classes and organized a day care center to earn money for university expenses. Only two women had their first children after receiving their Ph.D.s. One took the new baby to her university office in a little box; the other had a zigzag career that finally settled into place when she was forty and her younger child in school. Most of these tales are told with a humor that masks the hard work, late hours, and determination required.

After graduate school, some contributors embarked directly and easily on their professional careers; others sacrificed good opportunities in order to maintain a stable family life or personal relationship. Some followed a husband whose work took him elsewhere; occasionally a husband moved to help his wife's career. The academic market influences both a student's need for help in finding employment and a professor's ability to provide it. The painful search for jobs in the mid-sixties described by two women contrasts with the early seventies, when openings were more abundant. Canadian universities are portrayed as begging promising students to accept positions in the early seventies. If only that were true today! Not until the mid-seventies did affirmative action begin to help women. Still, many authors remain on the periphery of their profession, with careers in research institutes rather than academic departments, or in departments other than sociology.

These accounts provide the human stories behind statistical reports of academic women: their paths to graduate school and degree completion, their job searches and career advances. Some of the emotional costs and benefits apply to all graduate students, some primarily to women. A few of these pioneers remember those Berkeley years with anger, their early careers with bitterness. Most, however, seem to agree with the author who would not trade her own life story for any other.

Notes

1. Berkeley's departmental rank for reputation in sociology was sixth in 1957; first in 1964 and 1969; fourth in 1980. William Rau and Wilbert M. Leonard II, "Evaluating Ph.D. Sociology Programs: Theoretical, Methodological and Policy Implications," *American Sociologist* 21 (1990): 251.

2. See Wini Breines, *Young, White, and Miserable: Growing Up Female in the Fifties* (Boston: Beacon Press, 1992).

3. See Ellen Fitzpatrick, *Endless Crusade: Women Social Scientists and Progressive Reform* (New York: Oxford University Press, 1990); and Lynn D. Gordon, *Gender and Higher Education in the Progressive Era* (New Haven, Conn.: Yale Univ. Press, 1990).

4. Elaine Showalter, ed., *These Modern Women: Autobiographical Essays from the Twenties* (Old Westbury, N.Y.: Feminist Press, 1978).

5. Saul D. Feldman, *Escape from the Doll's House: Women in Graduate and Professional School Education* (New York: McGraw-Hill, 1974), p. 11.

6. Neil Smelser provided access to these data, and Elsa Tranter compiled summary statistics from department records of 1,003 students (19 of unknown gender were excluded).

7. In the United States, women comprised 16 percent of full-time social science faculty in 1974, 21 percent in 1985. However, in 1981, in sociology departments, 14 percent of full professors, 24 percent of associate, and 40 percent of assistant professors were women. See Mariam K. Chamberlain, ed., *Women in Academe: Progress and Prospects* (New York: Russell Sage Foundation, 1988), pp. 228–29.

8. Glen H. Elder, Jr., *Children of the Great Depression* (Chicago: University of Chicago Press, 1974).

9. Bennett M. Berger, "Looking for the Interstices," in *Authors of Their Own Lives, Intellectual Autobiographies by Twenty American Sociologists,* ed. Bennett M. Berger (Berkeley: University of California Press, 1990), p. 152.

10. Norman L. Friedman, "Autobiographical Sociology," *American Sociologist* 21 (1990): 61.

11. Robert K. Merton, "Some Thoughts on the Concept of Sociological Autobiography," in *Sociological Lives,* ed. Matilda White Riley (Newbury Park, Calif.: Sage, 1988), p. 19.

12. Barbara Laslett, "Unfeeling Knowledge: Emotion and Objectivity in the History of Sociology," *Sociological Forum* 5 (1990): 416.

13. Jessie Bernard, "A Woman's Twentieth Century," in Berger, *Authors of Their Own Lives;* Alice S. Rossi, "Seasons of a Woman's Life," *ibid.*

14. C. Wright Mills, *The Sociological Imagination* (New York: Grove Press, 1959; Evergreen, 1961), p. 6.

15. George Herbert Mead, *Mind, Self and Society* (Chicago: University of Chicago Press, 1934).

16. Erving Goffman, *The Presentation of Self in Everyday Life* (Garden City, N.Y.: Doubleday/Anchor, 1959).

17. John Updike, *Self-Consciousness: Memoirs* (New York: Fawcett Crest, 1989; Ballantine Books, 1990), p. xv.

18. *Ibid.,* p. xvi.

19. Jill Ker Conway, ed., *Written by Herself* (New York: Vintage Books, 1992), pp. vi–vii.

20. Barbara Laslett, "Biography as Historical Sociology: The Case of William Fielding Ogburn," *Theory and Society* 20 (1991): 515.

21. Barbara Miller Solomon, "Historical Determinants and Successful Professional Women," in *Women and Success: The Anatomy of Achievement*, ed. Ruth B. Kundsin (New York: William Morrow, 1974), p. 192.

22. Arlie Hochschild, "Making It: Marginality and Obstacles to Minority Consciousness," in Kundsin, *Women and Success*.

23. For a complete chronology of FSM events, see "Chronology of Events: Three Months of Crisis," in *The Berkeley Student Revolt, Facts and Interpretations*, ed. Seymour Martin Lipset and Sheldon S. Wolin (Garden City, N.Y.: Doubleday/Anchor, 1965), pp. 99–199.

24. Neil J. Smelser and Robin Content, *The Changing Academic Market, General Trends and a Berkeley Case Study* (Berkeley: University of California Press, 1980), p. 67.

25. *Ibid.*, p. 63.

26. *Ibid.*, pp. 64–65. One student with a 1960 Berkeley Ph.D. remembers Blumer as "bent on making [the department] the best in the world, as he repeated at the beginning of each academic year." Guenther Roth, "Partisanship and Scholarship," in Berger, *Authors of Their Own Lives*, p. 403.

27. Department lore includes the story of one student who sent Goffman a letter stating that "your services as advisor are no longer required" when he failed to acknowledge her completed dissertation after many months.

28. See Berger, *Authors of Their Own Lives*; Paul C. Higgins and John M. Johnson, eds., *Personal Sociology* (New York: Praeger, 1988); Riley, *Sociological Lives*.

Chapter 2

Varieties of Sociological Experience

DORRIS W. GOODRICH

My academic career in sociology was so short-lived as to be virtually non-existent. I retired after two years on the UC Berkeley faculty and have not resumed professional life. But does one need to be professionally active if one is to be a sociologist? Is there not a sociological attitude, a way of looking at the world, that is different from that of a farmer, or a physician, or a politician? I believe there is. For half a century I have had an abiding interest in the influence of social institutions on individual behavior, in the ways the individual is shaped, nourished, frustrated, perhaps even defined, by social configurations.

My Berkeley mentor, Robert A. Nisbet, once wrote: "Fundamental changes in culture cannot help but be reflected in even the most primary of social relationships and psychological identifications."[1] An awareness of this interplay between the individual and the cultural does not require a professional environment (although that certainly helps) and may even be enhanced by participation in that most primary social relationship—the family.

To what degree this perspective was created by my Berkeley training is hard to say. It is perhaps no accident that in 1947, the year when I first enrolled at Berkeley as a graduate student, the department was called Sociology and

Social Institutions. This was the first year the word "sociology" appeared as a department title in the campus catalog—an unusual situation for a major state university. I had been the half-time secretary in the sociology department while an undergraduate at what is now the State University of Washington at Pullman. When my duties involved canvassing sociologists elsewhere, I was instructed to exclude Berkeley, "where no sociology is taught." (This was not quite true, of course. Dorothy Thomas, the well-known demographer, taught in the School of Agriculture, and Judson T. Landis taught courses in marriage and family—in the home economics department.) Thus, when I applied to graduate school in 1942, after receiving the A.B. degree, I did not even consider Berkeley. Entirely dependent on my own earnings, I also ruled out private institutions. I needed a tuition waiver as well as a stipend to cover living expenses, and these were more likely to be available at a state university. Even so, I had few illusions about my ability, as a young woman from a small western state college, to compete successfully with male applicants from better-known institutions.

Following Pearl Harbor, however, rapid military mobilization thinned the ranks of young men in graduate school. While still an undergraduate, I had replaced a teaching assistant called up for military service. Before my graduation, each university to which I applied had offered me a job. The one I accepted was a teaching assistantship at the University of Minnesota.

This was a period of great opportunity for women. Male graduate students were scarce, and many faculty members were on leave for war-related reasons. As a result, women graduates were put in charge of undergraduate courses, particularly during the summer sessions. My secretarial experience led to an additional job as editorial assistant for the *American Sociological Review*. At the end of my third year at Minnesota, I was promoted to a lectureship.

It was always clear, however, that it was the wartime situation that had created these opportunities. Few women believed that a level playing field existed so far as male competitors were concerned. Furthermore, I think few of us objected. There were enough women professors around to assure us that academic life was not impossible. The real question was the feasibility of combining a career with marriage and children. In my personal experience, it was not unusual for women to work outside the home. My mother had been a teacher and, in later life, a businesswoman like her spinster sister. A great-aunt on each side of the family had been an educator; one was married, the other was not. For me to embark on a professional career was hardly remarkable. It was a family tradition. I had no fixed goal, no great calling or burning ambition. I simply loved the idea of living an intellectual life. How that was to be combined with a family only time would reveal.

The year 1942, my first at Minnesota, was a watershed in several ways. Not only was it the first year of full U.S. participation in World War II, it also marked the end of the Great Depression. When I had started college in 1938, unemployment rates ran as high as 25 percent. I had been fortunate to find a job that defrayed my college expenses. (I once applied for a small scholarship and was ruled ineligible on the grounds of being employed!)

Under such conditions it is not surprising that questions were raised about employing married women. With too little work to go around, was it fair that a family have more than one wage earner? If not, then why did women go to college? Intellectual curiosity was a strong incentive for me, but other women classmates were more interested in prospective husbands or a broader experience of the world before settling down to domestic life. We talked about acquiring a skill and becoming economically independent. We assumed that we would eventually marry, but our choice was to be unrelated to financial necessity. The liberated woman of my day scorned anyone who married a "meal ticket."

We knew it was possible to have both marriage and a career, but we questioned the cost—both personally and for society. Most of the students I knew had been conditioned by the heritage of the American West: we were WASPs, often of pioneer stock, with a rural or small-town background. We saw a distinction—not necessarily invidious—between men's work and women's. We believed our mothers to be playing roles essential to the social fabric. We were daughters, after all, of the suffragette generation. Our fathers might scorn "women's work," but we were certain that every man needed a wife if he was to take his proper position in the world. Running a household was a serious responsibility. Husbands might sometimes help with dishes and diapers and laundry, but wives were in charge. It was our daughters who saw this differently.

Coming from this background, I regarded a career as enhancing life rather than being central to it. Introduced to the small band of "intellectuals" at Pullman, I had discovered a community that was both congenial and rewarding. My years as a graduate student at Minnesota confirmed this feeling.

When early in 1945 I married a man preparing for overseas military duty, it was assumed that I would continue graduate studies until the end of the war. When peace came, my husband and I would consider future plans. Naturally, his career would come first; it seemed only fair that he have the opportunity to make up the time he had spent in military service. On the day my husband left for his overseas post, these notions were severely tested: I learned that I was pregnant. All too soon, it became apparent that pregnancy put all my brain cells into hibernation. How do women in academia manage to work until just before the baby's birth?

On returning from the war, my husband decided to do graduate work in classical Chinese at Berkeley. I decided to be content as wife and mother. That decision was good for about a year. After that, the little gray cells started itching for exercise, and I began looking at the university catalog for appealing courses in which I might enroll. I had lost interest in sociology as I had known it. The Minnesota program had been heavily weighted in favor of quantitative methods, and although I found problems of methodology intriguing, I was not convinced that statistical procedures were appropriate to the sociological areas I wanted to explore. A new approach seemed to be offered at Berkeley in the proposal for a new department with the strange double title Sociology and Social Institutions. The birth of this department had been anything but easy. Many of the faculty questioned the legitimacy of sociology as an academic discipline, at least as practiced in the United States. Frederick J. Teggart, who had founded the Department of Social Institutions at Berkeley in 1919, was said to have likened sociology to the Dance of the Seven Veils: one after another the veils are removed until at last one discovers . . . *nothing.*

Teggart was an academic iconoclast, a historian who was also critical of traditional approaches to the discipline of history. I knew little about his work, but my interest was piqued when I learned that he dealt extensively with methods of studying the facts of human experience.[2] That these facts were primarily historical made the approach even more interesting.

The new department was to be staffed largely by people who had studied with Teggart—Margaret T. Hodgen, Robert A. Nisbet, and Kenneth E. Bock. The one newcomer was a recent Ph.D. from the University of Chicago, Reinhard Bendix, whose intellectual interests and German background added breadth and variety to the curriculum.

It was all virgin territory as far as I was concerned. My earlier studies had been in departments closely allied with graduate training in social work, public administration, urban affairs, criminology, and the like. Much of the theoretical work, consequently, was concerned with social problems and public policy. When I approached Nisbet, the graduate adviser, he made it clear that my previous training had little relation to the Berkeley program. He also firmly opposed my idea of taking "a course or two"; this was not a program for bored housewives. The more he described departmental offerings, the more interested I became. Taking the plunge, I enrolled as a full-time graduate student.

For most of the first year I was lost. Kenneth Bock offered a year-long course in the history of sociological thought so densely packed with information and insights that it was like preparing for a second M.A. In it, he gave an explication of Teggart's theories of historiography that opened new and exciting vistas for sociological research.

I can't remember the name of the course I took with Margaret Hodgen. Totally absorbed in her research, she was often late for class and sometimes failed to appear altogether. Her reading assignments were fascinating: the letters of Charles Darwin, a thick book on libraries of the world, articles in *Isis* on mnemonic systems, theories of geological formation, and so on. Her lectures were stimulating, but I could not see how they related to the readings. Then, in the next to last class of the term (she never attended the last meeting of any of her classes in case she would be, in her words, "clapped at"), she reviewed the semester's work. Suddenly, all was clear, like a picture that emerges with the last piece of a jigsaw puzzle. She had spent the term providing illustrations of the ways in which materials and ideas could be organized, leaving interpretation and synthesis to the final class.

I audited Nisbet's lower-division course on the history of Western social institutions and enrolled in his seminar on the same subject. His lectures were brilliant; his coverage of a broad spectrum of historical material was beautifully organized and full of insightful ideas. For the seminar, we were expected to do individual research on the sociological aspects of a topic spanning several centuries. I chose the Freemasons because of their influence on European political history but could find nothing about them in the library. Sheer necessity led me to the masonic guilds, and I found myself traipsing all over the library in search of books on architecture, church doctrine, monastic life, and an endless number of byways. It was a salutary introduction to the methods of research that I would subsequently use.

During my second year, Kenneth Bock asked me to be his teaching assistant for his lower-division course. Reluctant to accept financial help when others were in greater need, I was also concerned about my reliability. When I told him that in an emergency my first loyalties would be to my family, Bock said he was willing to take a chance. (I don't recall whether or not I mentioned a further concern: Did I have the capacity to do the job?) Bock's lower-division course, like Nisbet's, was designed primarily for sophomores. Compared with my previous TA experience, the course was extraordinarily demanding.

It was an exciting time to be at Berkeley. The GI bill had brought many veterans to the campus—young men (and some women) whose military experiences added depth and variety to the student body. What had been, for me, a predominantly feminine graduate school environment now became predominantly masculine. Returning veterans exhibited a maturity of interest and purpose that put us on our toes. Berkeley enrollments swelled to 23,000 students. Classroom space was at a premium; administrative staffing was minimal; and most of the faculty taught eight or nine hours a week, doing committee work and graduate advising on the side.

Things were running smoothly at home. My husband was actively pursuing his own studies and we had reliable household help. I had no feeling that our daughter was neglected, for I was able to do much of my work at home. We did not want to be a one-child family, however, so I went into another year of hibernation and in April of 1950 gave birth to a son. A few weeks later, just as I had finished nursing the baby, the telephone rang. It was Kenneth Bock, asking if I would be his teaching assistant in the fall. I held the telephone in one hand, burped the squirming infant with the other, and wondered about changing gears again. The temptation was too great. I re-enrolled as a graduate student, rushing home at intervals to feed the baby.

The sociology department had grown. Wolfram Eberhard, an ethnologist specializing in the peoples of China, had joined the faculty. He had left Germany in the early 1930s to teach in China and ten years after that went to work in Turkey. He once told me that before coming to Berkeley, he had never lived in an English-speaking country. His spoken English was the "reading-knowledge" variety, but his students were thoroughly disarmed by his candor in requesting help on the meaning of an English word or on a point of grammar.

I missed the collegial atmosphere that I had enjoyed earlier. With two children at home—one an infant—my time on campus was rationed. The university offered little encouragement to women seeking professional companionship. Once, when invited by a visiting scholar to have lunch with him at the Men's Faculty Club, I waltzed innocently into the dining room, only to be informed that it was reserved for men. Eventually I found my host in an alcove set aside for co-ed dining. The status of women was not of much personal significance, however, for I had little professional ambition. I was enjoying what I was doing and wanted only the opportunity to continue doing it.

There were counterpressures, of course. McCarthyism dominated the political scene, and academic freedom was a burning issue. A number of other universities had become targets of Communist witch-hunts. Apparently in an effort to head off similar attacks at Berkeley, the board of regents insisted that all faculty members sign oaths swearing that they were not members of the Communist party. Since, as state employees, they had already sworn to support the state and national constitutions, the additional requirement seemed to insult their integrity as well as their loyalty. Even the board of regents was divided over the issue. Eventually, twenty-four members of the Berkeley faculty were dismissed for failure to sign the oath. Margaret Hodgen was one of them.

The eventual reinstatement of nonsigners led David P. Gardner, the recently retired president of the university, to term the episode "a futile interlude."[3] This characterization, however, misses the point. As a sociologist, I saw the issue as one concerning the individual's relation to a social institution. A controversy that awakens individual members of society to the dangers of unbridled institutional authority hardly deserves the term "futile."

During the period in which universities were being labeled "hotbeds of Communism," questions were raised about the use of taxpayers' money for higher education. What criteria should govern admissions policy and allocation of funds? In England, as we learned when living there later, the question was bluntly posed: Who is entitled to higher education—those who deserve it or those who need it? Is it the government's role to recognize superior ability and reward individual endeavor or to encourage broadly based acquisition of skills and knowledge according to society's needs? This is by no means a dead issue today.

During this time I was preparing myself for the qualifying examinations for Ph.D. candidacy. The main distraction was a piece of research that had been stimulated by one of Nisbet's seminars. Working with de Toqueville's *Democracy in America* and Myrdal's *American Dilemma,* I began to understand the significance of historical background in studies of racial and ethnic minorities. Especially interesting to me were questions concerning the means by which such minorities lost or retained their original identities. What affects their integration into the dominant culture? What informs public policy on such matters? These were lively issues in the forties as the European colonial empires dissolved. They are with us today: witness the consequences of the dissolution of the USSR.

My own focus was on the Anglo-Indian community in India, a social group characterized by a heritage of mixed European and Indian blood. As individuals caught between two cultures, unable to identify with either, they had maintained a separate identity for several centuries. Influenced by Bock's discussions of Teggart's method for using historical data, I was eager to test its applicability to a subject of this kind. From Teggart I borrowed three principles. The first was that the research have a well-documented history, limited by time and geographic area, that would offer an opportunity for correlating dated events. The Anglo-Indians served these requirements admirably. Their history could be traced to the beginning of the sixteenth century; their existence was tied to a colonial system with extensive records; and events in India could be correlated with what was happening in the home countries of the colonial powers.

The second principle was to approach the topic with a mind as free as possible from preconceived ideas. A number of studies had investigated people of mixed racial heritage, and some had dealt with the Anglo-Indians. Most of the conclusions, however, were reductive, based on the rationale that "such-and-such a situation must have come about because. . . ." I wanted to follow Bock's dictum and start with "what really happened" rather than with "what must have happened."

This method called for a third principle: being exhaustive in the collection of data. Only then could serendipity operate to assure me that my findings were not limited to "what I was looking for." The university library proved to have an exceptionally good collection of materials on colonial India. Starting with the first applicable call number, I took one book after another from the shelf, leafing through each for any information about marriages between Indian women and European men, about soldiers fraternizing with native women, about concubines and prostitution, and so on. One thing led to another, and by the end of the year, I had investigated travel literature, orphanages, Christian missions, the East India Company, military organization, railroads, theories of miscegenation, French and Portuguese rivalry, the English Reformation, Parliamentary papers, and countless other areas.

As I took notes, I tried not to form an overall picture. My idea of "purely empirical" historical research was collecting data without a thought as to pattern or development. The activity was a little like a treasure hunt, in which one clue points to another. I had no assurance that this was not a wasted year of research. All I had at the end of the 1952 spring term was a file case of notes four inches thick. These I took to Nisbet as evidence that I had done something to earn the research units for which I was registered. He riffled through the box, pulled out a few pages, looked at them, and asked, "Now what are you going to do?" I could only answer: "I don't know."

With the end of the term, I was looking forward to a vacation with my family. I took the bus home, as usual, and looked forward to the half-mile walk to our house on the quiet, tree-lined streets so typical of Berkeley. On this particular day, I must have been half-consciously mulling over the interview with my adviser. Suddenly I found myself standing stock-still under the branches of a large walnut tree that spread over the sidewalk. In my mind's eye appeared a tapestry of dated events that demonstrated how the Anglo-Indian community had emerged from collections of individuals previously defined in other ways.

Rushing home, I sat down at the typewriter and a five-page outline virtually wrote itself. Almost without being aware of it, I had mapped out a dissertation.[4] I had not yet taken the qualifying examinations, however. Most of my study during summer vacation and the following year was devoted to preparation for that ordeal. In the meantime, I had been offered a job in the department as lecturer—on the understanding that I would have received my degree by the end of the first year of employment. The year-to-year nature of the appointments suited my interests very well. My husband would be job hunting soon, and we might have to leave Berkeley.

Pleased with the gesture of confidence, I failed to consider the amount of work I would be taking on. The courses I was to teach were relatively new to the department, which was expanding to include more conventional sociological subjects like social statistics, population, and ethnic relations. I sensed that there was a lingering departmental suspicion of such studies as being "typical American sociology," and I felt that I was expected to sustain the Berkeley approach to these subjects while the department was developing its distinctive character.

That year was exhausting. After preparing for the next day's classes, I sat down at the typewriter to add a few pages to the dissertation. Fortunately, the outline held up to its promise, and writing was mostly a matter of amplification. I did most of my work at home. With a little encouragement, the children were able to entertain themselves. Now and then I was interrupted by the baby, curious about the names of things. "Nose?" he would ask, pushing at his own, or "Chair?" patting the seat before my desk. One day he pointed to the typewriter and asked: "Damn?" So much for my typing skills.

Nisbet apparently had little difficulty putting a dissertation committee together, although the subject matter was not well-known. Eberhard, with his interest in ethnology, seemed a natural representative from the department. David Mandelbaum of anthropology, with whom I had taken a seminar on India, agreed to be a member, as did Murray B. Emeneau, professor of Sanskrit. They were kind and helpful, accepted the final version, and at the end of the spring term in 1952 I was awarded the Ph.D. We headed for Lake Tahoe for a family vacation. Only later did I come fully to appreciate my extraordinary good fortune in having had, throughout my university career, a number of attentive and encouraging mentors who were also models of scholarly distinction and intellectual integrity.

Spring 1952 was Nisbet's last term at Berkeley. He had been appointed a dean at the University of California's newly opened Riverside campus. During the summer, Herbert Blumer arrived from the University of Chicago to become chair of the expanding department. In addition to academic credentials, Blumer brought with him subtle arbitration skills honed by his wartime experience on the National Labor Relations Board. A particular memory concerns his presiding at a faculty meeting called to discuss standards for the Ph.D. candidacy. After a lengthy discussion of measures proposed as automatic disqualifiers for questionable candidates—required courses, preliminary examinations, foreign language prerequisites, M.A. thesis—the issue focused on a particular student. One professor after another cited instances of incompetent work, and all agreed that the student should be dissuaded from further graduate study. Someone asked, "Who is going to tell him?" Blumer looked around the table. His glance lingered on each person who had spoken. When no one responded, he slapped the table and said, "All right. I will. I am chairman." There was a sense of sheepishness in the room, and I realized we had witnessed a real example of the assumption of personal responsibility.

Blumer's appointment put the final seal on Berkeley's recognition of the legitimacy of sociology as an academic discipline. The department office was moved from a long narrow basement room in Wheeler Hall to the sunny top floor of South Hall. The chairman was given a room of his own for his office, as was the departmental secretary. In a decade, the department had moved from nonexistence to host of the national meetings of the American Sociological Society. By 1964, its graduate program was ranked first in the country.

I was not a participant in that florescence. By the end of my second year of teaching, evidence had begun to mount that I was working too hard. A bout of mononucleosis had taken its toll, but the final stroke was another pregnancy. Reluctantly, I asked to be released from my contract for the following year. A miscarriage a short time later may have been brought on by sheer exhaustion, but perhaps it was a symptom of ambivalence about abandoning an academic career. A year later, Blumer asked whether I would be interested in a part-time appointment. Although pleased to learn that I was still in the good graces of the department, I nevertheless had to say no. I was expecting a third child.

That was the end of my teaching career. By the time a fourth child was born, I had little time or inclination to think of returning to academic life. Later, when the children were all in school, the possibility of returning occasionally crossed my mind, but there always seemed to be too many other things to do. School affairs and youth groups required parental participation, and volunteer organizations always needed help, usually supplied by women like me. I became deeply involved in Adlai Stevenson's 1956 presidential campaign and in local Berkeley politics. I learned that although a man was inevitably named to head a campaign committee, the final decision rested on the willingness of his wife to do most of the work!

Always there were sociological situations to explore. My husband's career as a sinologist took us to Cambridge University for three years. There the youngest of our children started kindergarten and the oldest completed her college preparatory education. Concerned to know how they would be affected by the new school environment, I began studying the history of English schools and the contemporary efforts at reform. Comparing the several levels of the English system with our own, I came to a deeper appreciation of the effect of an educational ethic on individual development, as well as a better understanding of the way a system of schooling reflects prevailing cultural values.

High on my list of intellectual interests was the phenomenon of the baby boom (for which I felt fractionally responsible). I found it hard to believe that this was just a blip on the growth curve. My hunch was that our generation was experiencing the loss of a sense of community and that we were trying to create new communities of our own, beginning with the primary group. Most of us had been part of the mass population movements of the thirties and forties that had severed old neighborhood ties and replaced them with the anonymity of metropolitan centers. Durkheim had a name for the resulting feeling: *anomie.*

Betty Friedan (who graduated from college the same year I did) opened a new way of looking at this situation. In *The Feminine Mystique,* she described with great insight a new attitude toward domestic life that had begun to affect our generation. Picked up and exploited by the advertising and entertainment industries, this attitude fostered a set of images that came to dominate middle-class values. The hero-husband, back from the war, marries the heroine-wife, ready to create an ideal home with enough perfect children to make dreams come true. In an era influenced by this kind of image making, housewives were "homemakers," houses were "homes," and "togetherness" described the most rewarding marital relationship. The family unit was centered on super-mom, a model of skillful housekeeping, motherly sensitivity, and selfless devotion to others. This ideal American family lived in Suburbia, a new kind of community composed of people of the same age group, sharing similar racial characteristics and socioeconomic backgrounds. In this community, conformity was the ruling ethic; children were taught to subordinate their individuality to the welfare of the group.

The younger generation's sense of the phoniness of these images was captured graphically in the film *The Graduate*. They came to realize that Donna Reed was not a real mother; Ozzie and Harriet were not real parents; and Father didn't know beans because he wasn't around much. The new generation pleaded with their parents to "get real," found new images of reality in LSD and marijuana trips, and looked to Woodstock as a model for "togetherness." They began forming communities of their own—communes and ashrams, coeducational dormitories, centers for peer counseling. Our basic social institutions were challenged; both marriage and the family were redefined in terms of sexual equality and "meaningful relationships" rather than by law or tradition.

To my way of thinking, these changing attitudes were both influenced and reflected by changing demographic patterns. I had not been able to find the handle for a research project that would deal with the human face of the higher birth rate, but with the growth of the women's movement came other approaches to an understanding of what was happening. One is the changing conception of the role of women in society. In an earlier age, a woman found her identity and sense of self-worth in primary-group relationships, but in the urban, industrialized world she is forced to recognize less personal, more abstract criteria of her value—holding office, being promoted, winning awards, getting published, making money. The modern woman is forced to make a choice between two images of selfhood or else find a way of unifying them into a harmonious whole.

As I approached the age of sixty, it dawned on me that much of my life had been lived vicariously, dependent on an identity provided by my husband and children. This was a shocking realization, for I had taken pains to avoid interference in their private lives. The children had

embarked on interesting careers that had taken them to the other side of the continent. All were married, and some had children of their own. Delighted with what they were doing, and in frequent communication with them, I had no difficulty in honoring their independence. But I began to wonder about my own role in life, particularly since I had no aptitude for playing the matriarch or even the doting grandmother.

For the first time in decades, I had plenty of free time for exploring interesting questions. But I was paralyzed by the sense of having become an anachronism, out of touch with developments in my academic field and certainly beyond any possibility of returning to professional life. How does one present a curriculum vitae that terminates in 1953 at age thirty-three, then give an adequate answer to the question, "But what have you done *lately?*" No matter how much effort and attention one gives to the family, it can hardly be displayed as evidence of career development.

This bleak period, fortunately, was short-lived. An old friend returned from Europe, where he had spent many years as a Jungian analyst. Conversations with him revitalized my long-standing but sporadic interest in the writings of C. G. Jung, and brought me into close relationship with several professional women working in psychology and related fields. In casual and formal meetings we have delved into our inner lives, reassessing our roles as wives, mothers, and professionals and addressing the central question: the nature of the feminine. Our Jungian approach has taken us into studies of art, myth, and religion as carriers of the human spirit and as sources for understanding the communal experiences of womankind.

My own inquiries center on historical conceptions of two powerful images of the feminine, Aphrodite and the Virgin Mary. These images— the one often trivialized into a figure of erotic fantasy, the other exalted into a vision of female perfection—seem to me to represent a historic polarization of attitudes toward women that is by no means extinct. We are beginning to understand the social effects of the traditional patriarchal attitude, but I wonder if we should not be giving more attention to certain contents of the attitude itself, especially when they suggest an inherent ambivalence toward women.

Working with images of the feminine may not seem particularly sociological, but I believe that the approach rather than the subject matter defines the discipline. One effort to assess Jung's work from a sociological point of view concluded, "Society and the social experiences of history are ultimately the main suppliers of the contents of the individual psyche."[5] This assessment brings social, historical, and psychological ideas together under one umbrella, and it captures the interrelationship of the three areas of study that have occupied my intellectual life. It also harks back to Nisbet's observation that changes in culture are reflected in primary social relationships and psychological identifications. Perhaps social institutions and individual behavior can be seen as the two poles of a single axis, the comprehension of one pole requiring awareness of the other.

Writing this memoir has helped me distinguish some of the several strands that make up the axis of my own life. But it also calls to mind a bit of ancient Chinese wisdom: "Only after one has done one's study is one aware of one's inadequacies." I find it comforting to know that the future is full of things to learn.

Notes

1. Robert A. Nisbet, *The Quest for Community: A Study in the Ethics of Order and Freedom* (New York: Oxford University Press, 1953), p. vii.

2. Theoretically, in Frederick J. Teggart, *Theory and Process of History* (1941), and practically applied in his *Rome and China: A Study of Correlations in Historical Events* (1939). Both are published by University of California Press, Berkeley. A brief biography of Teggart written by Nisbet appeared in *California Monthly*, April 1976.

3. David P. Gardner, *The California Oath Controversy* (Berkeley: University of California Press, 1967), p. 251.

4. Dorris W. Goodrich, "The Making of an Ethnic Group: The Eurasian Community in India," Ph.D. dissertation, University of California, Berkeley, 1952.

5. Ira Progoff, *Jung's Psychology and Its Social Meaning* (New York: Grove Press, 1953), p. 163.

Dorris W.
Goodrich

25

Chapter 3

When We Were All Boys Together:
Graduate School in the Fifties
and Beyond

ARLENE KAPLAN DANIELS

It is startling to realize that one has progressed from enfant terrible to éminence grise in what feels like no time at all. In those now historic "bad" old days of the fifties, the issue of the differences between men and women in academic life never arose explicitly, so I made my way through college (1948–52) and graduate school (1952–60) at Berkeley without thinking about my experiences in terms of difference or discrimination. The feminist consciousness I developed in the growing women's movement of the sixties produced a rethinking of those experiences, but that didn't help me at Berkeley.

In my undergraduate years as an English major, I attracted some favorable, as well as quite a lot of unfavorable, attention from my professors. Some of them found me too strident and avoided me or turned me away. These experiences affected me deeply, for my professors were very significant figures to me. Having escaped my family in Los Angeles, I had come to Berkeley to find a new life.

My professors represented figures I wanted to identify with and to be guided by. I wanted them to befriend me and to offer assurance and acceptance. These were hardly realistic desires. I was passionately interested and very vocal in classes when discussion was permitted, but somehow I was never quite comfortable in the department. My grades were erratic and I had difficulty figuring out what mistakes I had made when I received low marks. Perhaps it was the fault of my undisciplined study habits and the uncurbed enthusiasm I felt for some subjects while resisting others. In any case, I entered my upper-division years with a sense of growing unease.

I came from a family of shopkeepers who struggled to make a living. My parents had suffered in the Depression, so I knew you had to work or you would starve. My experience at jobs like waitressing, cashiering, and clerking convinced me that I wanted a career that made work interesting rather than deadly. My aggressiveness and articulateness did not make me popular with boys, and I had no faith that marriage was an option. My experience as an undergraduate began to suggest that English was not a field where I could flourish. So what could I do?

How do we make the fateful decisions that shape our careers? There is a sociological literature on commitment to careers, and we form impressions also from biographical and autobiographical writings. Those that talk about the importance of some significant other touch a responsive chord in me; it is clear that I was pushed and pulled in my early years by way of attraction and repulsion. I did well in courses when I liked the professors and poorly when I didn't. These feelings were influenced also by the subject, of course—I found it difficult to care one way or the other in math or natural science classes. And I felt thwarted in courses if the subject matter was interesting but the professor boring. Through the desire to learn more from a brilliant or charismatic or sympathetic other, one can develop a sense of direction and purpose not otherwise attainable. Commitment to work, like conversion experiences in other areas, may come quite suddenly, especially after a long period of unsettling soul searching about it.

A lucky encounter with Tamotsu Shibutani in his first years at Berkeley gave me the sense of direction I had been longing for. Shibutani is a brilliant and absorbing lecturer. Always throroughly prepared, he began each class by outlining major points on the blackboard, then speaking in a lively and compelling fashion, without notes. His lectures, sprinkled with marvelous illustrations and anecdotes, were spellbinding. He was asking us to consider how people are embedded in group life, how they take account of one another in interactions, how a negotiated order is developed and maintained. Trying to understand these matters seemed a worthwhile career to undertake. It was almost like receiving the call to a profession in the old evangelical sense of a *beruf*.

I didn't fall down in a trance; but an experience I had one day before Shibutani's class crystallized the idea of the calling. I bustled up to a little knot of chattering young women who were talking about the class. "That Shibutani is so cute," said one. "Do you think he's married?" "I'd like to marry him," volunteered another. Pushing my way into the circle, I announced: "Not me—I want to *be* Shibutani when I grow up. Eliminate the middleman!" I mused over what I had really meant as we filed into the lecture hall for our class in collective behavior. What I wanted to be was a sociologist.

This idea was reinforced through the readings in Shibutani's courses. I was entranced by Helen Hughes's *News and the Human Interest Story* (1940) and became immersed in Karl Mannheim's *Man and Society in an Age of Reconstruction* (1940). Except for novels, no nonrequired reading had so tempted me to stay awake for more. If this kind of excitement was to be found in sociology, I wanted to be there.

In my senior year, I went to see Shibutani and poured out my hopes and my conviction that sociology was something I wanted and could do, despite my spotty preparation. I was accepted into the program in 1952, when Herbert Blumer came from the University of Chicago to chair the department. I have always been grateful to Tom Shibutani for sponsoring my application. I was bumptious and overeager, dogging his footsteps, chattering compulsively whenever I gained his ear. A shy, reserved person, he must have found it difficult to accept such a follower. But his acceptance of me as his student and his assurance that I could succeed played a major part in fixing my career choice.

I was elated but nervous to be in the impressive group of students welcomed by Blumer. They included my former readers and teaching assistants; many were much older, some of them returning veterans. I hoped for their acceptance and looked forward with trepidation to my first graduate seminars and my first statistics course, an area I had avoided throughout college. Most of all, I was anxious about taking Shibutani's practicum in research methods. Fortunately, I found that Elaine Hadley, my former reader in one of Shibutani's courses, and her future husband, Wally MacDonald, were also members of that class and willing to work as a team. We became great friends and, after their marriage, shared a house. Wally was a great influence on my thinking, as were other students like Tom Scheff and Seth Fisher.

We spent hours together, discussing what we were reading. Wally was an ardent follower of John Dewey and the American pragmatists. He introduced us to some of the more obscure followers of the school and I struggled with these new ideas. Tom Scheff helped me find my way through the obscurities of George Herbert Mead. I became close to Dick Colvard, with whom I studied for the preliminary examinations, and to Fred Goldner and Warren Hagstrom, who were especially kind, coaching me in statistics and survey methods. Through Blumer and Shibutani, I was becoming a symbolic interactionist with a devotion to fieldwork. Through Philip Selznick, I learned something about organizations, and from Reinhard Bendix, although I resisted it, I got a glimpse of social theory and political sociology.

But the courses and professors blur in memory before the excitement of meeting and becoming friends with the other graduate students. We were all boys together; there was no other choice. The notion that women might have different agendas or interests or problems was unheard-of. The male model was the only one, and women had to adopt it. Under the male model, the usual role for a woman was wife and helpmeet. Unmarried women in the cohort might find some parallel role to that of wife in their spare time. My choice was to make myself agreeable by baby-sitting for the married couples with children. It now seems that the women who were uncomfortable in that neutralized role dropped out: they had affairs with male graduate students and left in the aftermath of breakup; they married and chose to devote themselves to husbands and raising a family; they went off into the world of junior college teaching or business. So in the end, I was the only woman in my cohort who completed the Ph.D. program.

A few years later, the pattern changed; and in my last years, I came to know a number of women who went on to finish. But in my own day, I remember exhorting woman after woman, begging them not to leave me, to no avail. To me, it seemed wrong for them to give up just short of their goal. No one remarked, then, about the personal as political; and since everyone seemed to have a reasonable, individual rationale, I turned my attention and commitment to my male comrades and their families. Except for two women—Paule Verdet and Sally Cassidy, who became lifelong friends after they arrived at Berkeley from the University of Chicago for a fellowship year—I had no women's support group, nor did I notice the lack, because *we were all boys together.*

Earlier, I had had the friendship of women who then decided to leave the Ph.D. program—Elaine MacDonald and Isadora Ding, particularly. Elaine left after being told at the oral examination to return for further questioning. She was angry at her treatment and refused to do so. Isadora married a professor in the sociology department and then, somehow or other, did not finish the program. So I went on without them. I couldn't imagine any other course of action.

I was part of various graduate student projects that helped me forge an identity as a sociologist. Two that I remember with particular fondness were serving as a teaching assistant for Blumer's and Shibutani's large undergraduate classes and working on the editorial board of the *Berkeley Journal of Sociology*. Shibutani showed his assistants how to organize for section meetings by preparing discussion questions in advance, using examples from current events, literature, autobiography, journals, and diaries to illustrate the theoretical material he presented. The TAs prepared their material and then met with Shibutani. We, too, would have our sentence outlines to display on the blackboard, as he did in his lectures. I received my only systematic teaching instruction in this way. For the rest, I learned by doing. As we compared notes, observed one another meeting with students in the TA room, struggled with exams, I began to feel like a bona fide member of the graduate student group.

This feeling was reinforced as a member of the editorial board of the graduate student journal, started during those years. I learned to encourage potential papers, to edit, to negotiate with other editors for the acceptance of articles, and to pull a completed issue together. I added to my understanding of what a sociologist does, how theories and evidence are brought together to formulate a publishable argument. And I learned that I had a knack for editing and helping others turn papers into publishable manuscripts, skills that I have used throughout my career in the service of friends, colleagues, and students.

The graduate student community took an active interest in my courtship with my future husband. In 1954, I had been part of a car pool to the San Francisco Opera season, along with Richard Daniels. He was lively and knowledgeable about opera and had a quick wit and a sense of humor that appealed to me. Our eighteen-month courtship took place under the glaring lights of departmental concern. Shibutani kept asking when we would get married, as it would be an excellent excuse for a great Chinese banquet. My peers charted the course of our courtship so closely that I began to feel the oppressive aspects of gemeinschaft. When we married, our Chinese banquet was organized by Isadora Ding and hosted by my sociology department professors and peers. I had found many of my significant others within sociology and they rallied around us on our wedding day in June of 1956.

I was finding my place as a leader in the cohort: I was the student liaison to the faculty to register complaints about our treatment; I was the organizer of the symbolic interactionist clique in various arguments and debates with the organizational theorists and the structural functionalists; I led in choosing the next crop of editors for the *Berkeley Journal*. In later years, I was much amused by the reminiscences of

Dorothy Smith, who painted me as the class bully. Through her eyes, I could see myself as perhaps a bit silly, even if plucky and assertive. And it is ironic to remember that even if a bully, I had no enduring status.

Despite my participation and leadership in the thick of graduate student life, I had small indications that the faculty did not consider me a serious candidate for help in finding a job. With Nedra Belloc, an older student who later dropped out, I drove to the sociology convention in Seattle in 1957. I noticed that the men graduate students were squired about by their professors and introduced to colleagues from other schools. But even professors I knew rather well and who regarded me as a good student, like Leo Lowenthal, had no time for me. I was a little wistful when I saw Bennett Berger and Cesar Graña in Lowenthal's company, meeting other sociologists, laughing and talking together. But I didn't think about it very much.

However, there was no dismissing the disappointment I felt after finishing my exams; no effort was made to find employment for me while I wrote my dissertation. In fact, it was fellow student Fred Goldner who tipped me off to a research job in the Berkeley public health school that might also provide material for a dissertation. None of the men graduate students wanted or needed the job, so I was launched on my research into dentistry—and into a long career of choosing research projects through expediency.

In my earlier career, choices had been different. My master's thesis had been on folksingers and was a labor of love. I nearly killed myself watching them perform at all hours while trying to maintain class and work schedules, but I learned a lot. Shibutani guided me through various drafts and taught me to organize and discipline my work in the process. My first draft was a disorganized mess. Shibutani was unpleasantly emphatic about its shortcomings, but he told me how to fix it. Each week I was to make a complete-sentence outline of a chapter. Each week we would meet to go over it. When the outline was complete, I wrote from it, meeting Shibutani each week to go over another chapter. Friends locked me into my apartment while I completed the week's assignment, passing in food for sustenance. The thesis was finally finished, and my happiest moment in graduate school came when Shibutani said, "I'm proud of you." Turned into an article, the thesis was published in a German review, *Soziologus,* never to be seen again. Years later, I learned that my thesis had been highly regarded in the department.

By the time I was ready for the dissertation, Shibutani had left the university. Blumer was away on leave. In casting about for a topic and an adviser, I went to the late Hanan Selvin, then a young survey researcher fresh from Columbia University, who offered to help me in my pursuit of dentistry and the art of the survey. Selvin was a dear, and I shall always cherish his memory. With his help and with a lot of coaching from fellow student Warren Hagstrom, I became a survey researcher and learned to think in categories that could fit on a punch card instead of in the contextual and processual terms of symbolic interaction. The mailed questionnaire to dentists was a rather pedestrian effort, producing prosaic findings of interest only to the funding agency. But interviewing dentists and learning how they focused on various aspects of their work—the craft, the business management, the advancement of the profession—interested me more.

Relying on my training with Blumer and Shibutani, I interviewed key informants in the local dental world and learned a lot about the "vision" of dentistry. In fact, I got a bit overly immersed. I remembered to outline my chapters all right, but as Selvin teased me, my first draft was "a bit long in the tooth." I had to draw back and remember that I was a sociologist and not a proponent of open or closed panel dental insurance.

While completing my dissertation, I worked for two years as an instructor in the speech department at Berkeley, teaching undergraduates to read "great books" and to write essays about them. In 1961, when I was thirty, Richard and I moved to the wastelands of suburbia on the San Francisco peninsula, to be near his first job. Our home is there to this day. The move did not prove fortunate for me. The indifference of my department to my employment difficulties continued after I received my degree.

My only nibble came from sociology sister Sally Cassidy, who had landed a good job at Wayne State University as chair of sociology in a new and exciting experimental college. In those days, commuting marriages were unknown, and it was unthinkable to commute halfway across the country for a job, as I do now. I never considered that option seriously; it was only a bright, unattainable dream.

Even the professors I knew best were not really helpful. When I asked Erving Goffman for help, he was, in fact, scathing: "You're not really a professional. You're only a housewife looking for pin money." I remember his contempt vividly. Though we were later to become close friends (or as close as Erving would let anyone get to him), he was at that time another force against which I had to contend. It was hard not to see these failures as my own fault. Tied to my husband, I was not a "real" professional ready to compete in the professional market.

If I hadn't been lucky enough to find a spot in a nonprofit research institute in Palo Alto, I would have been defeated. As it was, I drifted for almost a year trying to accommodate to my husband's career. My journals piled up as I found it more and more difficult to read them; they seemed further and further from my life. In some inchoate way, I was afraid I was falling out of the sphere of sociology and was anxious about losing my place. I voiced my fears to Shibutani and heard his lack of comprehension for my anxiety. He implicitly chided me for my inability to take advantage of my position as a housewife: "I wish I could stay home and have someone support me. I could get so much more work done. You're lucky." And he said, "I never cared much about status." I was too abashed to remind him that we sociologists distinguish between status and prestige and that all I wanted was a toehold as a sociologist, at any level. I felt that it was my personal failing not to be able to work without some institutional support. I suffered further, because I was not only anxious, I was also ashamed of myself for being unable to surmount my difficulties.

Determined to stay in sociology, I set my sights for a career in research rather than yearning for the unattainable—a job teaching at a university or a college. The Mental Research Institute (MRI) in Palo Alto gave me my first taste of the rigors of this career: do your research where the money is. The eager research grant applicant learns to tailor her interests to meet the specifications of the funding agency, as research contracts have detailed and demanding specifications. Befriended by the MRI director, the late Don Jackson, I was fortunate, at first, to be spared the rigors of contract research. It was clear, however, that if I were to stay, I would have to bring in money. Initially, Jackson found me a contract with the Department of Defense to study military recruits and I was launched on the track of expediency tempered by personal bent and the vagaries of fortune.

For almost fifteen years, at MRI and later at Dorothy Miller's Institute, which survived under a variety of names, including Scientific Analysis Corporation, I kept my connections to sociology alive through grants and contracts.

I had a bad patch in the early sixties, however, when I began to despair of ever finding a reasonably stable niche in the profession. During that period, I became pregnant unexpectedly and, not knowing what the future might hold for me, finished my currently funded project without seeking another source. When my pregnancy proved unsuccessful and I started to recover my strength and health, I thought that surely my efforts to find funding—or by this time, an academic job—would prove easier. It was especially daunting to find that once again I had to start from scratch.

Profoundly demoralized, I suffered one of the most anxious periods of my life, casting about for a new way to stay in the sociology business. My anxiety was only intensified by the apparently untroubled, successful progression of my cohort brothers in their careers. Still, I had to do something. The late Morris Daniels, a colleague at San Diego State, knew about my interest in the ethical issues in psychiatry. He had studied certified public accountants and we had talked idly of comparing and contrasting our fields, but now I really needed help. I shall always be grateful to Morris, for he shouldered the task of writing with me a grant proposal for the National Institute of Child Health and Human Development (NICHHD). An administrator there, David Kallen, helped us construct a proposal to meet NICHHD requirements. Those were the days of lush funding, and in 1966 we discovered we had received the grant, shortly after I was offered a job at San Francisco State. It looked as if I was finally home safely.

However, I had only a short period as a professor and a researcher at a teaching college. I was a casualty of the student-faculty strike of 1969 and was denied tenure. Many professors in the local chapter of the union (American Federation of Teachers local 1352) supported the student strike over demands raised by students who wanted black studies and other ethnic studies on campus. Faculty who were sympathetic with their demands (including about half the sociology department) went out on strike in the winter of 1968. We picketed the campus, taught our classes off-campus, and gave speeches to local organizations to gain support for the cause. A few of us collaborated on a book about our faculty union and the faculty union movement more generally: *Academics on the Line* (1970), published by Jossey-Bass.

Fortunately, I had kept my hand in the research business and so continued my entrepreneurial career after 1970, when the axe fell. I found a home at Scientific Analysis Corporation (SAC), a research corporation that bore the imprint of its remarkable founder and mainstay, Native American Dorothy Miller. She provided a haven for all manner of marginal but lively researchers at odds with the establishment or "between engagements" at universities. Unfailingly creative, she assisted people with their grant applications, and I learned a lot from her.

I rocketed along, learning to snaffle grants and then to administer them and, ultimately, to produce the research that was supposed to emerge from them. The grant world was hard, but women could succeed in it, and I met many like myself who survived there in the days before academic positions were more widely available to women. Living from grant to grant, the terms of the trade were writing five or six applications for every one funded, working feverishly to meet deadlines, and producing huge, complex documents (generally useless for anything but applications)—to say nothing of collecting data and writing reports within the specified time. The development of publishable articles or books from report findings was done on your own time or on time bootlegged off the next grant.

Perhaps the most difficult part of the life was coming down to the zero hour when the last funding was due to run out and new funding had not yet appeared. If you ran an office, had a modest staff and a budget for photocopying, telephone, and travel, you faced the possibility of having to disband the working team so necessary to productivity. Even if you had someone to support you, maintaining a steady flow of funds became a major headache. So it was not surprising that the lure of an academic position remained, and the loss of the appointment at San Francisco State was devastating.

During this period, my feminist consciousness began to develop. I was becoming aware of the problems that were specific to women researchers. The turning point in that development came at the American Sociological Association (ASA) meetings in San Francisco in 1969 with the call for a women's caucus. Alice Rossi had organized the meeting with the assistance of the UC Berkeley women graduate students and alums. In the audience, I mused on how quickly I had been forgotten at my home school and how I would have liked to participate in the call for action. Still, I was glad the women's caucus had been proposed, for it focused and put a name to the amorphous feelings of discontent and resentment that we had experienced.

I became intensely involved in the outpouring of emotion by the speakers, who talked about their difficulties in finishing their studies and finding careers against the odds of institutionalized and explicit sexism. As they spoke, I experienced my second professional (and personal) conversion as my past was revealed in a new light. Suddenly, I recognized the larger pattern in all the slights, snubs, omissions, and patronizing acts that I had shrugged off as my paranoia or my just desserts. I felt rage at what I had endured and terrible sorrow for all that had hampered me. I resolved to help younger women, to protect them against the systematic frustration and neglect that I had experienced. These ideas were so tumultuous that I wondered if I could keep my composure. I was so close to tears that I needed to escape to my room to recover. Even then, I thought that perhaps I had been lucky in the past not to realize what had been happening. As long as I thought I was responsible for events, I could try harder; my fate was within my own control. If I had seen the system as stacked against me, I might have been overcome with rage and despair and thus immobilized. Without support groups or an ideology of sisterhood, the idea of patterned gender injustice would have been devastating.

I wanted to act in any way I could on the ideas that were then abroad. Already I knew that my days at San Francisco State were numbered; soon I would have time for active involvement. I resolved to participate in the formation of the women's caucus in sociology. The following year, when the ASA met in Washington, D.C., there was another organizing meeting and when Alice Rossi called for someone to take notes, I sprang to attention. That step marked my entry into organized feminism and changed my life.

My hard times were brightened by my entry into the women's sociology network. Because of my activity at the organizing caucus in Washington, D.C., Alice Rossi and I began to correspond and share our work. We talked about the early feminists included in her compilation, *The Feminist Papers* (1973). We planned our campaign to further the status of women in sociology by bringing them into the power structure of the ASA and by encouraging the rise of gender studies through the development of a new ASA section. It was a heady experience for me, having a friend in sociology who shared my excitement about women's issues—a woman I had admired from afar after reading her eye-opening article "Equality Between the Sexes." I was looking ahead eagerly to meeting her again at the first organizing meeting for the caucus. Only participants who had attended the preliminary meeting in Washington were invited, so we automatically became a select group.

Some women I already knew were there, but I met others who became lifelong friends. The meeting was planned by women at Yale. With high feminist principles, the rooms we stayed in were randomly assigned, to avoid the formation of elitist cliques. Not yet sensitive to issues of hierarchy, I pleaded with the organizers to let me room with Alice Rossi, my new and treasured friend, so that we could gossip together. Since I was one of the "august" women, I was not put in my place, as perhaps I should have been. It is interesting to note how thin our ranks were then, and that I, with no stable academic position or particularly distinguished publication record, should have been a personage. But I was developing a reputation for helping women by offering advice, writing references, and editing their papers. That may have spared me my just desserts.

That meeting was my first encounter with the heady and intoxicating sense of a working sisterhood and a working social movement. We incorporated and formed a temporary leadership until we could enroll members and hold elections. Alice became president; I was a vice president and editor of the newsletter.

One of the momentous aspects of the meeting for me was the discovery that I could be a leader. There were some difficult moments and spirited discussions as liberal and radical feminists tried to hammer out policies we could all live with. For instance, we debated whether men would be permitted to join the organization and what name for it would reflect more than a narrow concern for middle-class women's professional advancement. It was surprising how quickly consensus was reached on potentially divisive issues, and I was happy to be a useful voice in creating that consensus.

I was struck by what a diverse, even motley, crew we were. We older women all had some disguise or eccentric persona to mask our professional acumen, stressing the peacemaker skills of parents and wives rather than the authority of expertise. Jessie Bernard hid behind a presentation as a vaguely sweet and mild-mannered lady. (She was, of course, a sharp and incisive thinker.) Alice Rossi presented herself as a genteel lady with the accents of a middle-class Baltimore housewife, yet her brilliant organizational skill saved us from many pitfalls. The late Rue Bucher, without Rossi's cloak, used instead shyness and an ability to merge with the background—a key strategy for many professional women. In my capacity as joker and clown, I interjected jests and antics into any situation that was becoming too tense.

The younger women seemed to need no cloak. They were bright, pretty, self-assured; ready to speak up aggressively and forthrightly for their views. They were not yet entrenched, middle-class women. I was delighted to meet them and pleased to see how self-assured they were, confident of their place in the professional world.

Among the early friendships formed at that meeting, I count Jessie Bernard. We instantly struck an accord and she agreed to house me on my next stop in Washington, D.C. That was the prototype for a chain of friendships and an ever-widening network linking members of Sociologists for Women in Society (SWS) to one another and to sociology. We offered one another speaking engagements, consultations on writing and research projects, houseroom, consolation in hard times (when tenure wasn't granted or there were family misfortunes), and rejoicing in triumphs. An SWS sister, Pamela Roby, sent me flowers in 1987, when I became president of the Society for the Study of Social Problems, just as I had sent flowers to Alice Rossi when she became president of the American Sociological Association a few years earlier.

I acquired a modest grant from the National Institute of Mental Health (NIMH) to study women volunteers (Kirsten E. Joslyn's original idea for the project provided the impetus), and I was again able to keep my research outfit in business. SAC was willing to house my efforts as an organizer for SWS, and it was intoxicating to be in the forefront of that movement.

By the time the seventies rolled round, I could look back on ten years in the field. I had somehow survived my apprenticeship in nonprofit research and had managed, despite the setback at San Francisco State, to establish myself as a working professional. My publications were beginning to see light, I was recognized by appointments and committee posts in professional associations, and could feel that, even without an academic position, I was truly a member of the sociology tribe.

I was helped by the newly formed networks of women spurred by the organization of SWS. There had previously been informal networks of assistance, but the importance of women helping one another was now highlighted by our acceptance of feminist ideas of sisterhood. These ideas supplemented the ideas of camaraderie that sustained me in graduate school and beyond. For example, when I was fired at San Francisco State, members of my cohort and other colleagues I had met through my work wrote letters of protest to our colleague, Don Garrity, and other administrators there. My brothers formed a protective net to soften some of the roughest blows of getting sacked. I was invited to speak at their universities and received a few appointments as visiting professor. These attentions bolstered my professional sense of self.

Particular friendships also helped in attaining that sense of professional membership. Early on in my career as a nonprofit researcher, I was fortunate to have Rachel Kahn-Hut as a research assistant. She soon became indispensable. Together, we worked on the NICHHD grant and edited the book on the San Francisco State strike. Rachel was always a hard taskmaster with a keen analytic eye. I owe a great deal of my success in presenting my research to her assistance, and I have no greater sense of satisfaction than the one I get when Rachel finally says, "Yes, I think you have it now—ready to publish."

She was especially helpful in one of my most difficult assignments, a review for *Contemporary Sociology* of Everett Hughes's collection of essays, *The Sociological Eye* (1971). My most admired colleagues and teachers—Shibutani, Freidson, Becker, Goffman among them—had been Hughes's students. Hughes himself would be reading that review. Rachel painstakingly reviewed draft after draft so that the theory underlying Hughes's work would be clear. Hughes wrote to say he was pleased with my efforts. I told him how much I owed Rachel, and he wrote to her as well.

Of course, I have relied on many other friends to help me through various stages of my career. While the list is too long to include here, I am keenly aware that my career is embedded in a string of personal relationships and mutual debts of friendship. Perhaps this context is even more important to women who have spent so much of their careers on the fringes of the profession. Or perhaps the context is more clear to someone in that category, for almost every sociologist relies on colleagues for review and comment.

In any case, with the help of these colleagues, I began to carve out my research niche. Occasionally, a small grant even came easily to me. In 1973, as a spokesperson for feminism in sociology, I was funded by the National Science Foundation to write a piece on research on women's issues. That grant was an example of the uses of networking. I was a friend of NSF grants and contracts administrator Gladys Handy, who remembered me when the contract became available. I didn't know much about the issues, but I became an overnight expert and built a reputation as a knowledgeable key figure in a new field. Eventually, the paper I wrote for NSF appeared as an article in a book called *Another Voice* (1975), edited by Marcia Millman and Rosabeth Kanter. In a different form, it appeared in Bernice Sandler's publication for the Project on the Status and Education of Women, which was distributed by the thousands.

By the mid-seventies, I was beginning to prosper, but my blood pressure was going up, and grant application and report deadlines were not helping it. When John Kitsuse called me from Northwestern University to see if I would become the first director of the newly formed Program on Women, with a joint appointment in sociology, I was tempted. But how could I leave home and husband for a job so far away? Again, Richard came to the rescue. He persuaded me to embark on a giant commuting relationship with the promise that he would look for a position in Chicago. "We have followed my career for twenty years," he said. "We can follow yours for the next twenty." Although a handsome suggestion that emboldened me to embark on the commute, the joint move to Chicago has not come to fruition. Richard became chief executive

officer of his hospital—and averse to moving. I discovered how much I valued my work at Northwestern and didn't want to leave it. But commuting marriages are possible, even if not ideal, and we have continued as we began. I return home during school holidays and summers, and Richard visits Evanston for long weekends and even for several weeks at a time now that he is retired.

The appointment in 1975 at Northwestern, as a full professor, after years of rattling around on the margins, came at the same time as my selection as editor of the journal *Social Problems.* I was also elected to the SWS presidency and made a fellow in the National Institute of Medicine. All these honors and responsibilities coming at once, when I was forty-four, left me overwhelmed. But with characteristic insouciance, I took to rattling off my titles to all I encountered. Friends who had heard this litany would sometimes prompt me if I faltered at ticking the titles off, and those close to me grew quite impatient at all my crowing. I got my comeuppance, though. On an SWS panel at a convention, I was asked in apparent seriousness by an earnest moderator: "Tell us, Professor Daniels, how you attained your eminent position." I snapped out of control at the thought of so much serious regard and began to prance about in the manner of the silly little baritone in Gilbert and Sullivan operettas. In fact, I started to sing Koko's aria from *The Mikado:* "Taken from a county jail, by a set of curious chances. . . ." However, I quickly stopped when I saw I had mystified and possibly alarmed the audience. Still, the incident helped me get back my perspective about the extent of the eminence I had at last achieved.

Becoming an administrator for the Program on Women was particularly difficult. Ray Mack, then provost at Northwestern and a former member of the sociology department, helped me enormously. He launched me on my career there and took the Program on Women under his aegis. We worked together and became great friends in our efforts to build a women's presence among the students, faculty, and staff, and to develop a women's studies component in the research agenda. Little by little, we established a program. I built a publication series with generous funding from Ray and ran a surreptitious business selling publications on my various speaking trips. Sales eventually amounted to enough to buy my way out of the directorship. I was able to return to the sociology department full time.

I had learned the joys of being "all girls together" in the women's movement and in SWS and was now to learn the joys and limitations— once again—of being "all boys together" in the Northwestern sociology department. There were few other women, so I joined my male colleagues in maintaining the ambience for which the department was famous and in adding the components of diversity for which women and minorities were clamoring. We are still hard at work on that endeavor.

What has it meant to me to begin a career by participating in a man's world? Dorothy Smith, in her article in *The Prism of Sex* (1979), edited by Julia Sherman and Evelyn Beck, talks about "the fault line" over which women scholars traditionally have worked. Before the women's movement, we denied our own experience as we looked at the world through the eyes of our male colleagues and teachers. We learned to see the world as it appeared to them and to ignore or dismiss any contrary indications from our own experience. Those of us who were successful accepted the generic "he" and met the standards of our male professors even while, if only dimly, conscious of not fitting in.

Participating in that world as a male meant the habit of thinking male. It meant seeing men as the norm and women as deviant. It meant focusing on work without attending to how family interests affected work. It meant assuming the public world of men was more important to study than the private world of women. In the sociology of work, I actually thought of myself sometimes as "an occupations and professions man" and might thoughtlessly, or wryly, describe myself that way. I wanted to be as much like Shibutani as possible, as much a regular member of the graduate student male cohort as I could. The bitterness of realizing the limitations of those aims, the loss of position and status after graduate school, contributed to the sense of bafflement and frustration when all my striving to be a sociologist seemed in vain. The marginal success of my first efforts and the nerve-wracking struggle to stay afloat in the nonprofit research business left me feeling sociology was almost too difficult and precarious a venture. But the luck I had and the networks I formed helped me persevere.

My realization of the importance of others to me fueled my conviction, at the start of the women's movement, that we must pass on the help we had been given. My modest successes showed me how to help others, beginning the changeover from a thwarted leader of men to a more successful organizer and mentor in the women's movement. While my career bears an idiosyncratic, perhaps eccentric stamp, it seems that many women from my period have had parallel experiences. Perhaps we responded differently, but we have all known the difficulties of working across the fault line, of being boys together in the once all-male world of sociology.

Chapter 4

A Berkeley Education

DOROTHY E. SMITH

I've never been back on the Berkeley campus, though I've visited the Bay area often since I've left. Not so often recently because the people I knew well there, particularly my friend Miriam Foley and my ex-husband Bill Smith, are dead. I was there several times when Bill was dying. During all those times, I avoided the campus. Never contacted old friends. When years earlier I had picked up the piece of paper from the administrative office ratifying my doctorate, I wanted to walk up to the department, tear it up in their faces, and tell them "no thanks to you."

In the old days, the days when I first came, there would have been a place for that drama. Faculty desks were in one big hall—South Hall, one of the original buildings of the university. There I could have thrown a fit and had an audience. But sociology's later quarters were buffered against such drama. They were corridors of office doors indistinguishable from floor to floor except for the alternations of women's and men's johns. One Sunday, when I was on contract there as a lecturer and working in my office, I went up to the women's john on the next floor. Someone had gone the whole round of the corridors, ripping up the cards identifying the names of office occupants on every door (political scientists, if I remember rightly, not sociologists). Hate. It never surprises me to read a news story of a graduate student shooting a faculty member. So much of who we are, who we feel ourselves to be, so much pain, humiliation, anxiety, are woven into and hidden by the ordinary decorum of classroom, courses, office hour meetings, term papers, grades, exams.

I think back on my relationship with my husband. At various times. We went into graduate school together. I was hooked on sociology; he was not. He loved the life, the good talk, and was passionately interested in people, but had little interest in sociology as inquiry or in its scholarly side. We had it the wrong way round in terms of the proper husband-wife relations of those times. We were constantly involved in pretending it was otherwise; I worked on learning to displace, subdue, or conceal my interests, trying, though never very successfully, to acquire the styles of subordination proper for an American woman toward her husband. Never being successful, I was guilty and anxious; Bill impugned, angry, and embarrassed. Our pretenses might have been less corrupting of our relationship if we had not had also to pretend they were its reality.

Our good times were somewhere else. Exploring the coast north of San Francisco and the wineries of the Napa Valley, camping in the Sierra, listening to the poets reading in North Beach coffeehouses.

Bill and I had met at the London School of Economics when I was an undergraduate. He was there on the GI bill. We got married right after my final exams and came to Berkeley in 1955. As an undergraduate, I'd been an independent and autonomous person. My discovery of the life of intellect was an extraordinary gift; it delighted me. I felt it was beyond gender (peculiar delusion!). The combination of Berkeley and marriage took that delight and autonomy away. I was terribly unhappy. Call it homesickness. Intensified by the frightening dissipation of independent identity consequent then for women on marriage. I had other miseries. In my first year at Berkeley, I had a miscarriage in the fourth month of pregnancy. The fetus had died in utero and they had to fish it out piece by bloody piece. I got a hospital infection, hemorrhaged, was hospitalized again, got an allergic reaction to blood transfusions. Came back to our apartment weak and weepy. Bill's friend, a psychiatrist, staying with us at that time, coming back home one afternoon to find me crying, angrily told me that I was the one of whom emotional demands were made and I should not make them. The woman there always for men, never for herself.

I was in and out of various therapists' offices during the whole period of my marriage. I started with a counselor on campus. A friendly woman. She wondered whether my mother had not loved me for being a girl. I said I thought she had. But in those times, the gender ideology was dogma and enforced and hence gender diagnoses in therapy were immovable. Mothers were responsible for their children's proper gender identities; a woman who loves her scholarly discipline is not properly womanly; she had been defectively mothered. So from session to session, my therapist came back again and again to the same point. I suppose she thought that somewhere down the line insight would hit and I would be transformed into the woman who could treat her graduate work as a feminine hobby to be forgone as soon as her more serious business as wife and mother supervened.

She was the first of many.

I don't remember distinct experiences of sex discrimination. I can understand why women in academia might not have experienced it consciously. The gendered relations of the academy masqueraded as neutrality. But of course sex discrimination was there. Sometimes I see it only as a generalized feeling of being out of place. And was that at work when Philip Selznick put me down in class? Why was it all my male peers got teaching or research assistantships and I did not until very late in my graduate career (when John Clausen, bless his heart, gave me a job)? I was told by one faculty member, I don't remember who, that I'd have to wait until my doctoral thesis was finished to get a university job. But my male colleagues, in those days, got their first jobs before they finished.

Erving Goffman told me once that, unlike other women in the program, I was responsible. I couldn't figure out exactly what he meant though I think he meant it kindly. I've thought since then that it just meant that I was still stubbornly and stupidly in the program, while other women, who hadn't put up with the crap, had left. Later a faculty member, again I don't remember who, described, though not in these terms, the masculinist ideology of the Berkeley sociology department: the university was a place for men, and women's place was in the home, supporting and sustaining men through the desperate anxieties of academic work and career. Of course women graduate students weren't told this, but it was, so I was told, up front among the exclusively male tenure-streamed faculty. Women were to be there always for men; the men were for themselves.

After Bill walked out early one summer morning, I talked tearfully with John Clausen about my situation. Bless his heart again, he got me a job as lecturer for a year in the sociology department. I taught in the department for two years (1964–66). For one term Shirley Starr was there as a visiting professor. Shirley was one of the older generation of women scholars whose statistical brilliance had enabled them to establish themselves in research positions. On the margins. She gave me some advice. She saw me one day running off my course outlines in the departmental office. "Don't do your own mimeographing," she said. "People will think you're a secretary." Since I'd been a secretary, that didn't exactly freak me out, but I got the point. The department was a caste system; faculty were male. Forty-four men. And me, and an occasional woman sessional, and Shirley for one semester.

The secretaries were all women, of course. A secretary who sat in on the meetings at which faculty decided whether to advance students into the doctoral program or to give them the terminal M.A., told me that women were routinely dropped from the doctoral program because they might get married, or have children, or simply because they were women and it wasn't worth putting faculty time into them. Of course the men who decided such matters did not recognize the secretary as a thinking, feeling presence in that room—a woman.

During this period of my life at Berkeley, teaching in the department, I became more conscious of what was happening and being done to women there. I remember a conference on the potential of women at about that time in San Francisco. All but one of the speakers were men. But we women came together and talked to each other. I don't remember anything significant being said, but I remember talking with other women about ourselves; I remember an intensity that had more to do with that than with the topics of our conversation. I remember reading Jessie Bernard's book *Academic Women* (1964) and finding it wonderfully enlightening about my working life and world.

Impelled by the neediness of women students in the department who crowded my office hours, and by the secretary's story of what went on among men behind closed doors, and who knows, by an already-happening women's movement, still hidden, I decided to tell women graduate students some of the realities, as I now knew them, of women's situation in the Berkeley academy. I thought they shouldn't be as naive as I had been. That meeting was my first political move in this still-hidden women's movement that I didn't know I was part of, and I was terrified. My hands shook. I did a very simple thing. I took the university bulletin and just went through the lists of names of faculty in each department. There'd be departments, such as history, with sixty names listed and not one woman; commonly women, sometimes of some eminence, would appear as lecturers. Some of those in psychology were women of historical significance in the development of American psychology. They were lecturers too, tacked on to the end of the list of tenure-track professors, all men. It was an extraordinary and intimidating picture. It was astonishing even for me. Was this what I'd been up against all this time? I had taken for granted that merit and competence were the operative values in determining people's success or lack of success in the university. Now it was clear that this was only a facade, at least so far as women were concerned. And that the facade had its political uses in concealing from us women just how we were despised.

When I was teaching in the department, I came into my office one morning feeling very disturbed. I didn't know why. After a while, I remembered a dream I'd had the night before: I was in a washroom in an institutional setting. It was very large and the stalls had no doors. I was just taking my pants down when I saw a group of men over against the far wall by the washbasins. They were muttering, "What's she doing here? Get her out of here!" Somehow I was in the men's room. Remembering the dream that morning, I recognized my relation to the Department of Sociology. I was a woman trying to pee in a men's john. And having got my pants down, I was going to go ahead and pee anyway.

This was the regime that dominated our lives as graduate students, though it only began to be visible to me when I was teaching in the department, and even then only very partially. It must be hard for women in academic life today to grasp just how the institutional order of patriarchy in the university was taken for granted—more than that, how deeply it was implicated in the established gender order beyond as well as within the university. In writing this essay, I rediscover the multiple ways in which my relationship to my husband was mediated by our different paths in the university and in sociology. About a third of the way through, we took our comprehensive exams. Written in those days. In the time leading up to them, I was fearfully anxious. It was like a great leaden mass in my stomach. I knew that Bill was not studying for the exams. I was afraid he would flunk. And he did. But I passed. It was the worst possible outcome. He was deeply humiliated. He felt he could not show his face on campus or meet with any but his closest friends. He was desperate for a time. Decided to drop out of graduate school and try something else (later and after I'd left Berkeley, he was able to return and finish his doctorate). He suffered as much from the gendered regime of the university as I did. Perhaps more. Hardly surprising that he walked out on me early one morning some three weeks after I handed in my thesis.

Odd, all the time underneath this, my love for sociology. Strange obsession. I thought about this when our disaster happened. I thought about giving up. But I just couldn't do it. Hard to express why. I'd un-expectedly discovered that this was for me when I'd gone to the London School of Economics at the age of twenty-six, after five or six years as a secretary, to do an undergraduate degree in sociology. I had expected at the end of that to get a better level of secretarial job. I had not expected to be enthralled. But I discovered myself in the discipline; this was my thing; it wasn't in me to give it up; it wasn't a matter of choice.

Shortly before the examination debacle, I'd thought I'd leave my marriage. But after that Bill was desperate and I couldn't do it to him. So I stuck with it, keeping my part of the marriage going, looking after my young son, bringing in at least a part-time income through my research assistantship, doing household chores in a somewhat haphazard way, going dutifully to my therapist once a week, and somehow, sometimes working on my thesis.

I'd make lists of what I had to do and stick them on a notice board in the kitchen: pick up Bill's jacket and pants from cleaners, do grocery shopping, Dave's (my son) dental appointment, iron shirts, ask Miriam if she can baby-sit Saturday, wash sheets and towels, finish thesis.

I was on my own with my thesis. The nightmare writing in which you know not who you write for, what it is you might be saying, and what it would be proper, correct, sociological, to say. Round and round. Thesis supervision as it was practiced then left the candidate to herself. If she had anything for her supervisor to read, she brought it to him. I was supervised by Erving Goffman. He was no exception. He told me at the outset that there was nothing new to be written about state mental hospitals, the topic of my research.[1] I handed in three chapters for comments at one point; he met with me, discussed the footnotes, and insisted that I translate a quotation because it was pretentious to quote in the original French. That was it. Later I handed in a complete draft. I didn't hear from him, though I talked once on the phone to his wife. She said something nice.

I don't remember Erving's ever commenting on that draft. And my relationship to the department was so contorted by the complexities of my relation to Bill and his relation to the department that I never thought of taking initiative. I waited to be told I existed and when the call to exist didn't come, I didn't realize that I could announce my existence myself.

I decided that the thesis was all wrong. I'd tried to write two theses in one. I didn't want to give up either, though I can't now remember what the other one was. But in order to write the one thesis that I decided should be written, I needed to understand organizational theory.

I dropped writing for a year to read organizational theory. I did that on my own. And when I'd done, I rewrote my thesis very rapidly. My youngest son was then about six or seven months old. I'd put the kids to bed in the evening and about nine o'clock I'd go down to my office in the Institute of Human Development, where I worked as John Clausen's research assistant. I'd write for three hours and then come home. Bill baby-sat. As the custom was in those times, he did not undertake to relieve me of household work or child care to enable me to do my thesis work. And I did not expect him to.

At some point I'd begun struggling out of the falsification of my life, of our lives, that had become so deeply implicated in our relationship and its daily practice. I didn't consciously think like that, but I became preoccupied with the problem that I wasn't at all how I represented myself. Of course I'd no idea who that other was—she was only then struggling into existence—but I could tell who she wasn't and I worked from that. I remember, not long before I finished my thesis and not long before Bill left, being at a dinner party where the host made a sexist joke. I said what I remember as "I'm not going to put up with this kind of shit about women any more" and walked out. Here, too, surfaced that hidden women's movement before the women's movement.

So much of our lives as middle-class women went into keeping the appearance of good marriage, of being right women, of properly dedicated mothers, of pleasure in responding to husband-initiated sex, of being responsible for good relations in the home and with friends and neighbors, of sustaining our children's appearance in school. Like the psychotherapists, we were engaged in this endless chore of trying to produce the perfection of home, marriage, and children that we thought we saw others achieving (we had only to look around us), that we thought could be achieved, and that we thought only we (each one in isolation from others) were failing to achieve. These were the relations that were sustained and ratified in the sociology department. That women weren't encouraged, that some were actively discouraged, that some were actually discarded was an extension of the gender ethos that trapped Bill and me in a relationship that was painful and damaging to both. And he was especially hurt by it, for when he failed the comprehensive exams and I did not, he felt hurt as a man among men.

At some point, somewhere in here, I became committed to the long struggle against this institutional imaginary,[2] though I didn't know at that time I'd made this commitment.

I learned from the student movement and the anti–Vietnam War activities on campus a great deal about that institutional imaginary. Bill and I had picketed to protest the police handling of people demonstrating outside the meetings of the House Un-American Activities Committee in San Francisco. I'd brought my son along, pulling him in a little red wagon as we walked. I was astonished when a car stopped and the driver leaned out to ask me how I could expose my child to such violence. What violence? We were peaceful. The violence there had been yesterday's police attack on the demonstrators outside the committee room. An English friend's arm was broken and she was later deported.

My Berkeley education, the real education I got, was lessons in recognizing—in the society, the university, my life, my marriage, and myself—the institutional imaginary. I came to grasp how I participated in and sustained pretense masquerading as reality and power masquerading as justice and neutrality, and also to understand the difficult but compelling importance of telling the truth. In those times, the solid became insubstantial, see-through. When Chancellor Clark Kerr spoke to the members of the university at the Greek Theatre during the early stages of the Free Speech Movement on campus, his institutional authority had been stripped away. He looked small, diminished, on the platform. Whatever had made the pompous phraseology of such institutional speech credible before, was no longer there. It was vacuous. After the dignitaries had left the platform, Mario Savio walked onto it to take the mike and speak. He was dragged off by campus police. The unveiling of pretensions to reason, justice, and truth as arbitrary power was enacted right there before us.

The university claimed commitment to those values but refused to allow freedom of political speech on campus. What we had thought were the real faces of institutional order turned out to be masks concealing powers and privileges ruthless in their own defense. Though I was not active in the movement—I was already over thirty, was not a citizen (and I'd seen my English friend deported), had a child—I was educated by it. I went to demonstrations, teach-ins, and lectures, and I learned that the received limits on thought, action, and organization that I'd accepted before were just that. It was possible to make things over, do things differently, think differently. Nothing could be taken for granted.

These things worked on what was already at work in me, whatever it was that wanted to come into being. Sylvia Sussman introduced me to the work of R. D. Laing on mental illness. Its preoccupation with authenticity and inauthenticity fascinated me. I don't remember taking it personally then, but it was good for me to think with. Laing wasn't a feminist but he located mental illness and its so-called treatment in relations of established powers and repressions. It must have spoken to me. Using John Clausen's research material on "paths to the mental hospital," I wrote a long paper in which I drew on my own experience of inarticulate misery and of symptomatic behavior as an outcome of being denied effective modes of action. I remembered one night sitting in my nightclothes on the back steps of our home. I wanted desperately to get away but I had nowhere to go. I used this experience as a model of symptomatology. Sitting on the back steps was neither acting on my desire to escape nor refusing to act; I was acting and not acting. What I was doing, however, failed to make ordinary sense. I could see that if my neighbors or the men in the firehouse across the street had seen me sitting there, they'd have thought it strange. It could be read as symptom. Being able to act, so far as others were concerned, only in symptoms would mean that every move to change the situation and escape would be read in a way that invalidated the impulse to change. You'd get further and further out and more disorganized because you'd be cut off from the ordinary feedback of society (I thought). Being treated as "sick" was itself a source of sickness. About this time, I stopped going to male or masculinist psychotherapists.

I think now that this was one step in breaking with the deep inauthenticities that were woven into my life and into my relation with Bill. Of the therapists, mostly men, I remember mainly how hard it was to tell the truth and harder even to be believed. We worked together in their offices to sustain the sacred versions of male and female and marriage as an actual practice in my own. An ever-renewable resource for the therapist since even the practical simulacrum of the sacred forms set up a deep internal war in me. I routinely, and never successfully, worked at repressing that unruly and profoundly selfish me who didn't want to be only for my husband and child. After Bill left, I did go for a while to a therapist of a different kind. She was an Afro-American woman and, I believe, a feminist, though we did not name ourselves so in those days. With her I began to learn my strength as a woman. Age has lost her name to me—much to my regret. I would like to honor her here. I still have the brooch she gave me when our therapy sessions concluded.

I can see now that the anger I experienced when my doctorate was awarded had sources deeper than career frustrations, bitter as these can be. Of course, there had been good things I'd got from teachers and courses. My thinking was transformed by Tamotsu Shibutani's brilliant course on George Herbert Mead; Bernie Cohen's teaching of mathematical sociology and small group research was wonderful (both of them were gone by the time I started on my thesis). And though we'd not much in common as sociologists, John Clausen gave me strong moral and practical support. Yet looking back on the department, I see it as withholding what it might have offered—sustenance and recognition for this oddball woman's passion for the field. Writing my thesis was uphill work, done in loneliness, entirely without support, and against practical and moral odds in my domestic life. But I think that anger came from the deeper insults I hadn't even consciously experienced, the deeper insults of the gender regime preserved by the male faculty of the department that became visible to me only later.

I was struggling slowly to the surface of my life. The great institutional imaginary I contended with was, of course, written thoroughly into sociology. And as I worked blindly away, being changed and changing, my discomfort with the discipline grew. My intellectual pleasures that had earlier enchanted me did so no longer. The world I encountered every day and night in the ordinary ways I went about in, didn't seem to be present in sociology. Even when it was addressed, it seemed to disappear. I was moved by Noam Chomsky's call for intellectuals to tell the truth. I wanted sociology to tell the truth, but I came to think that it didn't know how. The realities of people's daily lives were beyond anything sociology could speak of. Fix it, I thought. I imagined I would do this, though I didn't know how. Some have thought it not worth fixing.

During all this, I went on thinking a great deal about sociology. It ran through my life like the stream that then ran through the Berkeley campus—sometimes full of life and energy, sometimes almost dry, but constant. I became preoccupied with sociology's strange divorce from the local actuality of people's lives. When I was taking a course in sociological methods (mainly survey analysis), we did practice interviews. I interviewed in the "flats" of Berkeley. I thought it somehow odd that the interview topics had nothing to do with our respondents' lives; that sociology would use what people told us to speak somewhere else entirely; that it never had anything to say about what was going on in Berkeley, about the sharp racial divisions that were so visible on the flats and between the flats and the upwardly mobile hillside. How come sociology didn't talk about the world people knew as they lived it?

I would walk across campus with my young son, under the great gum trees, following the stream—a kind of underground life where the dogs went on with their doggy lives alongside ours—and wonder about the lack of connection between the everyday world and the sociology of the classrooms and the books.

Dorothy E. Smith

———

55

I thought something could be done about this. I didn't know what. When I finish my dissertation, I thought, I'm going to find a way of doing sociology differently.

It seems to me now like a child's story. My image comes from *Alice in Wonderland*: a wanderer in a world that isn't hers, being the wrong size—sometimes amazingly enlarged, and sometimes minute—always somehow out of whack with the proper dimensions of what and who were around me. Not connecting properly. But lacking Alice's confidence in the rectitude of her own consciousness. Or her being able simply to walk away from it all unchanged, from dream into waking life. I was changed. And changing myself. A ten-year struggle with everything I'd learned how to be, how to think, how to see, and how to value began then and was the beginning, in me, of the women's movement. I thought at that time that I was alone. And indeed I went through these changes by myself. But in writing this I am learning that my individual trajectory was a dialogue with and within an extraordinary political process, a late—and it now sometimes seems final—coming-to-fruit of the Enlightenment. For me as for many others at that time, change was in ourselves as much as in what was going on in the society, not a matter of doctrine or conviction, but a reshaping of self that was necessarily political and a politics necessarily expressing who we were becoming.

Acknowledgment: This essay was written while I was visiting scholar at the Center for the Study of Women in Society, University of Oregon. I'm deeply appreciative of the sanctuary it provided.—D.E.S.

Notes

1. His own work, *Asylums* (New York: Aldine, 1962), had transformed thinking on mental hospitals.

2. This term, as used in contemporary cultural theory, has a force that connotes more than "masquerade." It introduces the notion of what goes on at an unconscious level outside the scope of reason.

Chapter 5

Becoming an Ethnographer

SHERRI CAVAN

This is the story of how I became an ethnographer. It is a story about marginality, some extraordinary experiences of everyday life, some phenomenal bad luck, some inexplicable good luck. It is about the tension between the bohemian and the bourgeois ways of life, relationships between home and school, parents and children, men and women; how cultural scripts are written and rewritten, how socialization to sex roles does or does not take place, the reproduction of mothering, second shifts—and other things as well. It is limited by memory, space, and the ethnographer's eternal dilemma: What must be told if an adequate account is to be rendered?

Before Berkeley: 1938–61

I began in New York, the only child of a petite bourgeoisie Jewish family. My parents migrated to California during World War II in search of new opportunities to make a fortune and fulfill their vision of the American Dream, intensified by the crash of the stock market and the Great Depression.

What I knew about being Jewish was nothing. Ancestors had migrated from the Middle East to Eastern Europe and then to America, where, in varied couplings aboard ship and in the Boston Fish Market, they mingled their respective cultural traditions along with their genes. By the time my parents were born, in the early years of the twentieth century, their families spoke only English, and they practiced a version of secular humanism that involved no ritual or ceremony other than lighting a candle for the dead on High Holidays. After my mother died, not even that was done.

I had my own personal lesson about being Jewish when I was six years old. (I already knew about anti-Semitism and the victimization of Jews in Europe.) One day I went to the corner store. "Jew girl!" the clerk said, "Come here and smell this." He held out an open bottle of ammonia. The fumes brought torrents of tears to my eyes and permanently impaired my sense of smell. But hideous and abusive as that experience was, I never told my parents.

We lived in a garage that had been converted into an apartment during the housing shortages of the war. It was on the edge of a light manufacturing district, upwind of the oil wells of Signal Hill. My bedroom was next to the kitchen, behind a makeshift partition. At night I heard my parents talking about "Jews" and "anti-Semitism" in muffled and sometimes incomprehensible words. I knew the grocer's "Jew girl" was derogatory. I worried that if people knew we were Jews, the Gestapo would come to our house. Even more, I worried that if my parents thought I was in danger, they would take away my independence as a latchkey child.

Fifteen years later, working on a master's thesis at UCLA, I would return to the question of Jewish identity: how it is socially constructed and the disjunctions between public knowledge and private secrets. But as a child I was merely adventurous, curious, and secretive. I had a private life.

In Long Beach, my mother managed a millinery shop, my father was a salesman—of insurance, appliances, real estate—in complex "deals" that he expected would make him a fortune at any minute. I was enrolled in an elementary school a block from home; the store my mother managed was about a mile away. Though anti-Semitism lurked in the shadows, there was little violent imagery on the airwaves, no television except for the rich. As a port city, Long Beach was subject to a variety of cosmopolitan influences brought by shipping and the navy. But it was still a small town, and I was free to explore it.

My early sex role socialization was as deficient as my religious education. My mother had worked for as long as I could remember. I knew from those muffled kitchen conversations that she was the one who brought in a steady income; for my father, it was feast or famine. He was often indisposed, subject to various undiagnosed ailments that exempted him from looking for work, from household chores, and from leisure outings. If things got done, Mom did them. I had no brothers or sisters, cousins or near relatives to compare and contrast. My mother loved to sew for me and to dress me in ruffled velvet, but I was on my own much of the time, dressed casually in sneakers, jeans, and a T-shirt (the kind of clothing I am still wearing as I write these words, forty-five years later). I grew up thinking of myself neither as male nor as female. Much of my youthful activity reflected that uncorrected view. At ages seven, eight, and nine, often on my own, I would pack a large handbag with a favorite doll or two, a toy tea set, and a book (*Mutiny on the Bounty* and *Tarzan of the Apes* were favorites), a peanut butter sandwich, and set out for Signal Hill. Climbing to the first platform of one of the abandoned oil derricks (rarely further), I would take out my dollies and my doilies, read and play house, ironically oblivious to the odor of petroleum that I now find so offensive.

After school and on Saturdays (since Mom worked six days a week), I roamed through the alleys of the manufacturing district by circuitous routes that avoided the corner grocery store. These alleys provided a cornucopia of discarded objects that I took home and used to build dollhouses, ships, or a city of cardboard box houses perched on bed-pillow hills, surrounding a dishpan lake full of sailboats made of walnut shells, popsicle sticks, and bubble gum. I might play with my dog or spy through people's windows. I liked being home alone.

Two other places near home were important in those formative pre-pubescent years. One was the Long Beach public library, an imposing neoclassical building set in a lush green park, ringed by a farmers' market on Tuesdays and Saturdays. I liked school well enough, but school meant assignments, and the library was à la carte. The library had open stacks, and the librarians let me browse and check out books from the adult section, even when I was too young to do so under library rules. I read all of Nordhoff and Hall along with Edgar Rice Burrows; much of Steinbeck and a lot of Hemingway. Often, I went to the library after school and then to Mom's shop just before she closed up at 6:00 P.M. We would walk home together to fix dinner. Once we even took a cab. (That was really living!)

The second influential place in my childhood was the Pike, a shoddy amusement pier on the waterfront where, from 1944 to 1948, one could ride on a huge wooden roller coaster (although I didn't) or visit tattoo parlors, gambling rooms, and one of the last remaining public freak shows. I did not always tell my parents where I spent the afternoon. Indeed, I would often stop by the library, check out a book, and head directly to the backstage area of the freak show, where I enjoyed the company of contortionists, dwarfs, a fat lady and a very skinny man, a bearded lady, dwarf albino twins (sometimes made up to look like they were Siamese), two men with flippers for arms, and a black woman with an extra leg and foot growing between her hip and groin. In the summer time, especially, her protuberance was uncomfortable, and I would bring her talcum powder to ease the discomfort. In return, she taught me to knit. I ran errands, shared my library books, and generally hung out, listening to their insightful observations about the world and making whatever contributions I could from my ten-year-old perspective. Later, I understood these experiences as a subculture of outsiders. But at an age when I was still discovering everyday life, the freak show was normal.

Evenings, my parents often went to the Pike to play poker and low-ball in the gambling rooms, hoping to strike it rich and be freed from their oppressive (although not squalid) conditions to enjoy a more respectable (i.e., bourgeois) way of life. Sometimes I stayed home alone, sometimes I went with them, bringing my books, sitting or sleeping on plastic couches with bent chrome arms and legs. Sometimes I went to visit my friends at the Tent, as it was euphemistically called, and my parents would pick me up there when they were ready to go home.

When I was almost twelve, my mother died very suddenly, and my life changed dramatically. Long before, my father had severed relationships with everyone in his family except his unmarried older sister in New York, whose presence was felt through her airmail letters. Their arrival inevitably caused bitter conflicts between my parents sitting at the kitchen table in the evening after I went to bed. When my mother died, my father cut off relations with my mother's family as well. He referred to my mother's mother as "that foreign woman" (his own mother having been born in Boston) and only grudgingly invited my grandmother to California for the funeral service. After my mother's funeral, I never saw my grandmother again.

I was a motherless child in the company of a madman father, an angry, frustrated man whose sometimes diabolical schemes to achieve the American Dream never succeeded. His failures only made him more angry. We moved away from the old neighborhood into an apartment complex across town. My father was physically and psychologically abusive, openly boasting of his plans to assault me sexually. I taunted him and practiced various versions of contempt. At night I constructed makeshift alarms to wake me if he tried to enter my room. My escape from home was school, where I immersed myself. Six years later I left home permanently, enrolling as a freshman at the University of California, Los Angeles.

Getting there had taken a Herculean effort. No one in my father's family had completed high school. He himself had not gone past the sixth grade, and could not see why I should do so. My mother's five brothers had all gone to the university and some to medical and law schools. But my mother's father had prohibited her any education beyond high school because she was a daughter and not a son. My father insisted that if the two of us put our differences aside and our brains together, we could make a fortune. Who needs college? Still, I wanted to go, and finally, with the aid of two small scholarships and my father's promise of fifty dollars a month (sent more or less faithfully until I married two years later), I left for UCLA. In one of his rare gestures of affection, he offered to drive me to Los Angeles, and he did—no forgotten appointment, no vague chest pains.

In Los Angeles, I immediately fell in with what was known as a fast crowd, mostly Muslim students from Saudi Arabia and the Sudan who were studying subtropical horticulture or filmmaking and living a life unthinkable at home—dating Jewesses and drinking brandy. By the end of my freshman year, my grades were so bad that I lost both of my scholarships and was forced to take stock of my life. I needed stability and I thought marriage might be the answer. After all, this was the fifties, with its explicit prohibitions of sex outside of marriage and its implicit promise of marriage and family as the solution to existential angst.

I met my husband at one of the international student dances, though it turned out he too was from Long Beach, not foreign but exotic —Mexican and Filipino—beautiful, a graceful dancer, well-traveled, romantic.

I had a lot of sexual energy and having a steady date helped. I lived at the Co-op, worked in the library, and brought my grades up. Despite the protestations of my father, horrified by Phil's ethnicity, we were married at the start of my junior, his senior year. Our son was born at the end of the spring semester.

The year before Adam's birth was full of young married student activities. We were involved with the Council for Mexican American Education. We spent time in the barrios of East Los Angeles encouraging Hispanic youths to think about college, registering voters, drinking tequila, dancing to "La Bamba." I was majoring in international relations, Phil in business administration. We met some sociology students who told us about ideas like "social order," "scientific revolution," and "the rules of the sociological method." Young and idealistic, we changed our majors and thought we would change the world.

After Adam's birth in 1958, everything changed in our personal world. Unplanned (though well timed), I had the summer to deal with the amazing fact that I was a mother; I had a baby—neither a doll nor a dog. This was real. I also had a marriage that began to unravel as my husband faced his homosexuality in the days before the Stonewall demonstration made gay liberation a social movement rather than a dilemma of individual identity.

My father's checks had stopped when Phil and I married, but thanks to Phil's GI bill benefits, the part-time jobs we both had in the library, and later to my teaching assistantship, we managed to stay financially afloat. Interpersonally, we did not fare so well. We had devastating scenes and there were ongoing recriminations. Phil left for San Francisco. I stayed on in our tiny apartment in the veteran's housing complex with a baby, a job, and a semester's worth of term papers. When a lover from anthropology moved in, my mother-in-law reported me to the police. Still, it wasn't much more insane than my version of life with father. In spite of everything, I managed to finish my senior year (1959) and complete my master's (1961).

I had done well as a student of Harold Garfinkel, whose unique perspective of ethnomethodology made sense of my freak show childhood. Garfinkel introduced me to the phenomenology of Alfred Schutz (most memorably his essay "On Making Music Together"), the prodigious writings of Talcott Parsons, and the interactional framework of Erving Goffman. Garfinkel had no idea of my family situation other than that I occasionally showed up at his office with a plump, curly-haired baby on one hip and a bookbag on the other. He encouraged me to continue graduate work at either Harvard or Berkeley and promised to write letters of recommendation for me.

Harvard seemed far too bourgeois for my bohemian tastes. Besides, Phil had been writing and telephoning. While he wanted his independence, he also wanted his family, and I wanted that, too. Going to Berkeley would allow me to study with Erving Goffman and salvage my marriage as well. Or so I thought when I packed books, dishes, diapers, and plants into a Volkswagen bug, strapped the baby in his car seat, and started north on Highway 1. Twenty-three years old, I had been accepted to the Berkeley Ph.D. program in sociology for the fall semester 1961.

At Berkeley: 1961–65

These were heady years both for me and for society. While we started with naive enthusiasm, within four years, harsh, violent realities would be exposed.

Living in San Francisco; taking classes at Berkeley; working in the Behavioral and Social Science Project at the School of Public Health; being student, wife, and mother; knitting, reading murder mysteries— these were the major axes of my life. The murder mysteries were a respite from fieldwork. They described another world, complete and wrapped up, an antidote to the incomplete, partially documented world that I was struggling to describe as a fledgling ethnographer. But knitting was my ultimate escape. In that minute world, circumscribed by two stitches, one a variant of the other, complex designs emerged from the methodical application of attention, stress, and relaxation. It was a form of meditation I had learned backstage at the freak show as a child. I did a lot of knitting.

In San Francisco, Phil and I had mostly gay friends. We lived a demi-monde kind of life evenings and weekends. By day, Phil worked for the State Department of Employment; Adam was tended at the nursery school down the street. I drove to Berkeley to South Hall (now demolished), a beautiful Victorian building full of buttery, smooth-grained wood, badly scarred by partitions and fluorescent lights. This was the physical space the sociology department occupied, where students, faculty, and staff, coming and going, created a sense of "department."

I applied for, and received, a predoctoral fellowship with the Behavioral Science Project at the School of Public Health, directed by Andie Knutsen, who taught in the psychology department. Knutsen filled the offices of the building that had been the Odd Fellows Hall in the twenties with scholars from anthropology, sociology, and psychology. There, in the name of public health, we were encouraged to apply the theories we read about to the lives of people in the everyday world. Under his sponsorship and encouragement, I proposed to study "normal" drinking behavior by observing what people did in bars, cocktail lounges, taverns, saloons, and nightclubs. I read almost everything that had been written on these social institutions from historical and cross-cultural perspectives, then spent more than two years making observations in one hundred licensed establishments in San Francisco. I learned to make notes in a systematic fashion, to organize observations into conceptual categories, to see relationships between the categories, and between categories and theories: I spent my time learning empirically grounded inductive reasoning.

My association with Harold Garfinkel served as an introduction to Erving Goffman and the bright, passionate graduate students who had gathered around him in his early years at Berkeley: Harvey Sacks, Emmanuel Schegloff, Marvin Scott, Carl Werthman, David Sudnow, Roy Turner, occasionally Jackie Wiseman and Joan Emerson. Jackie is the only one of them with whom I developed a lasting friendship, though not until years after graduate school, when we were both teaching at San Francisco State University.

My gang was mainly guys, and frequently there was as much sexual tension as there was intellectual excitement. We tore into ideas in classes with Goffman and David Matza and Jerome Skolnick, the bright new faculty of the early sixties. In Sunday seminars that we organized at Harvey's apartment, we questioned the meaning of ordinary talk, the ways meaning was constructed and value allocated, the rules by which the social order made itself visible to the social actor and the observer, who is perforce outside the action. These were intense experiences. They influenced me profoundly.

When I first arrived at the sociology department, I requested that the statistics requirement be waived, arguing that I had completed equivalent material at UCLA. Naively, I ignored the paperwork necessary to record that initial permission. I discovered the omission four years later when I filed to be advanced to Ph.D. candidacy. "That's it," I thought. "I'm about to be swept out of the refuge of the ivory tower and onto the streets." Armed with my UCLA notebooks, I made an appointment with Hanan Selvin to explain my dilemma. He reviewed my notebooks— William Robinson's lectures all neatly typed; excerpts from assigned readings, integrated where relevant; artistic little charts and graphs— and told me that though I had not covered all the topics he taught, I demonstrated considerable command of the subject and he would waive requirements in my case. He made sure that I filed the correct forms. Selvin's generosity made a deep impression on me. As a teacher, I have tried to follow his example and extend special consideration when I can.

The language requirements were another obstacle. Representatives of the sociology department agreed that I would be exempted from the statistics requirements, but no one would accept the results of the foreign language exams I had passed at UCLA only after four tries. Herbert Blumer read my Berkeley Spanish exams; he made me take them three times. It seemed a minor miracle that I passed French on the first try. I remember going to Goffman's office to find out the results of the French exam he had read. "You passed," he said, adding, "but just barely." On top of that, I had studied two romance languages, prohibited by the rules, which were, thankfully, not enforced in my case. I was barely slipping by.

At home, everything was deteriorating. The marriage I had expected to save was going from bad to terrible. From the first time he had almost thrown me off the balcony of our Los Angeles apartment until the last time I barricaded a room in fear of being beaten or worse, I was constantly afraid of making Phil angry, an emotion that could be engendered by something as innocuous as a late dinner or being too quick to express an opinion. Under similar circumstances I had left my father's house. Now, however, I had a child, and it was hard to believe I could make it on my own. Eventually—like many other women in my position—I came to realize what I had to do, and I filed for divorce. But before that I coped with my situation by developing a second persona— an invisible woman. I found walls I could lean against and conversations I could overhear without needing to express an opinion. I learned to be *in* a social setting but not of it. This invisibility gave me a role in the various gay scenes Phil frequented, supporting the illusion that we were a couple. It also was the characteristic role of the participant-observer.

Always looking for a term paper topic, I transformed some of these observations into a small seminar paper for Goffman. David Sudnow published it in 1963 in an exciting issue of the *Berkeley Journal of Sociology,* where words like "ethnomethodology" and "conversational analysis" were bandied about. The paper, "Interaction in Home Territories," addressed the methods by which private definitions of exclusivity ("home territory") were superimposed on public space, and in particular how ordinary bars were transformed into gay bars.

Expanding my observations from gay bars to bars in general, I began my dissertation. I became a denizen of licensed public drinking places and after-hour establishments. It was the world of the Tenderloin and Skid Row, as well as the Top of the Mark and the neighborhood tavern. I explored sexual marketplaces, bars that fenced stolen goods, bars where drugs other than alcohol were sold and used, where drunks lurched for various parts of my anatomy, fights were occasional, and guns sometimes flashed. It was a world of easy camaraderie, witty conversation, entertainment, banality, and danger. Socialized by my childhood experiences at the Pike, I never gave my safety a second thought, although Goffman was impressed with my adventurous character, and the other guys in the department were a little impressed as well.

Erving made me promise not to get arrested and become an embarrassment to the university. He recommended that I take a fieldwork course in the anthropology department, taught by George Foster (which I did), and then left me alone to discover ethnography as I attempted to practice it. Fortunately, I had plenty of training for independence. Indeed, for a latchkey kid, it was the perfect existence.

How did I manage motherhood? Well, I had only one child, a good-natured, cooperative kid, so when he was still portable, I took him along to class (to be left with a secretary or a willing graduate student). When he was a preschooler, I took him to bars where he was cooed over by transvestites and earned silver dollars for busing dishes. When he was seven and eight, I occasionally left him alone, as I had been left alone as a child, with a list of telephone numbers in case of emergency and some money for food. It hardly fit the ideal image of motherhood, but it certainly reproduced my own mothering.

Of sisterhood I knew little. Before my mother's death, she, the women she worked with, and occasional visits from my grandmother created a world from which men were excluded. These were strong women who worked six days a week, nine and ten hours a day, then went home to domestic chores. At Mom's shop, I tried on hats and posed in front of the mirror, listening to women talk about their husbands' abuse, how they were deprecated and degraded by the men in their lives, secrets they hid in mixed company. After my mother's death, there were no women in my home life. My father banished my grandmother, so my world consisted of him, his friends, and his business associates—sleazy, greasy guys whom I avoided like the plague. Occasionally, my father brought a woman home for a night or a week or a month, situations more awkward than enlightening. Sometimes, he left a name and a phone number where he could be reached if anyone called with a deal. He did not remarry until after I left home, so there was not even a stepmother to learn from or bond with.

My mother-in-law was a mystical Mexican woman with exquisite taste in furniture and flowers. She taught me to garden and to appreciate objects that had a history, but we were never close. Sometimes I was afraid of her (as young brides often are); sometimes I found her foolish. I was learning about the scientific method; she lived in a world of magic. I wanted to live as a bohemian; she had more bourgeois aspirations.

However, throughout my youth and into those early years at the university, there were always models of self-supporting, independent women, even though they were the exception rather than the rule. While I had no female professors of sociology at either Berkeley or UCLA during the years 1955–65, women with Ph.D.s held appointments in various other departments. From 1959 to 1961, I worked as a research assistant for Eleanor Sheldon, a Ph.D. in sociology, who headed a research grant on the evaluation of treatments for mental illness. However, her academic appointment was in the School of Nursing. Similarly, Miriam Morris, also a sociology Ph.D., held an appointment in the UCLA School of Education. At Berkeley, Gertrude Selznick was always a significant force in the backstage region of the department, but I had no opportunity to work with her until years later, when we were both involved with the Pacific Sociological Association. The presence of professional women was felt only indirectly in those years.

In the underground world of the San Francisco gay subculture in the early sixties, the ideas and practices of men and women were tangled, tormented, diverse; sometimes perverse, often witty, always arch. I had not learned the conventional scripts for "femininity" as a child, and certainly was not being socialized to conventional norms in this new environment. I improvised my way through graduate school, noticing that my behavior was different from the guys' only when I had to get home to domestic chores that the others' wives were doing. At that point, "second shift" was an unquestioned assumption of my life.

Being female affected my chances as a sociologist, of course, as when I applied for a job at San Francisco State University. Although my qualifications were respectable and fit their needs exactly, I was ranked fourth, behind three male candidates. In this case, however, being in last place was not disastrous. Always in a state of financial crisis, the university could not get a commitment on funds for the position until late in the spring, and by then, all the male candidates had accepted jobs elsewhere. I began as a tenure-track assistant professor in 1965, the first woman in that department. In the next few years, the number of women in my department grew; by 1975, almost 50 percent of the tenure-track positions were filled by women.

The changing demographics of my department reflected the changing beliefs in the larger society. While working women had been the exception in my childhood, they were now coming to be the rule. While I had no women professors as instructors at UCLA or at Berkeley, now women were bringing a new perspective to the discipline, revealing the biases of gender that had been taken for granted a few years earlier.

Beyond Berkeley

San Francisco State University was the ideal place for me. It was in the city of my childhood dreams, where gingerbread houses perched on rolling hills like the toy cities I used to make with boxes and pillows and a dishpan for my boats. The lake represented by the dishpan turned out to be the Bay. Second, San Francisco State was more laid back than Berkeley, less competitive, less driven. I could have a life beyond academia, gardening and knitting and, eventually, sculpting. I could follow my own research interests without having to consider whether they were fundable, without ever having to write a grant proposal. So when the hippies appeared in my neighborhood, I could study how they articulated a unique ideology and the trials and tribulations they had in self-consciously applying those beliefs to their everyday lives, without having to convince a review committee that an ethnographic analysis of an emergent counterculture was a worthwhile project. When Watergate appeared on the front page of my newspaper, I could investigate the relationships of the beliefs and practices of the ruling class as well as how history and biography interconnect, without needing to prove that my credentials as an ethnographer of deviant practices of the counterculture certified me as competent to study the political elite.

Divorced, with one child, a dilapidated Victorian house and an unruly dog, I was saved by the fact that school and work were the same. School had always been a refuge, an escape—the ivory tower—and now I was in the fortunate circumstances of being able to support myself and my child, pay off a mortgage, and even afford a professional trainer for the dog. I was promoted to associate professor in 1969 and full professor in 1974. Without conscious design, I had drifted into a very bourgeois way of life unlike either my petite bourgeoisie origins or my bohemian aspirations.

The student-faculty strike at San Francisco State University (1968–69) provided an opportunity to rekindle my political consciousness and reassess my priorities. I turned my research interests away from the outsiders, the disenfranchised and the discredited, toward those of power and influence, those who make and enforce the rules and images that comprise the dominant culture. I also went back to school, taking classes in fiber art and ceramic sculpture, hanging out with artists, eschewing the conventional.

All of these experiences are old ones, yet here I sit writing about them at the same desk where I wrote my first lectures and worked on my first research projects. I have stayed in the same job and the same house, which I continue to restore at about the same rate it deteriorates. Like my house, my neighborhood in the Haight Ashbury has undergone various transformations from the working-class, ethnically diverse neighborhood it was when I was a graduate student at Berkeley. Now,

there are aging hippies, nouveau hippies, up-and-coming professionals, established celebrities, artists, musicians, radical office workers, punks with pierced nipples, a sizable homeless population, and a continuous parade of tourists from all over the world, including contingents of middle-aged (mostly) men telling their adolescent children where they did what, way back when. Given my childhood, I feel right at home in this milieu of urban diversity, like a small town as Federico Fellini might conceive it, not unlike the Pike of my childhood.

My son is grown, his things stored in my basement while he lives in Tokyo working in the computer industry. His father, now retired, lives in London. How dispersed is that nuclear family of graduate school days. How international, too. I have traveled to Africa, the Middle East, South America, the Caribbean, the American Southwest. Once I sat in the cafeteria at the Greyhound Bus Depot in Long Beach, a smalltown adolescent yearning to be a cosmopolitan world traveler; now I have a ticket to Bali and Java, with a return via Japan.

So what can be made of this fragment of the life of one of the women with a Berkeley Ph.D.? Much has been omitted from this account— some of it forgotten, some too complex to fit the time and space, some not clearly relevant.

I came to graduate school at Berkeley preformed by a variety of experiences, some from childhood, some from UCLA. Many of these were unique (not everyone gets a chance to hang out in the backstage of a freak show); some were quite common (many women are abused by fathers and husbands). I arrived at Berkeley at a historic time—the early sixties. The entire social order was beginning a tremendous upheaval. The week before my oral exams, President Kennedy was assassinated and my son came down with the chicken pox. As if that were not enough, my husband had invited friends for Thanksgiving and the rest of the weekend as well. At my exams the week before, Herbert Blumer, the chair, had told me that the committee had "magnanimously" agreed to pass me, although I had not done as well as they expected. I felt an abject failure and would have thrown myself off the Bay Bridge on my way home if I had not had so many other things on my mind—a sick child, a turkey dinner, a dead president. Between the concerns of home and school there was a fine line, and I felt I was balancing on it in a precarious fashion.

The optimistic person who had driven up Highway 1 on her way to graduate school was not the dejected person driving across the Bay Bridge after her exams; the Bay Bridge person was a rough draft of the rather contented author of this piece. Graduate work gave me the opportunity to make school my profession. At Berkeley, my professors and the other students I hung out with gave a special cast to the creation that was part me, part them, part the historic time.

Chapter 6

Gold and Blue
in California

KATHRYN P. MEADOW ORLANS

In the language of Sign, "California" is made by placing the tip of the extended third finger on an ear lobe and twisting the hand quickly away from the face, representing a gold earring from the Gold Rush. For me, California was golden indeed: golden poppies, the Golden Gate bridge, golden years for my children growing up, and in 1967, a gold and blue doctoral hood worn in a University of California convocation. But California was also blue-gray summer fog until noon, blue anxiety about graduate school requirements, my daughter's psychiatric hospitalization, a broken marriage.

That California story began in a somewhat unlikely setting: Joplin, Missour-uh, Gateway to the Ozarks, home to chat piles and Bonnie and Clyde. I was the older of two daughters of a rock-solid, middle-class, Republican, Protestant church-going couple. Electrical engineer father and homemaker mother were both graduates of the University of Oklahoma. My maternal grandparents were homesteaders on a farm where they often saw cotton destroyed before picking and wheat prices drop after a good harvest. When her husband died in the 1916 flu epidemic, that grandmother moved to Norman, where her two daughters earned degrees. She supported them by sewing and washing clothes for neighbors. My mother never used her teaching credential because Dad had to be the sole breadwinner—or suffer permanent damage to his ego. Bad enough that he had no sons, that I found fishing a bore and was afraid of guns.

Dad's family, the Pendletons, sneered at Mother's humble background. His mother, née Miss Lucia Freeman, had packed her lace tablecloth and mahogany whatnot into a covered wagon when Grandfather set off for the Oklahoma Territory. Grandmother Pendleton became the grande dame of Talala (population fifty, halfway between Tulsa and Nowata), where she lived to be 103.

As a child, I spent a lot of time reading (the Oz books, the Five Little Peppers, Nancy Drew); I enjoyed early fame as editor of the Joplin High yearbook and acclaim as a character actress in school plays. One legacy of my mother's education was the assumption that I would also go to college, and in 1947 I made a dramatic escape from Joplin by going East to school: Denison University in Granville, Ohio. At last, my chance to become an urbane sophisticate.

Indeed, Denison provided a good undergraduate experience. Paul Bennett gave tough but encouraging critiques of creative writing efforts; Ed Wright ran a top-rated theater department, training Hal Holbrook and other successful actors (he was astute enough to discourage my thespian aspirations); Juanita Kreps (later U.S. Secretary of Commerce) gave us a lucid introduction to Keynesian economics; Leonard Downs assigned Eliot, Pound, Joyce, Stein; two years of Denison French got me through the Berkeley Ph.D. language exam.

But it was Kenneth Underwood, in my sophomore year, who set me on the road that led to California Gold. A Yale Divinity School graduate with a strong social action approach to social science, he drew up a syllabus for the core course that included a varied assortment of primary sources from sociology, political science, social philosophy, labor economics. Term papers and exams required synthesizing an enormous range of material. It was my most demanding and exciting course. Among the readings were several community studies. *Middletown* (1929) was a revelation, the Lynds might have been describing Joplin. By my junior year I had married sociology, for better or worse.

It seemed that it might have been for worse when, about to graduate and needing a job, I found that the best offer was a secretarial position. A Denison sociology professor suggested graduate study at Columbia or the University of Chicago. My parents agreed to help and Denison provided a fellowship. New York seemed too foreign so I applied to Chicago and enrolled in 1951. My plan: a master's degree, then a job.

With a Denison friend, who had earlier transferred to the university,

I rented an apartment. Daughter of Chicago genetics professor Sewell Wright, Betty had visited my home during Denison school holidays and thought my parents concerned and warm, a wonderful contrast to her own. (Mine were actually quite reserved, rarely expressing any strong feelings.) I understood her view better when I read a story about her father in the Chicago alumni magazine. Going from his laboratory to a classroom one day, he had absent-mindedly carried a guinea pig under his arm. In class, needing to erase something from the blackboard, he retrieved the little animal and wiped the slate clean. No wonder he seemed to pay little attention to his children!

Betty introduced me to her many friends, mostly students in economics, geography, and city planning, some in psychology and anthropology. One of them became my first serious boyfriend, whom I married soon after receiving my degree.

I was caught up in the campus atmosphere, intimidated by the political, social, and sexual liberation, awed by the intellectual sophistication of late night discussions over beer at Jimmy's where a copy of the *Encyclopedia Britannica,* kept behind the bar, was used to settle disputes.

I had enrolled in a full program, never thinking I might take more than a year to get a master's. The lectures and class discussions were at the same high level as the informal conversations. While this was exciting, I remained quiet, certain that my feeble ideas were better left unsaid. Afraid of incomplete grades, I turned in every paper and, to my never-ending surprise, got As for most.

Some of the great Chicago sociologists taught those courses. Everett Hughes's sociology of work and Louis Wirth's urban sociology were favorites. Herbert Blumer's theory course was simply over my head, but I struggled in an attempt to understand George Herbert Mead, however difficult. Albert Reiss taught research methods. In nine weeks under Reiss, we designed a project on urban friendship patterns, constructed the interview schedule, drew a geographical sample, interviewed respondents, analyzed the data, and wrote a report—Awesome.

Electives were devoted to anthropology. Robert Redfield's lectures were disappointing but others were exciting. Still intrigued by community studies, I took two courses from "Mr. Yankee City," W. Lloyd Warner. He and William Henry taught together, assigning team projects on which three to five students were to collaborate. I petitioned to do an independent paper because the other members of my group wanted to take an incomplete grade. There were many students who had started in the lab school, continued in the college, were reluctant to finish a course, and seemed prepared to stay forever, imparting a strange flavor of eternity to the campus. Reluctant to be weaned from Chicago, they apprenticed to a professor for five, seven, even eight years.

I was among the student interviewers that Warner and Henry hired for their market research. Weekends, we rang doorbells and induced householders to report on their favorite brands of coffee and laundry soap. For a shy person, this was not the world's best job, and I soon shifted to coding at the National Opinion Research Center.

In addition to nine courses and the comprehensive exam, a thesis was required for the master's degree. In the spring, Louis Wirth met with students to outline topics for thesis projects with various community agencies. One possibility was a study of residents displaced by an urban redevelopment project, enlarging Michael Reese Hospital. I couldn't wait to claim this one since I was certain that everyone would want it. To my surprise, no one else was interested. Wirth was faculty sponsor for the thesis but the hospital's director of planning, Reginald Isaacs, was de facto adviser.

Locating and interviewing 120 former residents of the four-square-block site was an enormous task. The interviews took me to some highly unsavory slums as well as public housing projects. Once, while I was studying a street map in a tough neighborhood, a policeman tapped on my car window. "What do you think you're doing here?" "I'm a UC student interviewing for a research project." "Whose car is this?" "My boyfriend's." "Does he know where you are?" "Yes, he does." "Well, I want you to leave and don't come back down here. It's too dangerous." That time I was glad to be sent home. Isaacs had tried to persuade me not to interview alone; with uncharacteristic stubbornness, I persisted.

Eventually, after I had fallen behind schedule, I recognized that the project was too complex for one person. Another student, Howard Heller, became my partner, and we submitted a coauthored thesis. Before it was completed, Wirth died, and Joseph Lohman, a criminologist later elected Cook County sheriff, replaced him as faculty sponsor.

In December 1952, eighteen months after entering the program and six months behind schedule, I received a master's degree in sociology. Within a month, I married Lloyd Meadow and took a job with the Chicago Land Clearance Commission; within a year, I had the first of our two children and retired. So much for the rewards of a graduate degree. I gave not a single thought to the possibility that someone other than their mother might take care of my children so that I might pursue a career.

In 1954, Lloyd's new job took us to Detroit, where we lived in a neighborhood called Russell Woods. When black families began to move in,

I became active in a local association organized to maintain racial integration and discourage whites from fleeing to the suburbs. This led to a job with sociologist Richard Kerckhoff in the Merrill-Palmer Institute's community studies program. With my daughter in first grade and my son ready for nursery school, I was glad to escape the tedium of full-time housework. With a half-time appointment, my work schedule coincided with the children's school hours.

I designed a study of neighborhood cohesion in racially changing Highland Park, trained interviewers, analyzed the data, and published two journal articles, feeling like an untrained neophyte, an imposter among professional researchers. Fortunately, the project was completed on time because in June 1962 my husband accepted a faculty position at San Francisco State College. With our children (Lynn was eight and Rob, five), we set off for the Bay Area.

The first year, I worked part-time as a researcher with the Oakland Greater Cities Project, a federally funded program designed to improve conditions for inner-city residents. Then, with great trepidation, I enrolled in the Berkeley sociology department in 1963 to do the further graduate work that seemed necessary if I were to continue to conduct my own research. On-the-job training, always expected, never materialized. Also, Lloyd convinced me a Ph.D. would mean a better job that would help with the children's college expenses. His view of a working wife contrasted markedly with my father's.

The first semester, I took the required courses—theory, methods, statistics. Wanting to add something contemporary, I applied for Nathan Glazer's seminar on poverty. He said it "wouldn't be very good." I persisted. After asking about my work experience, he said, "You probably know more about this than I do. Anyway, I'm not really a sociologist." Having read several of his books, including one on urban housing, I was puzzled and unconvinced.

Reluctantly, he signed me up for the seminar, and I began immediately to worry about the oral presentation. As I hurried out the door on the scheduled night, my six-year-old baseball fan shouted, "I hope you win, Mommy!" For me, to "win" was to complete the course. The paper analyzing the Oakland project as a failed antipoverty program got an A, but I assumed the absence of comments meant that it had no merit. Two years later, however, Glazer asked if I had published it. The question astonished me and I wondered why he had not suggested publication earlier. Berkeley faculty seldom offered suggestions about publications, jobs, or careers. Even the entering graduate students enjoyed more professional socialization at Chicago.

By the end of my first year, I was engrossed in new ideas, reading, friends, conversation. A group of women students met often after classes, discussing theory and methods: Nancy Achilles, Shirley Hartley, Kathleen Herman, Connie Holstein, Lucy Sells, Metta Spencer, Mely Tan, Mary Taylor, Sister John Baptist (now Ruth Wallace), Jackie Wiseman. Most were older than the men students, having enrolled after the birth of children or in search of a second career.

They were important to me, providing an accepting forum for discussion as well as staunch, often lifelong friendships. Several of the most brilliant stopped short of a Ph.D.; some had only a brief professional career. Mary Taylor suffered gross mistreatment by male colleagues at California State University, Hayward; others suffered a lack of self-confidence. Nancy Achilles collected masses of data from leading rock stars, including the Beatles, for a dissertation on the sociology of fame, left uncompleted. Another refused to submit a dissertation that didn't meet her own high standards, but had a remarkable career teaching sociology.

Along with the other women, I complained that professors did not take us seriously. Though there were many women sociology students, no woman held a tenure-track appointment in the department. If women were good enough for graduate school, we said, at least *one* must be good enough for a faculty position. When Dorothy Smith was appointed a lecturer in 1964, we cheered. I learned a great deal from her courses on mental health and on health and medicine. Hers was not a tenure-track position, however, and she moved to a British university two years later.

A frequent topic of intense conversation was the relative merit of qualitative and quantitative methods. Most members of our informal group were enrolled in the required methods course, where the approach was quantitative. Charles Glock, who ordinarily taught this course, was on sabbatical, and David Gold, visiting professor, took his place. One day an insulting note appeared on a department bulletin board: "David Gold is a radical empiricist." Part of Gold's next lecture was devoted to his outraged response, including a statement of his admiration for Erving Goffman's work.

An aura of mystique surrounded Goffman. His students seemed members of a charmed but closed circle, envied by some of us outsiders. They contributed to that view by alluding to UCLA sociology professor Harold Garfinkel's "secret" lecture notes on ethnomethodology that were passed among them, with the understanding that no one outside the circle should see them.

The university's age-based discrimination aggravated its gender discrimination. Anyone older than thirty-two was ineligible for a university fellowship, so that avenue of financial support was not available to me. The combination of coursework and family responsibilities made a half-time research or teaching assistantship seem impossible. Fortunately, I received a fellowship in John Clausen's Personality and Social Structure training program, funded by the National Institute of Mental Health. The mental health, medical sociology, and social psychology content fit my interests. Contact with Clausen brought more cohesion to my courses and a perspective that continues to inform my research. Clausen's own work leaned toward the quantitative end of the methods continuum, but he welcomed a variety of approaches and incorporated them into a special course for trainees.

A more questionable benefit of the training stipend was pressure to proceed rapidly toward the Ph.D. To renew the grant, NIMH needed evidence that trainees finished promptly. I saluted, took the minimum number of courses, and got my degree in precisely four years. I envy Jackie Wiseman, who enrolled in or audited almost every course offered by every professor.

Juggling family responsibilities and studies was fairly easy, though I felt occasional twinges of guilt about the time I spent away from home. The children were old enough to be somewhat self-sufficient, and I did manage a few stints as "Hot Dog Mother" and assistant Cub Scout leader. The training stipend helped pay a part-time housekeeper. With a flexible academic schedule, my husband was willing to help at home, and he raided the San Francisco State library for me. (This saved hours of waiting for required books on two-hour reserve at Berkeley.) I learned to concentrate amid chaos, typing term papers and dissertation on the dining room table. My Chicago habit of avoiding incompletes led to more than one term paper written in only a weekend.

Perhaps most important to my steady progress toward the degree was a single-minded focus on coursework and family. When President Kennedy was assassinated, I was studying for a methodology midterm. After the first rush of shock and grief, I wondered if the exam would be postponed. (It was.) Except for a rare late-afternoon class, I was home when the children returned from school. My presence there meant, among other things, that I missed some of the hectic events of the Free Speech Movement in 1964. (In any case, I believed that my professors' feelings would be hurt if their classes were boycotted.)

Coursework and two foreign language exams completed, I took three months to study for the oral comps. The examination committee included Nathan Glazer for race relations; John Clausen, the family; Dorothy Smith, health and medicine; Herbert Blumer, contemporary theory and committee chair. Anthropologist George DeVos was the outside member.

I always preferred writing to verbalizing my ideas. Anxiety made my heart race and I had visions of physical collapse. So I asked the Student Health Service to help me through the three-hour ordeal and was given a prescription; apparently such requests were not uncommon. On the morning of the exam, I took a pill. Arriving at Barrows Hall, I took another. Still palpitating, I took a third just before the committee convened. The combination was effective. Spinnaker unfurled, I sailed through all questions, engaged in a lengthy verbal battle about the dangers of survey research for determining prevalence of mental illness, and performed uncharacteristic verbal acrobatics. The committee's decision: "Pass with Distinction." I barely made the drive home without an accident, and I still don't know the name of the magic potion. (I strongly advised Shirley Hartley not to take an untried medication before her exams.)

Throughout my coursework and exam preparation, I considered possible dissertation topics. The intersection of personality and social structure, especially the socialization of children, was the point of departure. The notion of the emerging self or self-image intrigued me; George Herbert Mead provided a fuzzy theoretical framework. Goffman's work, particularly *Stigma* (1964) and *The Presentation of Self in Everyday Life* (1959), fascinated me as they did so many other Berkeley students. I wanted to include some aspect of an interest in racial and ethnic relations. My husband's field (rehabilitation psychology) seemed relevant, and a related topic might lead to future collaboration. At first I thought of comparing the socialization strategies of black parents with strategies of parents of handicapped children. Reading about handicapping conditions, I decided to limit my research to deafness, partly because of the hostility that white researchers faced in black communities in the mid-1960s. A visit to the California School for the Deaf (CSD), a few blocks from campus, brought a warm welcome. Soon I was preparing a full-blown proposal and had a sign language tutor.

Learning languages has never been easy for me, and Sign is as difficult as any other. One day at CSD, I was introduced to Bernard Bragg, a deaf teacher at the school, now well-known as a mime and member of the National Theater of the Deaf. "Hello, happy to meet you," I signed. He smiled and replied, "Thank you very much," a gracious response to what I later realized I had signed: "Sorry to meet you." When I met Hilde

Schlesinger, a psychiatrist serving as mental health consultant at the school, she urged me, "Say something sociological." Nonplussed, I became both sign- and speechless. Despite that introduction, Schlesinger and I became close friends and collaborators.

My dissertation compared deaf students of hearing parents with those of deaf parents in terms of self-image, academic achievement, and family climate. Data for 112 students included school achievement records, self-image and lip-reading tests, teachers' ratings of social adjustment, and interviews with eighty sets of parents (half conducted with the help of a sign language interpreter). Every phase was exciting—dampened only slightly when I overheard a professor say that the Berkeley sociology department had never awarded a doctorate for a dissertation with negative results. Fortunately, mine were positive. As predicted, deaf students with deaf parents outperformed those with hearing parents in academic achievement scores and self-image tests, with family climate an important variable. Copies of the dissertation were collated by the entire family, trotting around the basement Ping-Pong table.

In 1967, oral-only methods, excluding sign language, were favored by teachers of the deaf. In most state residential schools (which many deaf children attended), the prohibition of sign language was relaxed only in the seventh grade, at age twelve or thirteen. Thus, the only children with early exposure to sign language were those whose parents were deaf. My findings, therefore, had important implications for deaf education. Sign language proponents quickly adopted me; invitations to lecture were frequent and the enthusiastic audience response helped propel me into further research with deaf children. I remember, somewhat ruefully, my response to Mary Taylor, planning her next research as an extension of her dissertation: "Once I finish this project, I'll never think about deafness again." Mary has since investigated a wide range of topics; this book is my first departure from the subject of deafness.

Before the ink was dry on the dissertation committee's signatures, Hilde Schlesinger and I had begun to write a grant proposal to establish coordinated mental health services and research in the Department of Psychiatry at the University of California's medical school in San Francisco. She had been encouraged in this application as the only child psychiatrist in the country who knew sign language. I gave no thought to a teaching position. At Nathan Glazer's invitation, I had served as part-time lecturer in the Berkeley Integrated Social Science Program, an experience that confirmed my preference for research. I worried from one lecture to the next about dealing with student questions: free to ask anything, the devils were certain to pick what I did not know.

At that time, research money was relatively plentiful. Hilde and I received a three-year grant from the U.S. Vocational Rehabilitation Administration, later supplemented by grants from a local foundation and other federal agencies. The research was fascinating, especially a longitudinal study of the effects of deafness on mother-child interaction. In addition, my dissertation research was extended to public school students, and we surveyed the behavioral problems of deaf children. We offered the first mental health services for deaf children in the United States, mounted a project introducing preschoolers and their parents to sign language, and provided counseling services for deaf adults. At its largest, our staff numbered fifteen, all supported by grants.

Sign language became more widely accepted, especially in the form of Total Communication, which combined speech and simultaneous, English-based Sign. Schlesinger and I were among those responsible for this remarkable shift. For eight hectic, productive, frustrating, exciting, rewarding, maddening, exhausting years, 1968 to 1976, we survived on soft money that grew progressively softer and leaner.

Whatever vague dissatisfactions I had felt as a female graduate student at Berkeley, I had had no deep or conscious sense of gender discrimination. It was only at UC San Francisco that I learned what it meant to be a woman in the academic world. Working in a competitive medical school department, responsible along with Schlesinger for a complex operation, trying to keep my family flourishing while working full-time, I realized how free and easy my graduate student years had been. The Department of Psychiatry would not give a woman with a mere Ph.D., nor even Schlesinger with an M.D., a precious tenure-track position; deafness lay outside the department's central interests. Despite many publications, including the influential *Sound and Sign: Childhood Deafness and Mental Health,* written with Schlesinger in 1972, I remained an adjunct professor in the psychiatry department, totally dependent on outside funding.

At home, the cooperative, indulgent husband of a graduate student wife, whose classes close to home did not disrupt his routine, found a wife with a full-time job and a long commute more aggravating. Conflicts about the time I spent at work and the division of home chores increased. Our daughter's serious problems, culminating in one stint with the Moonies and another in a psychiatric hospital, led to insolvable rifts that forced my first hard appraisal of the marriage. In 1974, after two years of therapy and much emotional trauma, I struck out on my own and filed for divorce.

Lloyd saw our breakup as "just a case of women's lib." For me, his inability to see beyond "women's lib" was a symptom of more basic problems. In a way, of course, he may have been right. Without the emotional power of the women's movement and the earning power of a Ph.D., I might have remained in the marriage. While singleness was a peaceful release, it was also difficult and lonely. John and Suzanne Clausen were among those who were kind and helpful during this period.

Responsible for my own support and half of my son's Ivy League college tuition, I found that the strain of living from one grant to another had become too much. The notice of an opening for research director at the Kendall Demonstration Elementary School on the Gallaudet College campus in Washington, D.C., was propitious. I almost didn't get the job, as the search committee thought my application was merely a ploy to earn a promotion at UC San Francisco. However, I was frank about my personal situation and soft-money position. As the successful candidate, I moved in 1976 to a hard-money research appointment at an institution that fully credited my previous research.

Subsequently, the college became Gallaudet University, with a Research Institute where I was named a senior research scientist. With a tenured faculty appointment, I have occasional teaching and committee assignments, but am primarily a full-time researcher. I have studied the attachment and separation behaviors of deaf toddlers and the impact of a child's deafness on the family, developed social-emotional inventories for assessing deaf children (translated into eight languages), and, most recently, directed an investigation of the linguistic, cognitive, and social development of deaf and hearing infants. Talented younger colleagues with diverse academic backgrounds are members of my research group; Gallaudet's support of our work has been extraordinary.

Deafness poses many unusual research issues. The deaf community, especially around Gallaudet, is tightly knit and has an incredibly efficient grapevine. The maintenance of rapport and strict confidentiality are constant concerns. The pool of potential research subjects is so small that a boycott could be disastrous for a research group. The low incidence of deafness creates other challenges. Since only one in a thousand children is born deaf, and early diagnosis of those with hearing parents is difficult, recruitment of young deaf children is arduous. As visual communication is vital, videotaped data are helpful. The analysis of communication through signing is slow and very expensive, requiring a native (deaf) signer. My Berkeley background has helped me to remain eclectic about research approaches.

Gallaudet is a unique institution with strong training, service, and

Kathryn P. Meadow Orlans

81

advocacy functions, funded almost entirely by the federal government. It prepares deaf students for work, and it serves the interests and promotes the welfare of deaf people of all ages throughout the nation, and indeed, throughout the world. Research conducted at Gallaudet becomes part of the daily lives of deaf people, their families, teachers, and friends. This intensive connection between the real world of deafness and the world of research makes work at Gallaudet more satisfying than it might be elsewhere; the constant political intrigue, however, and the need always to consider the responses of the deaf community make the work often frustrating as well.

A student revolution in 1988 caused the board of trustees to appoint the institution's first deaf president, I. King Jordan, replacing a hearing woman who resigned after six days in the position. This astoundingly successful student uprising was a polite contrast with Berkeley's Free Speech Movement of 1964. The Gallaudet events have brought growing pressure to appoint more deaf faculty and staff, to require greater sign language proficiency, and to shift from English-based Sign (often used simultaneously with speech) to the more "pure" American Sign Language, native to children of deaf parents. "Deaf Power" is a popular slogan. The current situation could hardly differ more from that existing when I signed "Sorry to meet you" to Bernard Bragg.

My appraisal of the Berkeley experience is entirely positive, as I acknowledge somewhat reluctantly. From a 1990s perspective, that evaluation would seem to reflect a failure of perception or an absence of consciousness about our environment as women graduate students. Despite the unavailability or aloofness of some professors, the department offered a rich and varied sociological education. Compared with the University of Chicago, where a certain cohesiveness in courses and in faculty views reflected a true school of thought, Berkeley represented every sociological approach, evident in visiting lecturers as well as regular faculty. It is hard to choose between the two departments. Chicago may have been more congenial, Berkeley more exciting. Each contributed important dimensions to my education.

To compare student life at Chicago and Berkeley is equally difficult. At Chicago, I was young and single; at Berkeley, almost middle-aged, very married, with two school-age children. At Chicago, the university was the center, while at Berkeley, only a fraction of my life. Chicago parties included union song fests and intense discussions of McCarthy-era concerns. During my second semester at Berkeley, the Free Speech Movement erupted; students protested the war in Vietnam and Cambodia; the backdrop to graduate school was created by Patty Hearst and

the Symbionese Liberation Army, the Black Panthers, Haight Ashbury flower children, public marijuana use. Neither at Chicago nor at Berkeley did those events greatly affect classroom lectures or discussions. Berkeley students seemed more concerned about preparing for future jobs; those at Chicago enjoyed their academic grove; at neither campus were professors eager to incorporate current events into their lectures.

John Clausen's program and personal investment in his students were very important to me. He and his wife were among the few faculty couples who invited students to their home. His proposal of my name as author of a chapter for a review volume sponsored by the Society for Research in Child Development led to my 1980 book, *Deafness and Child Development.*

My Berkeley education gave me intellectual and methodological frameworks that continue to inform my research. Understanding early socialization experiences helps to explain later behaviors; the life course is a vital context for understanding individuals, as are family and community influences; study of minorities can illuminate the lives of the majority.

My major professional affiliation has been the Society for Research on Child Development. Although I served on their program committee for four years, I am something of an outsider, as most members are developmental psychologists. I drifted away from the American Sociological Association, rejoining only recently, partly because of a newly formed section on the sociology of childhood.

Anticipating retirement, I wonder if I should have achieved more professionally. Usually, but not always, I conclude that avoiding over-commitment to career activities was wise. My husband, Harold Orlans, provides peerless companionship, occasional collaboration, tireless editorial advice, and daily dishwashing services. With two healthy, happy, and productive children plus four beautiful, talented, intelligent grandchildren to enjoy, and an avid interest in weaving, my life is satisfying and full.

The blues of California have receded, leaving golden memories of bridges, small children, absorbing studies, and lasting friendships.

Chapter 7

Indonesian Odyssey: Jakarta, Cornell, Berkeley, Jakarta

MELY G. TAN

Jakarta

My first attempt to study society was a self-assigned project in meeting and interviewing people, although I had no training in methodology or fieldwork. As a third-year student in the Department of Sinology at the University of Indonesia in Jakarta, I had a chance to participate in a science writing competition organized by the Catholic Scientific Circle. The Dutch Franciscan priest who told me about the contest had a degree in ethnography and edited a Catholic weekly. He encouraged me to participate and was an invaluable adviser on the study. The paper I submitted, a study of the ethnic Chinese in Jakarta, was also my end-of-third-year thesis. (At that time, the university followed the Dutch system, with an exam after the first year and a thesis at the end of the third and fifth years of study.)

To my utter delight, my paper won the prize. Admittedly, there were only three entrants, and I learned that the paper had won because it was based on original empirical research. The contest made me think that perhaps my abilities lay more in social science than in the humanities. I had become bored with Chinese studies, which at the time emphasized the classic literature. Another turning point was the arrival in Jakarta of G. William Skinner, a professor of anthropology from Cornell University, who wanted to study the ethnic Chinese in Indonesia. He contacted the head of the department, Tjan Tjoe Som, an eminent sinologist, to inquire if there were students who would like to work with him. Thus began my training in systematic and rigorous fieldwork, with Skinner a precise and tough taskmaster. Many times I considered him to be an outright slave driver, but he was himself a real workaholic, like my father.

My eighteen months as Skinner's apprentice paid off handsomely. I learned as much about fieldwork and research methodology as would be gained from a graduate degree. In fact, the work I did on the ethnic Chinese in Sukabumi, a town about 120 kilometers south of Jakarta, became my Cornell M.A. thesis. The opportunity to study at Cornell was also a direct outcome of my work with Skinner. From the outset, the three of us who worked with him were told that there would be a fellowship for the one who did the best work. I was elated to receive the Cornell Southeast Asia Training Fellowship. I also received a travel grant from the Rockefeller Foundation. I left for Ithaca soon after finishing my studies in the sinology department and receiving the Dra. degree (*doctoranda,* Latin, meaning entitled to become a doctor).

I was the first woman in the family to study abroad. My mother probably had some misgivings about my going to Cornell, since I was almost thirty years old at the time and still unmarried. Yet she supported my desire for further study, adhering to the high value placed on education that prevails in Chinese culture and among those of Chinese descent. My sister and I were the first women in the family to get university degrees. After finishing medical school at the University of Indonesia in Jakarta, my sister received a World Health Organization fellowship for a master's in public health at the University of Pittsburgh.

Neither of my parents had much formal education. My mother never went to school. Her father, an immigrant from Fukien Province in South China, was a wealthy shopkeeper who owned the largest store in the small town in South Sumatra where he had settled. He did not think it proper or necessary for his only daughter to go to school. However, she had a native intelligence that made it possible for her to operate the store when her father died. She was then in her early twenties.

After finishing elementary school, my father went on to get a diploma in bookkeeping. Also of Chinese ancestry (probably fifth generation), he left his hometown in North Sulawesi when he was barely twenty years old and went to Java. After receiving his diploma, he took a job in a Dutch company and ended up in Batavia (the name for Jakarta in colonial times). There he met relatives of his future wife, who arranged for them to meet.

My parents were strict and took the education of their five children very seriously. Every afternoon, our homework was done under the supervision of a Dutch woman, a teacher hired for the purpose. Although my mother did not speak Dutch, she understood it and insisted that we speak it well. So at home we children were bilingual, speaking Dutch with my father and among ourselves, and Indonesian with my mother. My mother did know some Fukienese, the dialect of her father, but she never used it with us children. (I learned Mandarin at the Department of Sinology, but having no one at home to use it with, I never really mastered it). In high school we learned three other foreign languages, English, German, and French—useful when I took the foreign language exams required for the M.A. and Ph.D. degrees.

In the evening, when my father had time from his work (he had his own business), he had us look up Dutch, English, French, and German words in dictionaries. From the time we were young, we were familiar with foreign languages, were used to having books around, and were motivated to get as much education as possible.

Cornell

I flew into Ithaca in January 1959, in the dead of winter. The sky was sunny and clear, and the snow on the ground sparkled like diamonds. This was my first view of a winter landscape and its beauty overwhelmed me.

At Cornell I enrolled in the Department of Sociology and Anthropology, the beginning of the long road toward becoming a sociologist. In the first semester I took the required courses in theory and methodology—my first systematic study of sociology—and had some good professors: Robin Williams for theory and J. Mayone Stycos for methodology. I also took a course on Southeast Asia from Lauriston Sharp.

Like many other foreign students from a completely different society and university system, that first semester I had to overcome a (fortunately, slight) case of culture shock. That shock was cushioned by the "Indonesianists" of the Cornell Modern Indonesia Project.[1] The project was located in an old building, fondly remembered by all who worked there as "102 West Avenue." The first floor accommodated the project office, the office of the director, George McT. Kahin, the library, and the meeting room. On the floors above were a number of study rooms for graduate students working on Indonesia and other Southeast Asian countries.

My study room was on the second floor, shared with an American student in the government department who was working on her Ph.D. on the politics of the ethnic Chinese in Indonesia. Later my office mate was a young American woman studying the history of Thailand. They were dedicated students, both becoming well-known in their respective fields. There were other Indonesianists, Indonesian and non-Indonesian, and other Southeast Asianists. There was a sizable number of Indonesian students, since the project was considered the best on Indonesian studies in the United States. The "old-timer" students were very supportive of newcomers. I benefited especially from the presence of Selo Soemardjan, a remarkable student who earned a Ph.D. in sociology without any previous study at the university level. He is today considered the doyen of sociologists in Indonesia.

The mix of American, European, and Southeast Asian students generated a cross-fertilization of knowledge and understanding that was beneficial to all who were part of it. There was a weekly luncheon meeting, usually with a speaker from the group in the building. Not infrequently there were visits from high officials of Southeast Asian countries.

My two and one half years at Cornell, in the company of such serious students, motivated to study Southeast Asian societies because of the concern about what was happening there, were some of the happiest and most intellectually stimulating years of my life. Many of those former Cornell colleagues have continued working in academia and are dispersed across the whole world. Some come to Indonesia regularly to keep up with events. In the winter of 1989, a number of us met at the University of British Columbia at a symposium on Southeast Asia. Another reunion occurred in the summer of 1990, when a symposium on ethnic Chinese in Indonesia was held at Cornell.[2] For me, it was also a reunion with some of my former professors: G. William Skinner, Lauriston Sharp, Robin Williams, J. Mayone Stycos (whom I had first encountered at the World Population Conference in Bucharest in 1974, then again at a WHO Task Force meeting in Geneva, Switzerland).

The last six months or so at Cornell I concentrated on writing my thesis, with Skinner as supervisor. I finished it in early summer, 1961. In 1963 the Cornell Modern Indonesia Project published it in the monograph series with the title, *The Chinese of Sukabumi: A Study in Social and Cultural Accommodation*. I was thrilled to see my name and my first brainchild in print.

Berkeley

I returned to Jakarta in July 1961 by way of Europe—my very first trip there and a memorable experience. Back home, I began teaching sociology at the Catholic University in Jakarta. In 1963 I was recruited as a researcher by the Center for Economic and Social Research of the Indonesian Council of Sciences. (In 1967 the name was changed to Indonesian Institute of Sciences). I was one of twelve (the only woman) recruited as part of the institutional development program of the center, partially funded by the Ford Foundation. We were the nucleus of the center's full-time researchers, all of whom were sent to universities in the United States for further study.

The first half of the sixties were the last years of the Soekarno government. When I left for Berkeley in August 1963, the economic situation in Indonesia was deteriorating rapidly and the Indonesian Communist party was gaining ground. Then the killing of six generals on September 30, 1965, triggered the country's explosion.[3]

For Indonesian students abroad, that was a terrible time of anxiety and uncertainty. The anxiety had begun in 1963, when Indonesia was leaning toward the left, the Eastern bloc. We students in the leading country of the Western bloc heard many rumors that our fellowships would be canceled. (There were grounds for this rumor since the Ford Foundation had left Indonesia in 1964.) Fortunately, our fellowships remained in effect, and Indonesia shifted to the Western bloc after 1965.

The sixties were turbulent years in the United States and at Berkeley as well. Etched most clearly in my mind is the day President Kennedy was shot. I was in my apartment getting ready for the first test of my first semester. Suddenly the music on the radio stopped and there was an announcement that Kennedy had been shot. Not long after came the terrible news that he had died. I was stunned. I left my apartment to look for people, but there was no one in the building. I tried to call people on the phone but kept getting a busy signal. It was a frightening sensation, wanting to reach out to people and being unable to communicate with anyone. I was struck with the full meaning of the truth that we are indeed social beings. I decided to go to the university. My apartment was on a main street leading off the campus, but it was deserted and there was a strange silence even though it was the middle of the day. I learned later that everybody was huddled in front of a TV set. I learned something else: the power of television. For three days the entire nation was transfixed, watching incredible events unfold on the TV screen.

But life goes on, and eventually things went back to normal. My first semester at Berkeley was not easy. I had to adjust to life on a big campus with a population of about 27,000 students. I was the only Indonesian student in the sociology department. Neither faculty members nor students were interested in Indonesia as an area of study, completely different from the situation at Cornell, where I had been welcomed by the sizable group of Indonesiaphiles. With only 10,000 students, the atmosphere at Cornell had been less impersonal than that at Berkeley. At one time I seriously considered going back to Cornell. I was taking a course from Reinhard Bendix at the time and consulted with him about it. He was very nice, advising me to think about it carefully and to stay at least until the end of the semester. Eventually, I was glad that I had decided to stay.

Another memorable experience at Berkeley was the tumultuous days of the Free Speech Movement. I was completely on the students' side and participated actively in various sit-ins. However, when foreign students were warned that we could be deported if arrested, I decided I should not jeopardize my studies. Afterward I watched from the sidelines, taking hundreds of slides. Those were exciting but also scary times, and for a sociologist in the making, the campus was a natural laboratory of student politics.

After four semesters of coursework, during which I took courses from Reinhard Bendix, Neil Smelser, William Kornhauser, Wolfram Eberhard, Herbert Blumer, and Robert Blauner, I decided I was ready for the oral examination. Taken prior to beginning the dissertation, this was the most dreaded event of graduate school.

Thus I entered the examination room, adjacent to the department office, with trepidation. A rectangular table was in the center, with the five examiners sitting along one end: Eberhard (committee chair), Blumer, Blauner, Smelser, and Daniel Lev from political science as the outsider knowledgeable about Indonesia. I sat at the other end, facing the windows. I had the uncomfortable feeling that I was on trial (basically I was, of course). When it was Smelser's turn to question, I could not grasp what he was getting at, and he did not help me one bit. After several tries, I stopped. There was an awful silence, and I don't remember what happened after that. (I was reminded then of the exam in linguistics at the end of my first year at the University of Indonesia. The Dutch professor, a well-known poet, looked out the window when I was unable to respond immediately. Fortunately, that was the only time I flunked an oral exam.) After about two hours of questions, I was released. I waited in the next room, since one might be asked to return for further questioning. When I was not recalled, I knew that I had passed!

Still I had the feeling that something had not been right. I thought the situation utterly unfair: facing those five examiners, separated by that long table. It was more a test of performance under stress than of the candidate's knowledge and comprehension of sociology. The next day I went to see Smelser and told him, rather emotionally, how I felt. He looked surprised: "But you passed!" Then he asked me how I would change the conditions. I told him that the exam should be given in a smaller room, with easy chairs arranged in a circle, and that the objective should be to elicit what the candidate knows. As I recall, Smelser was responsive to these ideas, and I believe that subsequently the exam environment became more "examinee-friendly." As an examiner myself, I still remember that experience and always try to put the candidate at ease.

After clearing this big hurdle, I began to think about my dissertation, not realizing that I was embarking on a long and rather lonely road. I had planned to do a study of the ethnic Chinese in the United States to add to my knowledge of Chinese communities outside China, which I had decided would be my area of specialization. I was fortunate to get help from a project on family life in San Francisco's Chinatown, sponsored by the UC Berkeley School of Social Welfare. The study population was Chinese youths with adjustment problems who were registered at the juvenile delinquency office. The two persons who were most helpful in introducing me to the Chinatown community were Elisabeth Abbott, née Lee, a Chinese-American, and her husband, Kenneth Abbott. I also consulted with George DeVos, a professor of anthropology, who had worked on Japanese and Korean studies and was part of the Family Life Project.

The primary objective of my study was an examination of the relationship between social mobility and assimilation. My main hypothesis was that social mobility had not led to structural assimilation on the primary group level among the Chinese—that is, to full assimilation. To test this hypothesis, I had to do two things: first, show that indeed there was a high degree of social mobility among the Chinese, and second, show that there was an absence of assimilation on the primary group level. The basis for my demonstration of social mobility was the U.S. Census for 1940, 1950, and 1960. To investigate assimilation, I did a study of high school students in San Francisco's Chinatown.

Conducting research in a society and culture different from my own increased my ability to do both secondary analysis and field research.

The fieldwork forced me to realize the handicap of not knowing the language of my subjects. Although I had no difficulty in communicating with the high school students, I had no access to some of their parents, who spoke only Cantonese.

Eventually, I spent months scrutinizing the U.S. Census and immigration data, more months doing the fieldwork, then processing and organizing the data. Altogether, these steps must have taken more than one year. Everything was done manually, using keysort cards, since I had a sample of only 102 respondents. After several more months for data analysis, I was ready to write the report. That was a period of really hard work, concentration, and perseverance. My major adviser, Wolfram Eberhard, was very accessible and helpful, but Ph.D. candidates basically must work on their own, always feeling that what has been written is inadequate. Many times I felt like throwing everything out the window. Fortunately, Eberhard and my other advisers, Robert Blauner and Daniel Lev, gave me the moral support I sorely needed. When I finally submitted the dissertation (approved on June 13, 1968), I was relieved but utterly drained. For the record, I was the first Indonesian to receive a Ph.D. in sociology from UC Berkeley. Back in Indonesia, I became the first woman with a Ph.D. in my field.

My parents attended the 1968 commencement exercises, the occasion of the one hundredth anniversary of the University of California at Berkeley. It was a manifestation of their belief that the best they could give their children was a good education. I still cherish the picture of me in my cap and gown, flanked by my mother on one side, my father on the other.

Jakarta, 1968–92

When I returned to Jakarta in August 1968, the New Order government under President Suharto was in its third year. It was still a period of recovery and stabilization after the upheaval of September 1965, the abortive coup attempt attributed to the Indonesian Communist party. The killing of the generals had brought immediate and devastating retaliation against the Communists and their allies. The terrifying time of uncertainty and unclear leadership had come to an end on March 11, 1966, when the presidency was transferred from President Soekarno to President Suharto.

The first thing the New Order government did was to put the economy in order. It was a shambles, with an inflation rate reported as around 650 percent.[4] Remarkably, by 1968 this rate had dropped to manageable proportions, and foreign investment, from the West and from Japan, was pouring in.

The phenomenal recovery of the economy is attributed to the team of economists headed by Widjojo Nitisastro, the first Indonesian to receive a Ph.D. in economics from UC Berkeley. This team, appointed by President Suharto, became the key people of the National Development Planning Agency, the powerful agency entrusted with the development of Indonesia.[5]

As other members of the team also had Berkeley Ph.D.'s, the group became known as the Berkeley Mafia, an epithet that first appeared in an article on Indonesia in *Ramparts* magazine. It was extremely critical of the economic planners and accused them of being instrumental in the emergence of a "military-bureaucratic complex," committed to growth at all costs.

The article was distributed widely among Jakarta intellectuals, a small but significant group of educated people, including university faculty and students, scientists, journalists, artists, and novelists. Ironically, the term was adopted by Indonesians themselves to refer to the economists (who were by then recognized as technocrats), but not with the negative connotation intended by *Ramparts*. When people learn that my Ph.D. is from Berkeley, they immediately say, "Ha, the Berkeley Mafia!" I always deny this, countering that only economists are members of that mafia.

In 1969 Indonesia started its first five-year development plan. From its inception, the emphasis was on economic growth. However, beginning in the seventies the United Nations, in proclaiming the second development decade, introduced the concept of social development and the International Labor Organization in Geneva came up with the concept of basic needs. These concepts were also adopted by the development experts in Indonesia.

In the early seventies, I was involved in a discussion on development, a discourse that still continues.[6] The big issue, then and now, is the dilemma of growth and equity. The economists insist that growth is a necessary and sufficient condition for development. I was in the camp of those who argue that growth is necessary but not sufficient for development; that the strategy should be growth *with* equity. This discussion became a rather heated debate, with one of the top people of the National Planning Development Agency, now the state minister for population and environment, and a number of noneconomists, including myself, as the major proponents.

At the time, Indonesia was riding high on revenues from oil, gas, and timber. In other words, Indonesia was extracting its natural resources to the limit.

There was consensus among planners and big business that growth should come first, that is, the development cake must grow before it can be divided. I countered in an article in the major national weekly, *Tempo,* that we should determine, first, what kind of cake is to be made, and that the process of making it is as important as the product. I suggested that the cake should be of the local variety, using local ingredients, local equipment, and local producers. This kind of cake is much cheaper and is to the liking of most of the people; thus development is participatory and the emphasis is on the process.

On the other hand, if the cake is of the "modern" variety, such as a Black Forest cake, imported ingredients, like high-technology equipment and technical assistance, will be needed. The cake will be expensive, with low local content and low participation of local people, and the product will not suit the taste of most.

As expected, the technocrats were inclined toward the modern cake, and growth continued to be the overriding consideration. However, toward the end of the seventies, the importance of equity was increasingly recognized.

In the 1978 General Guidelines of State Policy, formulated every five years by the People's Consultative Assembly, the highest legislative body, the strategy of development is stated as the trilogy of development: equity, growth, and stability. These three dimensions of the strategy are interdependent. Recognition of the importance of equity was generated by the high economic growth rate that Indonesia was able to sustain in the seventies. No doubt the success of the family planning program, begun in 1967, also contributed to the relaxation of the emphasis on growth and stability. Population growth decreased continuously, and by 1990 it was reduced to 1.97 percent. (With 179 million people counted in the 1990 census, Indonesia was the fifth largest nation in the world. Since the breakup of the USSR, it has become the fourth largest).

However, the high economic growth came to an end with the oil bust of 1982, and Indonesia could no longer rely on oil and gas as the major sources of revenue. The strategy became the export of nonpetroleum commodities, which was quite successful. Toward the end of the eighties, Indonesia turned more and more toward an open economy with the deregulation of key economic activities, the most important being finance and banking. Today Indonesia is very much part of the global market economy.

Another important phenomenon is the recognition that environmental considerations should be central to the development process. In 1982 an environmental law was passed, introducing the concept of sustainable development.

Nevertheless, there is a concern that, although the policies and the rhetoric of the leaders emphasize equity, the growing gap between the very poor and the rich makes implementation of the policies a different matter. There is also the basic criticism that although the economy has been opened up, the political field is still a closed sphere. The switch to an open economy, to a market system, has not been followed by an increased openness in the political system. This situation has led to criticism from various nongovernment agencies and from intellectuals.

Where does a sociologist, trained in the most advanced industrial country, stand in a country that, according to the World Bank's *World Development Report 1993,* still is in the category of Low Income Economies, with a per capita GNP of U.S. $570 in 1990 (in 1992 estimated at around U.S. $650)? The first thing I realized was that many of the tools I had acquired for studying society needed to be modified. Within a few months after returning to Indonesia, I became head of the subdivision of social studies of the division of economic and social research of the Indonesian Institute of Sciences. I was also involved in setting up the subdivision of population studies, now one of the institute's strongest research centers.

My appointment and involvement in the development of the institute indicate that anyone, man or woman, who has the qualifications and the inclination can get into a leadership position. Of course, this is also an indication of the scarcity of qualified people: not even my triple minority status—as a woman, an ethnic Chinese, and a Roman Catholic— has hindered the use and development of my abilities. (Women make up only 6.5 percent of the top echelon of decision makers in Indonesian government service, according to 1989 figures, although they account for almost 51 percent of the population; ethnic Chinese are estimated at about 3 percent of the population; and Catholics account for only 5 or 6 percent [Indonesia is about 85 percent Moslem].)

One of my first projects was the study of social and cultural aspects of food habits, in cooperation with the Ministry of Health and UNICEF, as part of a program of applied nutrition. This research brought me to rural areas in five provinces after an absence of five years, and made me realize that in Indonesia priority should be given to applied and policy research, and that in-depth studies should be conducted in addition to large-scale quantitative studies. I sometimes identify myself as a cultural sociologist, the equivalent of social anthropologist.

Under today's realization that we should be more concerned with basic research, many of us are now involved in the global discourse on development, searching for theories and methods relevant to developing countries, especially Indonesia.

Over the years, my interests evolved to include social change, focusing on development indicators and changes in social stratification and on women and health. I also continue work on my main interest, the ethnic Chinese in Indonesia and other ASEAN countries.[7] These interests led to my nine-month stay as a visiting scholar at Kyoto University in 1986–87, a teaching assignment in Kuala Lumpur, Malaysia, in 1989, and membership in a World Health Organization task force from 1977 to 1981 and from 1990 until the present. Nevertheless, there is a continuing demand from government, for social scientists especially, to emphasize applied and policy research, and to provide instant solutions to problems that are inevitable in a society undergoing rapid change. This demand is a constant pressure, at times frustrating and stressful. As a government agency, receiving most of its budget from the government, our institute is expected to support government policies and to give priority to research that contributes to the development process. Fortunately, there is some leeway in our acceptance of requests for research from outside agencies, including international agencies like the World Health Organization.

There is no doubt, however, that a strong government with a president in power for twenty-six years feels secure about its strategy and leaves little room for dissent or alternative ideas. (As predicted in the presidential election of 1993, Suharto was reelected for another five-year term.) This curb on dissent (usually construed as antigovernment) is a dilemma faced by many social scientists and other intellectuals in developing countries. It is a matter of the natural desire to be effective, to be included, yet to maintain one's intellectual integrity as a concerned social scientist. In the many meetings I have attended, in Indonesia and twenty-two other countries, I have met many people struggling with this dilemma. In the last analysis, however, each of us must resolve the dilemma for herself. As my Indonesian odyssey unfolded, the Berkeley portion added an important dimension of learning and experience, widening my horizons even more. It has enabled me to lead a rewarding life as a social scientist and to feel that I am part of the immense challenge of a developing Indonesia.

Notes

1. The October 1989 issue of *Indonesia*, the journal of the Cornell Modern Indonesia Project (CMIP), contains a comprehensive history to commemorate its thirty-fifth anniversary. It was written by George McT. Kahin, initiator and first director. When the CMIP was established in 1954, Kahin was already well known as an Indonesianist through his now-classic book, *Nationalism and Revo-*

lution in Indonesia (1952, Cornell University Press). This book is based on his research of the Indonesian revolution, which he witnessed, in 1948–49. Indonesia proclaimed its independence on August 17, 1945, after three and one-half years of occupation by the Japanese during World War II. However, after the defeat of Japan, the Dutch, who had colonized Indonesia for 350 years, returned. A bloody revolution ensued, and the Dutch finally transferred sovereignty to Indonesia on December 27, 1949, after prolonged negotiations and international pressure. Other scholars affiliated with the CMIP produced highly acclaimed books, including Ruth McVey, whose *Indonesia* (New Haven, Conn.: HRAF Press, 1963), is an edited collection of basic articles covering all aspects of society by eminent scholars. In 1971 CMIP published the controversial *A Preliminary Analysis of the October 1, 1965 Coup in Indonesia,* which questions the official government version condemning the Indonesian Communist Party as instigator of the coup. As a consequence, the main author, Benedict Anderson, present director of the CMIP, has been banned from Indonesia.

2. The proceedings of this symposium, entitled *The Role of the Indonesian Chinese in Shaping Modern Indonesian Life,* were published in a special issue of *Indonesia* in 1991. My paper, "The Social and Cultural Dimension of the Role of the Ethnic Chinese in Indonesian Society," is included (pp. 113–27).

3. For a book on this coup attempt, see *Indonesian Upheaval* (New York: David McKay, 1967). This is an expansion and reworking of articles for which the author, John Hughes, Far Eastern correspondent of the *Christian Science Monitor,* received the 1967 Pulitzer Prize for foreign reporting.

4. In the words of Heinz Arndt, an astute economist of the Australian

National University in Canberra and a longstanding expert on the Indonesian economy: "The country was literally bankrupt. . . . Inflation, which had been chronic since the early days of the Republic, had got completely out of control." *The Indonesian Economy: Collected Papers* (Singapore: Chopmen Publishers, 1984), p. 29.

5. For an analysis of the period of rehabilitation and stabilization of the economy and polity and the role of the economists in this endeavor, see Arndt, ibid., chap. 2, "Five Years of New Order." For an analysis that is critical of the more recent development of the Indonesian economy, see Richard Robison, *Indonesia: The Rise of Capital* (Sydney: Allen & Unwin, 1986), and Yoshihara Kunio, *The Rise of Ersatz Capitalism in Southeast Asia* (Singapore: Oxford University Press, 1988).

6. In the foreword to Arndt's book (n. 4), written in 1981, M. Sadli, a professor of economics and former minister of manpower and minister of mining, wrote: "During the 1970's the Indonesian economy did fairly well, with an average real growth rate of GDP (Gross Domestic Product) of 7.5 per cent per annum, but there is controversy about the quality of the development. I presume that this debate will continue during the 1980's. As a member of the government during much of this time, and at the same time also still teaching at the university, I can remember vividly the uncomfortable times we had trying to explain things to gatherings of students."

7. ASEAN, or Association of Southeast Asian Nations, includes the six countries of Indonesia, Malaysia, Singapore, Thailand, the Philippines, and Brunei Darrussalam.

Chapter 8

Transformation from Sacred to Secular

RUTH A. WALLACE

My arrival at Berkeley in 1963 represented not only the first page of a new chapter in my life, but also the first step into a new world. My apparel, a religious habit, suggested that I was not a typical Berkeley student. However, because its sociology department was considered the best in the country, this campus represented a formidable challenge and a key to the future.

Born in 1932 in a small Indiana town near Chicago of an Irish Catholic father and a Swedish mother, a Catholic convert, I attended the local Catholic grammar and high schools. In second grade I wrote an essay about becoming a Sister so that I could help the poor. In those days, young women did not have alternative service organizations, like the Peace Corps, to consider. Although I dated a lot during high school, at no point did I entirely dismiss the notion that someday I might join a religious community.

My father played football under Knute Rockne and had a law degree from Notre Dame University. He made it very clear to his three daughters that he expected us to do well in school and to go to college. We had no thought of following in his steps and enrolling in law school, however, since like playing football, we thought it inappropriate for women. My mother, who had completed two years of college before she married my father, also encouraged us to excel in school. She died suddenly when I was twelve, and six years later, after my father remarried, the family moved to California. We lived in Glendale in 1950, and I attended Immaculate Heart College in Los Angeles. The first year of college convinced me that the women professors, Sisters of the Immaculate Heart of Mary (IHMs), were a wonderful group of professionals. They also seemed very happy in their community life. It didn't take long to decide that this was the group I had been searching for, and I joined their ranks in September 1951.

How, then, did I end up in sociology? During my freshman year, I was advised to major in something that really interested me. Until then, my work as a counselor at a Catholic Youth Organization camp for two summers had been the most interesting and enjoyable thing I had done. I knew sociology had something to do with group interaction, and, in my estimation, that's what camp was all about. I thoroughly enjoyed my sociology courses, and was convinced that they made me a better teacher.

Graduate Student at Notre Dame

By 1961, when I finished my bachelor's degree, I had been teaching for nine years in California Catholic schools, six in grammar schools and three in high schools. The head of our IHM community instructed me to apply to graduate school because a Sister in our college sociology department was nearing retirement. Under my vow of obedience I went wherever I was sent, so off I went to Notre Dame in September 1962 to begin work on a master's degree, completed in August 1963.

At that time Notre Dame was exclusively male, but nuns were accepted at the graduate level; I was one of thirty women among 6,000 male students. The Notre Dame sociology department was small, and as at Berkeley, all the professors were men. Two, Bill D'Antonio and Don Barrett, stand out in my memory: they were excellent teachers and convinced me that I could succeed in graduate school.

How did I end up at UC Berkeley for doctoral work? First, I discovered that Notre Dame did not have enough course offerings for a student to complete both an M.A. and a Ph.D. in sociology. My religious superior asked me to send her the names of four or five universities with good doctoral programs. In my letter, I listed no Catholic universities. Although she was hesitant to send me to a secular campus, the Mother General (as she was called) instructed me to apply at Berkeley because there I could live with some members of my community who were teaching in a small parish school twenty minutes from the campus. When people, usually Catholics, stopped me on campus to inquire why I was studying at Berkeley, I sometimes replied, "Because of holy obedience."

Graduate Student at Berkeley

Ruth A. Wallace

What to call me was a perplexing problem for most of those in the Berkeley sociology department who had never spoken to a nun before. My name, Sister John Baptist, was awkward for them, and most settled on "Sister John." There were also awkward moments for me, accustomed to the language of the convent, which viewed the clergy as esteemed male authority figures. One day in Neil Smelser's office, I called him "Father." I was very embarrassed at my slip of the tongue, and I'll never forget his startled look. Later, when he was directing my dissertation, we joked about it.

Although a gregarious person, I felt I had to be especially outgoing because my clothing and name were off-putting for many colleagues. Some people who were uncomfortable with a nun tried to avoid me. Several graduate students kept their distance at first; my world was totally foreign to them, and they had no idea how to interact with me.

Faculty shared this problem. Once Seymour Martin Lipset asked if I minded answering a personal question. To my relief it was "Where did you get that name?"

I relaxed, thinking that was an easy question, but then I realized how complicated the answer was for someone unfamiliar with the Catholic world. I explained that religious communities tended to bestow the names of saints on their new members, and since the practice was to avoid surnames, they soon ran out of female saints' names. The custom was to allow new members to submit three names in order of preference. My first choice was John Baptist because my father's name was John. I can still see the look of puzzlement on Lipset's face when he remarked, "Oh, so you *chose* that name?" While he seemed relieved to hear that it hadn't been foisted on me, at the same time his expression suggested that he was still perplexed that any woman would choose a male name.

I was deeply grateful to the graduate students, mostly women but also a few men, who went out of their way to make me feel more comfortable by initiating conversations, joining me for a bag lunch outside the library, including me in study groups, and inviting me to their homes. I remember reflecting that Berkeley had lived up to its reputation of embracing minority students.

Women graduate students both felt and were in fact a minority in the department, as the introductory chapter of this book demonstrates. Also, during the entire period of my graduate training (1963 to 1968) no woman occupied a full-time tenure-line position in the sociology department. Although I had no women professors at either Berkeley or Notre Dame, I remember envying those who took Dorothy Smith's seminar, which was outside my areas of specialization. It was, no doubt, our minority position that gave women students the impetus to gather together for support.

At thirty-one, I was among the older graduate students because it had taken me nine years to complete my B.A. while teaching full-time. Some of us did not realize that many graduate schools rejected applicants older than age thirty. The rationale was that training older people was a waste of time since their contributions to the field would be limited. This policy was discriminatory in nature because most of those older applicants were women. In our case it was fortunate that Berkeley had not adopted that policy.

Female graduate students were supportive during the traumatic period of the oral comprehensives. I was touched when Kay Herman joined me at the Newman Center for noon Mass on the day of my exam. Another close friend, Kathryn Meadow, invited several female graduate students to a party for me held immediately after my exam at her home. And on graduation day itself, Shirley Hartley invited me and my family to celebrate the occasion with a party at her home. As I reflect on these friendships, it seems that the gemeinschaft I experienced among those women was akin to the feeling of community I shared with the Sisters in my religious community.

There were also some male graduate students who were important members of my network at Berkeley. I was virtually adopted by Whitney Pope and his wife, Christie, both as friend and as godmother to their children. I felt a particular affinity with Herman Blake, the only black graduate student in sociology during the time I was there. In my first year, Herman observed that he and I were two of the "most visible minorities" on campus.

Sam Kaplan, another good friend, jokingly told me one day during a seminar that in his estimation I had broken several "quotas" in the department, because I was a woman, a Roman Catholic, and a nun. As he put it, there were "very few women" graduate students, "hardly any Catholics," and "no other nuns." He felt I had accomplished a breakthrough. Although priests had enrolled in the sociology program from time to time, I was the first nun to do so.

On the campus as a whole, in fact, only a few nuns were sprinkled among the Berkeley graduate departments like economics, education, comparative literature, biology, and zoology. I knew most of the other Sister graduate students, having met them on campus or at liturgies and programs at the Newman Center. There was only a handful because most religious communities sent their members to Catholic universities for graduate degrees.

My effect on the faculty was less clear to me at the time, although it was they who had accepted me into the program, and the grades I received in their classes indicated that I would survive in this secular environment. Leo Lowenthal once asked me if I was expected to do manual work at the convent, in addition to the time I spent in communal prayer. He was surprised that I did my share of housecleaning and cooking. However, my time constraints were probably less than those of the married women and single-parent graduate students, most of whom did all their housecleaning and cooking, in addition to child care.

It was only after I returned to Berkeley during my first sabbatical leave from George Washington University in 1975 that I got an inkling of the effect of my former "visible minority" status on some of the faculty. I had arranged an interview with Herbert Blumer for a chapter I was writing on symbolic interactionism. Although I had taken a theory course from him in 1965, I felt I should reintroduce myself, so I began by reminding him that I had been the only nun in his course that year. He said that he certainly remembered me but added that there had been "at least five" Sisters around the department in the sixties, as he recalled "always meeting them in the hallways and the department office."

I carefully worded my reply to Blumer. (After all, he was the one who had coined the term symbolic interactionism, a perspective that focuses on the individual's everyday world.) I explained that, like Herman Blake, I had been the only one of my kind during the sixties and that what Blumer had seen, again and again, had been only one nun, who spent a great deal of time around the hallways and offices on the fourth floor at Barrows Hall. As I expected, Blumer had a good laugh about his mistaken perception.

The Vatican II Catalyst

During my graduate school years numerous historical events in the United States reverberated throughout the world: the Kennedy assassination, the passing of civil rights legislation, and on our own campus, the Free Speech Movement. During the semester following the completion of my coursework, a different kind of historical event took place in Rome: the final session of the Vatican Council.

In September 1962 Pope John XXIII convened the first session of the Second Vatican Council (Vatican II). A vatican council is an extraordinary event because all the Catholic bishops in the world participate in its meetings, while the pope presides. Only twenty ecumenical councils have been held in twenty centuries. One of the chief aims of the council was to bring about changes in the church that would allow for a better adaptation to modern society. To that end Catholic bishops met in Rome for three months each year for four consecutive years (1962–65).

These were exciting times for Catholics, and the media coverage was impressive. Few of the graduate students at Berkeley were Catholic, but all my friends rejoiced with me when they heard that I had been asked to join three American Sisters, each representing a different religious community, to organize discussions on topics being deliberated by the council. Our group of four was sponsored by a progressive Belgian prelate, Cardinal Leon Joseph Suenens. Both Reinhard Bendix and Herbert Blumer, who were following the press coverage of Vatican II, expressed great interest in my trip to Rome. Blumer, fascinated by reports of the bishops' lobbying during their coffee breaks, urged me to take field notes.

If I accepted the invitation, I would stay in Rome for the entire fourth session, from mid-September to early December 1965. I agreed to go provided I passed my comprehensive exams before leaving. If I did not pass, I resolved to remain at Berkeley and study for a second try.

Shortly before classes ended in June 1965, I was asked to join a theory study group of three other students, all male, who also were planning to take their exams in sociological theory in the near future. Our meetings took place in the parlor of my convent at a large round table, a quiet spot, conducive to study and concentration. Whitney Pope, Herman Blake, and Sam Kaplan attended regularly. These weekly meetings, where we analyzed assigned readings and mercilessly challenged weaknesses in conceptual clarity or argumentation, were decisive in my passing the oral examination.

My committee was chaired by Leo Lowenthal, who examined me in social stratification; the others were Neil Smelser (theory), Martin Trow (education), Nathan Glazer (religion), and a female professor from the Berkeley Department of Education. I was very nervous, but my most anxious period occurred when Glazer began to question me. As I was answering his first question, he interrupted me, and immediately moved on to a second question. Again, just as I was halfway toward completing my response, he intervened with another question, repeating this strategy throughout the session. Each time he interrupted me, I assumed that my response had not been satisfactory, and that he was introducing a different question to give me another chance.

When I left the examining room while the committee evaluated my performance, the first person I saw was Herman Blake, who was waiting for me. When I told him that I was sure I had failed in religion, he argued to the contrary, "They couldn't possibly fail a nun on religion." In spite of Herman's reassurance, I was surprised when I was told that I had passed the examination, with a high pass in religion! Later I learned that Glazer's strategy on the orals was to interrupt any student as soon as he was satisfied that the student was headed toward a correct response. No one had warned me, however, that his interruptions meant success, not failure.

Once the orals were over, another important chapter of my life began to unfold with the trip to Rome. It was a new experience for me to engage in discussions with bishops, priests, Protestant observers, and Catholic laymen and laywomen about the ideals that the council was introducing into the life of the church, such as co-responsibility, participation of the laity, and respect for religious pluralism. Vatican II was the catalyst that challenged religious communities to re-evaluate their constitutions and to bring them into line with the changes promulgated by the council. I was eager to become involved in the implementation of the council decrees, which would bring about many changes in the lives of Catholic people.

Researcher in Toronto

The Vatican II changes were not going to happen overnight, however, so back I went to Berkeley to face the reality of my dissertation. I immediately began work on the theoretical framework. The sociology of religion was my principal field of specialization, but I chose the dissertation topic, change of religious affiliation, for pragmatic reasons as well. In 1964 I had learned that the Catholic Information Center in Toronto had important data, to which I had been granted access by the director.

When I showed Smelser a sample of the data, unanalyzed questionnaires designed by a sociologist and filled out by 5,000 persons who had completed a course of instruction in the Catholic religion, he said it was a gold mine, and agreed to be my dissertation director. He suggested that I apply for a dissertation grant from the National Institute of Mental Health. Without his advice, I doubt that I would have applied for the grant, which was very helpful. Throughout the dissertation process, Smelser was consistently thorough in his criticisms and comments, always returning drafts of my chapters punctually. I usually came away from his office with several pages of single-spaced comments that challenged me to meet his high standards.

In addition to the quantitative analysis comparing those who became Catholics after the course with those who did not, I proposed to conduct face-to-face interviews with fifty subjects. This decision reflected the influence of Herbert Blumer and Erving Goffman. In discussing the details of my fieldwork with Smelser, the question of how I was to conduct these interviews arose. In particular, I raised the issue of a possible negative impact on the subject facing an interviewer dressed in religious garb. Smelser's response was, "Yes, unless you change clothes, it will be like a police officer dressed in uniform asking people about breaking the law." My religious superiors gave me permission to don secular clothes for the duration of my fieldwork, from April through August 1966. This would be the first time that I had dressed in secular clothes since the day I entered the convent, fifteen years earlier.

Erving Goffman, in particular, was fascinated by my impending transformation. During a conversation in his office, I admitted that I feared my transition would not be smooth, because, for example, I needed to relearn how to wear high heels, after fifteen years of sensible low-heeled shoes. His reaction was to lend me a copy of a manuscript he had just received from Harold Garfinkel, subsequently published as *Studies in Ethnomethodology* (1967). Goffman recommended that I read the chapter on the case study of Agnes, a transsexual who experienced the risks and uncertainties involved in learning to act and feel like a woman. Since Goffman lent it to me for only forty-five minutes, I barely skimmed the chapter, but it was enough to see the parallel. I was about to face the same constraints as I relearned how to behave while wearing secular garb.

Goffman also urged me to keep a journal during the entire five months of my fieldwork, carefully recording my observations, thoughts, and feelings when I changed to lay clothing, as well as the reactions of others with whom I interacted during this time. Although I was both surprised and gratified by his interest, I decided I didn't have the time to work on this project while gathering dissertation data. I undoubtedly missed a golden opportunity.

Graduate students who heard about my forthcoming change in appearance also offered advice. Max Heirich, who had observed the warmth with which I greeted people around campus, recommended that I adopt a less outgoing stance when I began to wear ordinary clothes. "You smile too much," he said. He was concerned that my friendly Sister posture would be misinterpreted once I was not distinguishable from other women. I immediately saw the wisdom of his advice.

Another novel experience was my living arrangement while collecting my data. During my fieldwork I lived in an apartment with two Catholic laywomen, the first time in fifteen years that I had lived outside a convent. It proved to be a beneficial experience as well as a rehearsal for the next stage of my life. Without these still-close friends, Bonnie Brennan and Betty Skuffham, my transition to the secular world would have been more awkward and troublesome. Their advice about clothes, hair, makeup, and appropriate behavior was invaluable.

From Sister to Doctor

My Berkeley friends did not witness my change of apparel in the spring and summer of 1966 because it happened in Toronto, but not long afterward I appeared on campus wearing a dark blue suit rather than my flowing blue habit with the black veil. Religious communities had been encouraged by the Vatican II documents to adapt to the modern world. My own community, a progressive group taking the lead in the reform movement, decided to ask Sisters doing graduate work to experiment with changes in dress.

When I arrived at the sociology department office for the first time in my tailored suit and sensible mid-heel shoes, a foreign student told me that he was sorry I no longer wore the habit, because now I couldn't be distinguished from any other woman on the campus. As a female and a Catholic, I was still a minority in the department, but without religious garb I was no longer, as Herman Blake had pointed out, a "most visible minority." Reflecting on his words, it struck me that I had only to change my attire if I was to blend in with others on campus, whereas Herman could not discard his visibility.

In 1968, the year I finished my Ph.D., our baptismal names were reinstated, and I became Sister Ruth Wallace. On the day when Neil Smelser signed my completed dissertation, he jokingly asked if I should be called "Doctor Sister" or "Sister Doctor." After graduation, I joined the Department of Sociology at Immaculate Heart College in Los Angeles. During my next two and one-half years of teaching there, the IHM Sisters were in conflict with the local archbishop over policy decisions inspired by Vatican II, including our changes in dress. Because we refused to back down on our position, the IHMs in the elementary and secondary schools of the archdiocese were told they would no longer be needed after the school year ended. This conflict was widely reported in the press, and some Sisters, chiefly those teaching at the college, spent enormous amounts of time preparing press releases and speaking to groups about our view of the controversy.

Partly because of the burn-out I was experiencing, and with much soul-searching, I made the difficult request for a dispensation from my vows. The decision was wrenching because I loved the community and was enormously grateful for my years with them. Living with those who ran colleges, hospitals, high schools, and grammar schools, it had never occurred to me to question women's leadership. But deep down I knew it was time to move on.

In my last semester at Immaculate Heart, the spring of 1970, I became Dr. Ruth Wallace. College Sisters, both faculty and administrators, urged me to stay, even though I was no longer a member of the religious community, but I remained for only one more semester.

During that time I had difficulty establishing my identity as a laywoman, since nuns too were wearing secular clothes, and I didn't look different from them. I still felt very close to many of them. In particular, I was indebted to Sister Helen Kelley, the college president—sociologist, friend, and role model—who had taught most of my undergraduate sociology courses and who was instrumental in the community's decision to send me to graduate school. The need to distance myself geographically in order to complete the transformation process and overcome my ambivalence became evident.

As a member of the religious order, I never worried about employment because there were many places where I could be sent to teach. For the first time, then, at age thirty-eight, I found myself on the job market. Once again Neil Smelser was very helpful. When I told him I wanted to locate in the Washington, D.C., area, he asked me to send him the names and addresses of the heads of all the departments where I would be applying. He wrote a letter to each one, introducing me as his student and presenting his reasons for recommending me. His strategy was to prepare the way before I even approached them. Only after his letters had gone out was I to apply for the position. I don't know what Neil said in those letters, but it worked. I interviewed in four departments with vacancies at the junior level and received three job offers. Other students told me that Neil had done the same for them.

Sociology Professor at GWU

My final transformation to this point in my life started in September 1970, when I began teaching sociology at George Washington University (GWU), where I am now professor of sociology. Because of my teaching load of three courses per semester, I was a slow starter with regard to publications. During the seventies I published a few articles, including one from my dissertation and one from my presidential address at the 1975 meeting of the Association for the Sociology of Religion. In the mid-eighties I was given a course reduction, and became more productive.

My career has been influenced greatly by outstanding Berkeley theorists. While undergraduate courses had sparked an interest in theory, that spark became a flame at Berkeley. An unintended consequence of the Free Speech Movement, during my second year, was Herbert Blumer's substitution for Neil Smelser as instructor for the required theory course. Neil was recruited to help in the chancellor's office as the special assistant for student political activity and relieved of his teaching duties during the spring semester 1965. In gratitude to Blumer for his willingness to help the department, many faculty members were guest lecturers for an unforgettable, one-time, star-studded course. In addition to Blumer's lectures on symbolic interactionism, Smelser lectured on functionalism, Phil Selznick on organizations, John Clausen on socialization, David Matza on deviance, and Leo Lowenthal on culture. A unique aspect of these sessions was that each of the theorists would follow up his presentation by a friendly debate with Blumer, then open the class to discussion.

Four other experiences—a course on the development of social thought with Reinhard Bendix, a seminar on Emile Durkheim by Leo Lowenthal, a course on Talcott Parsons by Smelser, and several conversations with Erving Goffman—convinced me of the value of diverse theoretical approaches for the explanation of sociological phenomena. This conviction has been played out in my teaching of theory to graduates and undergraduates over the past quarter of a century, in the publication of several theoretical articles and chapters in books, and in a text entitled *Contemporary Sociological Theory* (1980), coauthored with Alison Wolf, now in its third edition and translated into Italian and Japanese.

In 1987 I was elected chair of the theory section of the American Sociological Association (ASA). That Edith Kurzweil is the only other woman thus far to head the theory section is not surprising, given the gender expectations about appropriate fields of specialization. (I was told by a male graduate student at Berkeley in the early sixties that the areas of specialization for women were family, education, and religion.) Undoubtedly, the growing number of women now joining the theory section as active members will remedy that situation.

My graduate school days at Berkeley preceded the women's movement, but I joined Sociologists for Women in Society (SWS) and the American Sociological Association section on sex and gender early, and began reading the proliferating gender publications. During my first year at GWU (1970–71), my consciousness about gender inequality in academia was raised by several personal experiences.

A dramatic example occurred during a meeting of the College of Arts and Sciences. The faculty was predominantly white male, and the dean conducting the meeting referred to male faculty as "Professor," usually adding the surname. At one point in the meeting when I had the temerity to raise my hand, he referred to me as "Ma'am." (It's true that I was a newcomer, and he may not have known my name, but everyone in attendance was a faculty member.)

The dean's form of address really threw me, but more shocking was the reaction of the faculty. As soon as I started to speak, everything stopped. Every head turned toward me, and the rustle of papers ceased, as did the usual buzz of whispered conversation. In that deafening silence with eyes riveted on me, I found myself stammering while I tried to figure out what was wrong. Later I realized that their strange behavior was probably due simply to the sound of a female voice; I was the first woman to speak at that meeting. For subsequent meetings I prepared questions beforehand to insure a smooth delivery, determined not to be silenced by that experience.

Later, when I applied for promotion to full professor, I was unclear about the rules of the game. There were no female full professors in my department, and no advice was forthcoming. It was a woman from another department who told me to "go for it." Only after the promotion was approved did a male professor apologetically explain that they were not used to having women faculty, and their usual procedure was to "take the guy out for a beer and suggest that he ask for promotion."

Given these experiences and my interest in the new subfield of gender, my subsequent teaching and research on the sociology of gender is not surprising. Additional support and personal encouragement in this area of specialization came from a lively local SWS group that met monthly for a number of years.

It was at one of these SWS meetings that I first met Jessie Bernard, and was pleased when the ASA asked me to chair the first Jessie Bernard Award Committee. A few years later I persuaded Jessie to contribute a chapter to my edited book *Feminism and Sociological Theory* (1989), a project that gave me a chance to combine a longtime interest in theory with a growing interest in feminism.

In the mid-eighties my interests in religion, theory, and gender con-

verged in a new research project, a study of Catholic women administering priestless parishes, funded by the Lilly Endowment and the National Science Foundation. As I traveled to parishes throughout the country, I found that my experiences as both a nun and a laywoman facilitated the interview process, because approximately half of the women pastors were nuns. Once I revealed my lay and religious background to my interviewee, there was immediate rapport.

Because this was a cutting-edge phenomenon related directly to the increasing shortage of priests, there was considerable press coverage of my research on women pastors, even before the book was published. My chief findings, that these women were practicing collaborative rather than hierarchical leadership, and that parishioners' attitudes toward both female and married pastors were changing dramatically, presage profound changes that might eventually lead to a restructuring of the Catholic church. When the Religious Research Association invited me to deliver the H. Paul Douglass Lecture in 1990, I included some of the results of that research in my address. My book, *They Call Her Pastor: A New Role for Catholic Women,* was published by the State University of New York Press in 1992. My recent election as president-elect of the Society for the Scientific Study of Religion will enable me to focus on issues of gender and religion as the program theme for the annual meeting in 1995, when I deliver my presidential address.

In my new life, my commitment to Catholicism endures. One of my important communities is a small group of Catholic friends in the Washington, D.C., area, a link to earlier families. On three occasions I have been recruited by my friends in the IHMs to teach a course on gender inequality for their master's program in feminist spirituality. Other more heterogeneous communities include faculty from various departments at GWU and colleagues with whom I exchange working papers, some of whom are Berkeley friends: Kay Meadow Orlans, Shirley Hartley, Jackie Wiseman, Metta Spencer, Whitney Pope, and Max Heirich.

These reflections about the past have been very instructive. Taking time to revisit my transformation, recalling those who helped me journey from sacred to secular reaffirms a conviction that I have often voiced: "If I had it to do again, I would—with the same people, in the same places, in the same way."

Chapter 9

Multiple Roles,
Multiple Selves

SHIRLEY FOSTER HARTLEY

It's impossible for me even to think of my years at Berkeley without also acknowledging a pattern that began in early childhood. For most of my life I felt that I didn't belong. Yet, through a series of very small steps, through a multiplicity of roles and a willingness, even determination, to explore possibilities, a transformation occurred that allows me to celebrate the person I've become.

My parents grew up in extreme poverty in Allentown, Pennsylvania, a coal-mining, steel-producing area. My mother and her identical twin lived with their mother above a pawnshop. Grandmother earned money (and left-over food) by working at a boarding-house during the week, selling roach poison door-to-door on weekends. Neither of my parents went beyond the eighth grade; they met as child-laborers in a paper box factory. Mother married at eighteen, to get away from her mother and a despicable home life. It was not a satisfying marriage for either parent. My only memory of them together was evenings, after work, with dad in his chair and mother over a washboard at the kitchen sink. There were hours of bickering and no apparent joy in their relationship. They divorced when I was six, and mother and I moved into a room in the home of a family where I had a sense of warmth and acceptance. Mother remarried the following year, however, and we moved to a small apartment in Chicago.

My early memories are limited, perhaps because I led a robot-like existence. I was painfully shy: children were to be seen and not heard, and I was a good little girl (both unseen and unheard). Unhappy memories are often repressed; it was probably easier for me to forget than to resent my family. My stepfather was an alcoholic, and there were ten more years of pain and tension at home. I was a marginal person, even as a child. My only enrichment toys were colored pencils and paper dolls, and for them I created endlessly. There were certainly no books in my home, no parental interest in books or in anything beyond daily life that I remember.

How does a poor little girl with no sense of possibilities, a puppet-like child, become a Renaissance Woman in charge of her life: joyful, powerful, efficient? No sociologist would expect it. No marriage counselor would predict an ecstatically happy marriage for anyone from such a problem-ridden home. In retrospect, however, it's easy to recognize the small steps that expanded a series of marginal roles into a full life. At each step there were friends who facilitated the process and pushed the transformation.

My first positive sense of self developed with new friends following our move to California shortly after I entered ninth grade. Until then I had had no real friend—some casual playmates, but no one with whom there was reciprocal caring. In the small city of San Leandro, I experienced a sense of security and ability to trust. We lived on the second floor of an old farmhouse two blocks from the high school. My two new friends, whose families had real homes, accepted me and even included me in their family vacations. We became the Three Musketeers but had a larger group of friends at school, all of whom accepted me in spite of my alcoholic stepfather and lack of a real home in which to reciprocate visits. The sense of belonging and affection experienced during those typically difficult teen years allowed me to gain some self-respect.

At San Leandro High, girls were not expected to succeed. There was little intellectual challenge, and while I was in the college prep track (because all my friends were), I never expected to go to college. (In fact, I worked part-time and could hardly wait to work full-time so my mother could escape her miserable marriage.) Although I had straight As in math and science courses, I had no idea what a woman might do with those. Because I worked part-time as a bookkeeper, I assumed that was my only option for earning a living and being independent. I was class valedictorian and voted "Most likely to succeed," but thought this was a mistake, because I never saw myself as capable. Yet, since our English teacher had been drilling us in entrance exams for UC Berkeley (an hour and a half away by bus) and I was doing well, I took a small step and applied, without knowing the cost or how I might earn the money for books and tuition.

Berkeley, the First Time

I was accepted by the university—another small step. With no career counseling and no role models, my math ability and part-time jobs led me to accounting, and I registered as a business major. Little did I know that foreign trade, economics, and other traditionally male subjects were required. I commuted from San Leandro, still living in the old farmhouse with my mother and stepfather. I worked three days a week, made my own clothes, and even saved a little money. The long commute, however, meant that I had no time to make new friends or participate in campus life. Nor did I see much of my high school friends who had not gone to college; they were busy with work schedules.

Registering for fall classes my sophomore year, I met an acquaintance who asked if I had signed up for sorority rush. The process had already begun, but my curiosity and need to meet people on campus led me to register. I knew no one in a sorority or anything about the system, but with a map in hand I wandered through the open houses. It was great to meet friendly people, and I returned to several houses when invited. Meanwhile I learned that if I lived at home, the cost of belonging to the sorority would be only about forty dollars a month, with lunches and Monday night dinners included. Pledging revolutionized my campus experience. I stayed overnight at the sorority house two or three times a week; gained new friends and experienced a new aspect of college life. I volunteered for everything, with life turning into a smorgasbord of possibilities. Within a year, I was elected vice-president and president-elect of Panhellenic, the sorority system about which I had known nothing just twelve months earlier. Needless to say, I was sure I didn't fit, I still felt marginal, but I was definitely enjoying life.

About the time I started Berkeley, mother found a job selling yardage. Her husband had forbidden her working, claiming that would be "an insult to his manhood." Added to my part-time salary, the little she earned gave her the courage to end the trauma of her marriage. Financially, we were better off than when money was thrown away on alcoholic binges. I was juggling work, school, and extracurricular responsibilities, but I was learning about my own capabilities, opportunities, and alternatives to my mother's way of life. My high school friends were still supportive, though none of them went on to university. New friends boosted my self-esteem and let me believe that nothing was impossible.

Shirley Foster Hartley

115

Although I dated a lot, usually having different, but consistent, Friday, Saturday, and Sunday dates, I really thought I would never marry. Observing my mother's two failed marriages and the general dating games that people played, I could not imagine finding a trustworthy male who could also "light my fire." Fortunately for me, I dated many men willing to have an ongoing relationship without expecting that we jump into bed after the first or even the fiftieth date. The one person who had really created a spark had transferred to the University of Washington a month after our meeting at the end of my freshman year. Neither of us had the money to travel to see each other, but we did write, and he drove back with friends a couple of times each year. The more we saw each other, the more determined we were to organize our lives together. Our wedding took place two days after my graduation in June 1950. It seems that my life began with that commitment to and from a trustworthy, handsome man with whom I continue to explore possibilities for growth.

Traditional Wife and Mother

In those days, women were expected to "find fulfillment through husbands and children." So I set about learning to cook, to decorate an apartment and our first home, to sew drapes and bedspreads, and when pregnant, read all about babies, thanks to Drs. Spock and Gesell. What I really learned was that for me, self-fulfillment through others was not possible. Trying to fill my life with a husband and child felt more like stagnation and self-destruction than fulfillment. I tried the housewives' coffee-klatch, more sewing lessons, arts and crafts projects, part-time jobs, and more volunteer work. It was the "woman's role," and I didn't fit. I was sure there was something wrong with me. If I tried to discuss my discontent with other women, I felt their rejection; there were no consciousness-raising groups in those days. A minister suggested that I could "make a sacrament out of doing the dishes"! That didn't work for me. Part-time jobs included no real responsibility. So we planned another child. I read more, volunteered at our daughter's nursery school, sewed more for the children, played games with them, became a Brownie and Cub Scout leader, joined more volunteer organizations.

At the Retarded Children's Guild, I wanted to work with the difficult group, but the professionals had responsibility for them and clearly preferred that volunteers limit themselves to selling used clothing and raising money. I was not interested in the society pages of volunteerism, and estimated that for all women volunteers combined, only fifty cents an hour was earned for the charity. I also loved working with the foreign students at the university but again found myself wanting to be in charge.

My favorite activity for three years running was helping migrant farm laborers in their tent camps because it meant working with those who needed it most. We offered classes in first aid, legal rights, child care, sewing, and English at their two- to six-week campsites. In the fourth and fifth years, we tried serving them year-round in one area. But again I didn't fit, I was a marginal person. Social workers resented the volunteers, and we were often used as unpaid baby-sitters. I found myself looking for ways to reorganize the social service system, but a professional degree was needed to achieve the things I wanted to do.

Each time I discussed my restlessness with my husband, Dave, he was sympathetic. In fact, he could read my moods before I was aware of them myself. He was more conscious than most men that many doors were closed to women, and he encouraged me to push some of them open. So he made it easy for me to go back to school, taking a few classes at first, then a heavier load when I became really serious.

Graduate School

In 1961, at age thirty-two, I was the only "older" woman in my classes at San Jose State. I knew I didn't fit, but I was enjoying it so much that there was no way to stop me. I took any course that interested me in political science, history, and sociology, hooked on learning in general and on sociology in particular. Dave was delighted, but our families and friends didn't understand my excitement. I still had no women role models and no idea how I might use the courses I was taking, but one step at a time I moved toward a master's in sociology. When I began job hunting, I was told I needed a degree in social welfare if I wanted to work in social services. Meanwhile, I asked to meet the unemployed wife of one of my male professors. She encouraged me to continue graduate work, suggesting that even though she had not been able to get a job using her sociology Ph.D., women should be prepared when opportunities opened up. (Years later, she became president of San Jose State University.) With that one thread of encouragement, I applied to doctoral programs at both Stanford and the University of California, Berkeley.

I was more enthusiastic about Berkeley, based on what I had read about the faculty, but thought I should learn about the Stanford program as well. When I went there after applying, I was referred to a faculty member who made it clear that "Stanford doesn't accept middle-aged women [I was thirty-three] who just happen to live in the area. We expect our Ph.D.s to teach at Harvard and Columbia."

After that put-down, I was not inclined to attend Stanford when the university formally accepted me. My commitment to Berkeley was now complete, and Dave agreed that we would move the family closer, assuming that I would be accepted at Berkeley as I had been at Stanford. I was shocked when the sociology department secretary informed me that acceptance was not automatic simply because I had met all the requirements. Public universities have differential standards, too.

When I interviewed a Berkeley faculty member, he suggested that an older married woman might "add some diversity to the younger, radical students, who seemed to despise the society they were studying." Again I didn't fit, though accepted into the program, as faculty and graduate students were all males. Then I discovered that Mary Taylor, a San Jose friend, had decided to enter the Berkeley sociology graduate program. Although sociology was her first love, she had originally planned to go for a Ph.D. in anthropology, since Margaret Mead and Ruth Benedict served as role models. When classes began in September 1963, we did meet a few other women.

Our theory and research classes were amazingly large for a graduate program, and I felt I was in way over my head. I was an eager student but said not a word in class for fear of showing my ignorance. I made my experience more difficult by choosing term paper topics about which I knew nothing, instead of building on what I had already learned. One of my first papers was a comparison of Freud and Talcott Parsons, whose complete works I read at the pace of ten pages per hour. For a full year I felt intimidated by both faculty and students.

My multiple roles—student, wife, mother, daughter, friend, volunteer—entailed overlapping conflicts and frustrations. Except for family gatherings at our home, my role-partners were relatively isolated from each other and knew little of my difficulties. I was too busy to complain; the more tasks and roles I added, the more I was able to juggle.

In my second year at Berkeley, I finally had a small class, a seminar on Durkheim with Leo Lowenthal. The males took over the first few class sessions, but as the three women began to contribute, we discovered that our comments were valued by both the professor and our fellow students. I enjoyed the opportunity to know Ruth Wallace (then Sister John Baptist). Since I had never spoken to a nun, I was amazed at how open she was to all the students. (She continues to integrate and celebrate a diversity of friends and professional colleagues in her life.) The Durkheim seminar was a giant step toward acknowledgment of my intellectual potential. It helped me move beyond feeling that others were more competent than I and boosted my self-esteem in a new arena. I was moving toward finding fulfillment in myself rather than through my husband and children (a burden for them as well as for me).

During that second year of graduate work, I also enrolled in the population class taught by Kingsley Davis. His book *Human Society* (1949) had earlier drawn me to a fascination with sociology. Although I had no interest in population, that course was the only one he was teaching, so with thirty other students, I listened to lectures on a new subject. K.D. (as I've only recently been brave enough to call him) had very strict requirements for term papers. We had to explore significant international issues and do a full population analysis (fertility, mortality, migration, age-sex structure) of a country. I followed up a news report that births out of wedlock had doubled in England. Because I had accepted the stereotype of the English as superrational, cold, not very sexy, that increase seemed strange. My curiosity led to research that was intriguing and satisfying. K.D. returned my paper with the comment that it was "probably publishable." When I asked him where or how that might happen, he said curtly that it was up to me to figure it out, and I could search for some likely journals.

Shirley Foster Hartley

119

Finding a publisher was another learning experience, and I did figure it out. My article, accepted on my first attempt, was published in *Social Forces* in 1966. After that success, K.D. asked if I had any scholarship money. Because my husband was supporting me, I hadn't even thought of seeking any. Davis laughed and said, "Most of our male students have wives supporting them, but it doesn't deter their fellowship requests." K.D. did most of the paper work that made me the recipient of an IBM grant the following year.

With real money coming from IBM, I felt compelled to learn more about computer technology and its utility for social research, so I registered for the seminar in mathematical demography taught by Nathan Keyfitz. (He had come to Berkeley as part of a developing graduate program in demography.) I had none of the prerequisites and was again overwhelmed, sure that I didn't fit. But Keyfitz took off like we were headed for the stars. He totally ignored my dumbfounded expressions. Since he was developing a monograph-text, his lectures zoomed rapidly through the advanced principles of demography. It was clear that everyone else understood, so I began to ask how I could catch up. Compared with the others, I lacked about three years of math, and was so pitiful (the only woman in class) that Bob Redford and several other students began suggesting books on matrix algebra, logarithms, and calculus as aids. In some mysterious way, I made it through the course, completed some creative research and wrote another paper, published in 1970 in the *Journal of Biosocial Science.*

By then a small group of women was meeting to share concerns and support. Jackie Wiseman was one of those who loved to introduce her friends to one another. Kay Meadow was among the first of our cohort to move toward oral exams, and we began some review sessions together. For me, the feeling of belonging and achieving some respect from women I admired was important.

The Dissertation Phase

As I moved toward coursework completion, I searched for dissertation topics. Expanding on my first publication, I began research on childbearing out of wedlock in various societies around the world, collecting all the data on illegitimate births published by the United Nations and many individual countries. Since some had very high rates, others very low, some rising, some declining, I decided to examine level of births out of wedlock as a "social fact." This became a historical and cross-cultural study with special focus on Japan, Jamaica, and England: Japan because even though historically concubinage was legal, and a form of "recognized illegitimate" children existed, nevertheless they reported declining rates of illegitimacy; Jamaica, because more than 70 percent of children were born out of wedlock; England, because the pattern of increasing illegitimacy was like that in the United States. Kingsley Davis, chair of my dissertation committee, teased me about creating an encyclopedia of illegitimacy. Completed and revised, *Illegitimacy* became my second book (published by the University of California Press in 1975). I presented the theoretical framework at the International Sociological meetings in Varna, Bulgaria, in 1970.

The Role of Professor

I was fortunate to enter the job market in 1968 (before my dissertation was complete), a time when universities were expanding. The new California State University at Hayward, twenty-five miles from my home, hired five sociologists, including me, in a single year. The department already had a talented woman, Thelma Batten, who gave me a female role model at last. It became quickly apparent, however, that many of the men in the department were determined to make life difficult for her. Within a couple of years, Thelma succumbed to their tactics and resigned, but she had made it easier for two of the three newer women in the department. I cannot claim that the male leadership purposely made my life difficult. Perhaps I was an insignificant target: preparing nine classes a year, I didn't have time to get in anyone's way. In addition to teaching nine classes, I was assigned many of the odd courses no one wanted. In my first three years I prepared and taught seventeen different courses, ranging from social psychology and sociology of identity to population and human ecology. (Obviously, no one can be a specialist in all those areas.) The only time I actually took offense at attitudes toward my workload was when the chair of the Promotion and Tenure Committee asked if I had "really written" my first book. The implication was that with my teaching schedule, I must have been a workaholic or hired someone else to write it. The promotion went through, but the process was painful: some of the men even criticized the kind of car I was driving.

The publication of my first book (*Population: Quantity vs. Quality,* Prentice Hall, 1972), together with several articles and conference papers, contributed to my nomination to the board of directors of the Population Association of America in 1973. It didn't happen through the normal channels, however. By the early 1970s, women made up between one-fourth and one-fifth of the PAA membership and contributed at least that proportion of professional papers to the annual meetings. Yet the nominating committee proposed the names of eight men for four openings on the board of directors. Harriet Presser and Ruth Dixon collected signatures nominating two women by petition—a new provision in the by-laws. With Mary Grace Kovar, from the National Institutes of Health (NIH), I was elected to a three-year term. Since then, women have always been among the nominees. Indeed, Harriet Presser recently completed a term as president.

The following year, I was elected to a four-year term on the NIH Population Research Panel. Meeting quarterly in Washington, D.C., we reviewed between thirty and fifty proposals submitted each period. Since I was required to return my one-hundred-dollar-per-day honorarium to the university and make up any classes missed, the work of the panel left me exhausted, with little reward.

Continuing to carry heavy teaching loads with little recognition and no release time for professional activities, I was insulted when our university required faculty members to sign a loyalty oath. I refused. The relatively few of us who did not comply got some hassling. (I had a very nasty letter from the Wente winemaker who served on the university board of trustees. He was sure we were Marxists and guilty of shirking our duties until proven innocent.) None of the Marxists I knew were among the nonsigners. There was no plot, no "group"; we were too busy to organize. Our campus president used my protest letter in his discussion with trustees. I hope that it helped in getting the oath withdrawn two months later.

One of my greatest disappointments in the Hayward department was the rejection for tenure and promotion of my friend and coauthor, Mary Taylor, a brilliant woman who completed her Berkeley Ph.D. the year after I did. The circumstances of her hiring contributed to her non-retention. When one of the young men on the faculty left his classes for two weeks without informing anyone, Mary was hired by the acting chair (our only tenured woman) to replace him. She continued to teach, with strong student and faculty support, until time for tenure review. Although she had more publications and better student evaluations than a young male colleague who was recommended for tenure, Mary was not. The former department chair, Peter Geiser, who sat on the promotion and tenure committee for the School of Arts, Letters, and Social Sciences, supported Mary, knowing the quality of her performance, but the department committee's decision held. Several of us urged her to take the case to the university's grievance committee, but her pain was already too great. One of the men on the department committee later confessed to me that there had been a campaign to get at the woman who had hired Mary through the back door. It's hard to imagine that a career can be ruined by such a petty power play.

For the most part, I did not experience any direct sexism in publishing, although there was one instance of not-so-subtle sexism midway through my career, when William Petersen was organizing a book as a tribute to Kingsley Davis on his retirement from the UC faculty. Several women were to be included among the fifteen or so contributors. I was honored to be asked to write a chapter on American women as a minority. It seemed strange to me, however, that I, a middle-aged wife-mother sociologist, would be asked to write on a topic that I hadn't worked on, when Harriet Presser or Ruth Dixon would have been logical choices. However, I was excited about doing research on American women. It happened that some excellent data had become available from the U.S. Census, demonstrating that for six racial and ethnic categories, women were severely disadvantaged in income and on the job market compared with men of equivalent education. The data made the disadvantages of American women obvious. I was proud of the completed article, and amazed when Petersen wrote suggesting a different chapter, oriented to issues faced by middle-class mothers. Clearly, he rejected the feminist thrust of my research. (The paper was published

as the lead article in the second issue of the *International Journal for Women's Studies* in 1978.)

Yesterday and Today

Changes since I received my doctorate are so phenomenal that I can't imagine how my young students can appreciate them. At the time when I went back to graduate school, I was almost embarrassed to talk about it with my husband's colleagues. Twenty years ago I was the only spouse with a career; wives often asked how I could take time away from my family and the support of my husband's career. My enthusiasm for my studies and work didn't allow for guilt feelings. In fact, I believe my relationships with Dave and our children are better because of my many interests.

Today most of the wives of Dave's younger partners and colleagues have careers of their own. Those of my own age are now sympathetic and supportive because their daughters are embarking on or searching for meaningful jobs. Dave and I also meet men who are supportive spouses of the young women who have entered his public finance business.

In retrospect, even though I did not have a stable, secure home life as a child, my high school friends gave me security and a sense of belonging. In college, each small achievement made me a little more courageous.

My husband was more understanding than many. There were no complaints about late dinners or evenings spent studying. When I returned to being a student, I made time to participate in all the activities we had formerly been involved with together.

Through the even greater multiplicity of roles than there is space to discuss, the multiple selves and role conflicts that I have experienced, sociology has given me a framework for understanding my relationships, the social settings in which I've developed, and our interrelated world. National and international professional contacts help me appreciate my Berkeley education more than I did as a student.

Graduate friendships have developed over two decades into close personal ties. Our professors presented the full range of ideologies and activities available to men. It is our contribution to make that range available to women. My hope is that as women knock down walls that limit, push against cultural constraints and create new choices, men will be liberated too, so that together we may create a world of opportunities for all.

Chapter 10

Inside the Clockwork
of Male Careers

ARLIE RUSSELL HOCHSCHILD

An offhand remark made to me years ago has haunted me more and more ever since. I was talking at lunch with an acquaintance, and the talk turned, as it often does among women academicians just before it's time to part, to "how you manage" a full teaching schedule and family and how you feel about being a woman in a world of men. My acquaintance held a marginal position as one of two women in a department of fifty-five, a situation so common that I don't fear for her anonymity here. She said in passing, "My husband took our son to the university swimming pool the other day. He got so embarrassed being the only man with all those faculty wives and their kids." When the talk turned to her work, she said, "I was in a department meeting yesterday, and, you know, I always feel self-conscious. It's not that people aren't friendly. It's just that I feel I don't fit in." She felt "uneasy" in a world of men, he "embarrassed" in a world of women. It is not only the double world of swimming pools and department meetings that has haunted me, but his embarrassment, her unease.

This conversation recurred to me when I met with the Committee on the Status of Women, a newly formed senate committee on the Berkeley campus. We met in the Men's Faculty Club, a row of male scholars framed on the dark walls, the waitresses bringing in coffee and taking out dishes. The talk was about discrimination and about the Affirmative Action Plan, a reluctant, ambiguous document that, to quote from its own elephant-foot language, "recognizes the desirability of removing obstacles to the flow of ability into appropriate occupational roles."

The well-meaning biologist on the committee was apologizing for his department, the engineer reminding us that they were "looking very hard" for a woman and a black, and another reminding us that things were getting better all the time. But I remember feeling what many of us probably sensed but didn't say: that an enormously complex problem—one world of swimming pools, children, women, another of men in departments and committee meetings—was being delicately sliced into the tiny tidbits a giant bureaucracy could digest. I wondered if anything in that affirmative action plan, and others like it across the country, would begin to merge these double worlds. Such plans ignore the fact that existing academic career patterns subcontract work to the family—work that women perform. Without changing the structure of his career, and its imperial relation to the family, it will be impossible for married women to move up in careers and for men to move into the family.

I have heard two standard explanations for the classic pattern of underrepresentation of women at higher university levels, but I doubt that either gets to the bottom of the matter. One explanation is that the university discriminates against women. If only tomorrow it could halt discrimination and become an impartial meritocracy, there would be many more academic women. The second explanation is that women are trained early to avoid success and authority and, lacking good role models as well, they "cool themselves out."

A third explanation rings more true to me: namely, that the classic profile of the academic career is cut to the image of the traditional man with his traditional wife. To ask why more women are not full professors, or "full" anything else in the upper reaches of the economy, we have to ask first what it means to be a male full professor—socially, morally, and humanly—and what kind of system makes them into what they become.

The academic career is founded on some peculiar assumptions about the relation between doing work and competing with others, competing with others and getting credit for work, getting credit and building a reputation, building a reputation and doing it while you're young, doing it while you're young and hoarding scarce time, hoarding scarce time and minimizing family life, minimizing family life and leaving it to your wife—the chain of experiences that seems to anchor the traditional academic career. Even if the meritocracy worked perfectly, even if women did not cool themselves out, I suspect there would remain, in a system that defines careers this way, only a handful of women at the top.

If Machiavelli had turned his pen, as so many modern satirists have, to how a provincial might come to the university and become a full professor, he might have the following advice: enter graduate school with the same mentality with which you think you will emerge from graduate school. Be confident, ambitious, and well-aimed. Don't waste time. Get a good research topic early and find an important but kindly and nonprejudicial benefactor from whom you actually learn something. Most important, put your all into those crucial years after you get your doctorate—in your twenties and thirties—putting nothing else first then. Take your best job offer and go there no matter what your family or social situation. Publish your first book with a well-known publisher, and cross the land to a slightly better position, if it comes up. Extend your now-ambitious self broadly and deeply into research, committee work, and editorships, to make your name in your late twenties and at the latest early thirties. If somewhere along the way teaching becomes the psychic equivalent of volunteer work, don't let it bother you. You are now a full professor and can guide other young fledglings along that course.

Discrimination

When I entered Berkeley as a graduate student in 1962, I sat with some fifty other incoming students that first week in a methodology course. One of the two sociology professors on the podium before us said, "We say this to every incoming class and we'll say it to you. Look to your left and look to your right. Two out of three of you will drop out before you are through, probably in the first two years." We looked blankly right and left, and quick nervous laughter jumped out and back from the class. I wonder now, a decade later, what each of us was thinking at that moment. I remember only that I didn't hear a word during the rest of the hour, wondering whether it would be the fellow on my left, the one on my right, or me. A fifth of my incoming class was female, and in the three years that followed, indeed, three-quarters of the women (and half of the men) did drop out. But a good many neither dropped out nor moved on, but stayed trapped between the M.A. and the orals, or the orals and the dissertation, fighting the private devil of a writing block, or even relaxing within that ambiguous passage, like those permanent "temporary buildings" standing on the Berkeley campus since World War II.

Much of the discrimination argument rests on how broadly we define discrimination or how trained the eye is for "seeing" it. Women have acclimatized themselves to discrimination, expect it, get it, and try to move around it. It is hard to say, since I continually re-remember those early years through different prisms, whether I experienced any discrimination myself. I don't think so. I considered quitting graduate school to the extent of interviewing at the end of my first miserable year for several jobs in New York that did not pan out. Beyond that, my uncertainty expressed itself in virtually every paper I wrote for the first two years. I can hardly read the papers now since it appears that for about a year and a half I never changed the typewriter ribbon.

That uncertainty centered, I imagine, on a number of issues, but one of them was probably the relation between the career I might get into and the family I might have. I say "probably" because I didn't see it clearly that way, for I saw nothing very clearly then.

Women Cooling Themselves Out

The second explanation for the attrition of women in academe touches private inequality more directly: women sooner or later cool themselves out by a form of "autodiscrimination." Here, inequality is conceived not as the mark of a chairperson's pen, but as the consequence of a whole constellation of disadvantages.

Some things are simply discouraging: the invisibility of women among the teachers and writers of the books one reads or among the faces framed on the walls of the faculty club; the paucity of women at the informal gathering over beers after the seminar. In addition, there is the low standing of the "female" specialties—like sociology of the family and education—which some early feminists like me scrupulously avoided for that stupid reason. The real thing to study, of course, was political sociology and general theory: those were virtually all-male classes, from which one could emerge with a "command" of the important literature.

Women are discouraged by competition and by the need to be, despite their training, unambivalent about ambition. Ambition is no static or given thing, like having blue eyes. It is more like sexuality: variable, subject to influence, attached to past loves, deprivations, rivalries, and many events long erased from memory. Some people would be ambitious anywhere, but competitive situations tend to drive ambition underground in women. Despite supportive mentors, for many women there still remains something intangibly frightening about a competitive environment, competitive seminar talk, even about argumentative writing. While feminists have challenged the fear of competition—both by competing successfully and by refusing to compete—and while some male dropouts crossing over the other way advise against competing, the issue is hardly settled for most women. For those who cannot imagine themselves inside a competitive environment, the question becomes: How much is something wrong with me and how much is something wrong with my situation?

Models of People and Places

It is often said that a good female "role model" can make up for the pervasive discouragement women find in academe. By role model I mean simply a person whom a student feels she wants to be like or could become. It is someone she may magically incorporate into herself, someone who, intentionally or not, throws her a psychic lifeline. A role model is thus highly personal and idiosyncratic, although she may fit a pattern. I am aware of being part of an invisible parade of models. Even as I seek a model myself, I might be one to students who are, in turn, models to others. Various parades of role models crisscross in the university, each going back in psychological time.

There is a second sense in which we can talk of models—models of situations that allow a woman to be who she gradually gets to want to be. Among the inspiring leaders of this parade are also some sad examples of women whose creativity has cramped itself into modest addenda, replications of old research, or reformations of some man's theory—research, in sum, that will not "hurt anyone's feelings." The other human pinch is remaining single among couples, having one's sexual life an item of amused curiosity. For still others, it is the harried life of trying to work and raise a family; it's the premature aging around the eyes, the third drink at night, the tired resignation when she opens the door to a sparkling freshman who wants to know "all about how social science can cure the world of war and poverty." There are other kinds of models, too.

Women respond not simply to a psychological lifeline in the parade, but to the social ecology of survival. If we are to talk about good models we must talk about the context that produces them. To ignore this is to risk running into the problems I did when I accepted my first appointment as the first woman sociologist in a small department at the University of California, Santa Cruz. Some very strange things happened to me, but I am not sure that anything happened to the department or university. Sprinkled thinly as women were across departments there, we created a new minority status where none had existed before, models of token women. The first week there, I began receiving Xeroxed newspaper clippings and magazine articles praising the women's movement or detailing how bad the "woman situation" was in medicine or describing Danish women dentists. These clippings that began to swell my files were invariably attached to a friendly forwarding note: "Thought you'd be interested," or "Just saw this and thought of you." I stopped an older colleague in the hall to thank him for an article he had given me and inquired what he had thought of it. He hadn't read it himself. I began to realize that I was becoming my colleagues' friendly totem, a representation of feminism. "I'm all with you people" began to seem more like "You be it for us." But for every paper I read on the philosophy of Charlotte Gilman, the history of the garment union, the dual career family, or women and art, I wondered if I shouldn't poke a copy into the mailboxes of my clipping-sending friends. I had wound myself into a feminist cocoon and left the tree standing serenely as it was. No, it takes more than this kind of "model."

The Clockwork of the Career System

It is not easy to clip and press what I am talking about inside the square boundaries of an "administrative problem." The context has to do with the very clockwork of a career system that seems to eliminate women not so much through malevolent disobedience to good rules, but through making up rules to suit half the population in the first place. For all the turmoil of the sixties, those rules have not changed a bit. The year 1962 was an interesting one to come to Berkeley, and 1972 a depressing one. The Free Speech Movement in 1964 and the black power and women's liberation movements following it seem framed now by the fifties and Eisenhower on one side and the seventies, Nixon, and Ford on the other.

Age discrimination is not some separate extra unfairness thoughtlessly tacked on to universities; it follows inevitably from the bottommost assumptions about university careers. If jobs are scarce and promising reputations important, who wants a fifty-year-old mother of three with a dissertation almost completed? Since age is the measure of achievement, competition often takes the form of working long hours and working harder than the next person. This definition of work does not refer to teaching, committee work, office hours, phone conversations with students, editing students' work, but refers more narrowly to one's own work. Time becomes a scarce resource that one hoards greedily, and time becomes the thing one talks about when one is wasting it. If "doing one's work" is a labor of love, love itself comes to have an economic and honorific base.

The Social Psychology of Career Talk

It is often said that women do not speak up in class as much as men do, and I have noticed it, too, occasionally even in my graduate seminar on the sociology of sex roles. The reason, I suspect, is that they are aware that they have not yet perfected the proper style. (It is often older women, not yet aware of the stylistic requirements, who speak up.) Some say also that women are ignored in conversation because they are sex objects; I think, rather, that they are defined as conversational cheerleaders to the verbal tournament.

Even writing about career talk in cynical language, I find that, bizarrely enough, I don't *feel* cynical, even while I think that way; and I have tried to consider why. I think it is because I know, in a distant corner of my mind, that the very impersonality that competition creates provides the role of the "humanizer" that I so enjoy filling. I know that only in a hierarchy built on fear (it's called "respect," but that is an emotional alloy with a large part of fear in it) is there a role for those who reduce it. Only in a conservative student body is there a role for the "house radical." Only in a department with no women are you considered "really something" to be the first. A bad system ironically produces a market, on its underside, for the "good guys." I know this, but somehow it does not stop me from loving to teach. For it is from this soft spot, in the underbelly of the whale, that a counteroffensive can begin against women's second socialization to career talk and all that goes with it.

Situation and Consciousness

It is for a minority of academic women with children that the contradictions exist in their full glory. My own solution may be uncommon, but not the general contours of my dilemma. When I first decided to have a child at the age of thirty-one, my thoughts turned to the practical arrangements whereby I could continue to teach, something that means a great deal to me. Several arrangements were possible, but my experiment was a preindustrial one—to introduce the family back into the university, to take the baby with me for office hours on the fourth floor of Barrows Hall. From two to eight months, he was, for the most part, the perfect guest. I made him a little cardboard box with blankets where he napped (which he did most of the time), and I brought along an infant seat from which he kept an eye on key chains, colored notebooks, earrings, and glasses. Sometimes waiting students took him out into the hall and passed him around. He became a conversation piece with shy students, and some returned to see him rather than me. I put up a fictitious name on the appointment list every four hours and fed him alone or while on the telephone.

The baby's presence proved to be a Rorschach test, for people reacted very differently. Older men, undergraduate women, and a few younger men seemed to like him and the idea of his being there. In the next office there was a distinguished professor of seventy-four; it was our joke that he would stop by when he heard the baby crying and say, shaking his head, "Beating the baby again, eh?" Publishers and book salesmen in trim suits and exquisite sideburns were generally shocked. Graduate student women would often inquire about him tentatively, and a few feminists were put off, perhaps because babies are out of fashion these days, perhaps because his presence seemed "unprofessional."

One incident brought into focus my identity and the university's bizarre power to maintain relationships in the face of change. It happened about a year ago. A male graduate student had come early for his appointment. The baby had slept longer than usual and got hungry later than I had scheduled by Barrows Hall time. I invited the student in. He introduced himself with extreme deference, and I responded with slightly more formality than I otherwise might. He had the onerous task of explaining to me that he was a clever student, a trustworthy and obedient student, but that academic fields were not organized as he wanted to study them; and of asking me without knowing what I thought, whether he could study Marx under the rubric of the sociology of work.

In the course of this lengthy explanation, the baby began to cry. I gave him a pacifier and continued to listen all the more intently. The student went on. The baby spat out the pacifier and began to wail. Finally, trying to be casual, I began to feed him. He wailed now the strongest, most rebellious I had ever heard from this small armful of person.

The student uncrossed one leg and crossed the other and held a polite smile, coughing a bit as he waited for this little crisis to pass. I excused myself, and got up to walk back and forth with the baby to calm him down. "I've never done this before. It's just an experiment," I remember saying.

"I have two children of my own," he replied. "Only they're not in

Berkeley. We're divorced and I miss them a lot." We exchanged a human glance of mutual support, talked of our families more, and soon the baby calmed down.

A month later when John had signed up for a second appointment, he entered the office, sat down formally. "As we were discussing last time, Professor Hochschild. . . ." Nothing further was said about the prior occasion, but more astonishing to me, nothing had changed. I was still Professor Hochschild and he was still John. Something about power lived on regardless.

In retrospect, I felt a little like one of the characters in *Dr. Dolittle and the Pirates,* the pushme–pullyu, a horse with two heads that see and say different things. The pushme head was relieved that motherhood had not reduced me as a professional. But the pullyu wondered what the pervasive power differences were doing there in the first place. And why weren't children in offices occasionally part of the "normal" scene?

At the same time I also felt envious of the smooth choicelessness of my male colleagues who did not bring their children to Barrows Hall. I sometimes feel this keenly when I meet a male colleague jogging on the track (it's a popular academic sport because it takes little time) and then meet his wife taking their child to the YMCA kinder-gym program. I feel it too when I see wives drive up to the building in the evening, in the station wagon, elbow on the window, two children in the back, waiting for a man briskly walking down the steps, briefcase in hand. It seems a particularly pleasant moment in the day for them. It reminds me of those Friday evenings, always a great treat, when my older brother and I would pack into the back of our old Hudson, and my mother with a picnic basket would drive up from the suburbs to Washington, D.C., at five o'clock to meet my father walking briskly down the steps of the State Department, briefcase in hand. We picnicked at the Tidal Basin near the Jefferson Memorial, my parents sharing their day, and in that end-of-the-week mood, we came home.

Whenever I see similar scenes, something inside rips in half, for I am neither and both the brisk-stepping carrier of a briefcase and the mother with a packed picnic lunch. The university is designed for such men, and their homes for such women. It looks easier for them and part of me envies them for it. Beneath the envy lies a sense of my competitive disadvantage vis-à-vis the men to whom I am compared and to whom I compare myself. Also beneath it, I am aware of the bizarreness of my experiment with the infant box, and paradoxically aware too that I am envious of a life I would not really like to live.

Conclusion

To talk as I have about the evils of the system as they affect a handful of academic women is a little like talking about the problems of the suburb while there are people trapped in the ghetto. But there are problems both with trying to find a meaningful career and with having one on the system's terms. The two problems are more than distantly related. Both finding an academic job and remaining humane once you have had one for a while are problems that lead ultimately to assumptions about the families that lie behind careers. At present, women are either slowly eliminated from academic life or forced imperceptibly to acquire the moral and psychic disabilities from which male academics have had to suffer.

The very first step is to reconsider what parts in the cultural recipe of our first socialization to nurturance and caring are worth salvaging in ourselves, and the second step is to consider how to extend and institutionalize them in our place of work. The second way of creating social justice less often speaks up for itself: it is to democratize and reward that cooperative, caretaking, morally concerned, not-always-lived-up-to womanly virtue of the past. We need that in careers among our professors of either sex. My utopian university is not a Tolstoyan peasant family, but neither is it vita talking to vita. It requires a move in the balance between competition and cooperation, doing well and doing good, taking time to teach a child to swim and taking time to vote in a department meeting. When we have made that change, surely it will show in book prefaces and office talk.

A Postscript through a 1991 Prism

As I reflect on this piece written in 1973, I'm struck by what has changed—the increasing numbers of women in sociology and their impact; but also by what has not changed—the clockwork of male careers.

When I was a graduate student, there was no sociology of gender, not much work on women in the subfields where one might have looked: the sociology of change, sociology of the family, sociology of occupations. In 1962, little had been written that was explicitly about women. Between 1873 and 1960 fewer than 1 percent of all books in the *Subject Guide to Books in Print* were expressly on the subject of women. During that time only sixteen history doctoral theses concerned women, one of them, "Recent Popes on Women's Position in Society," written by a man. Today we have an independent subfield and, indeed, an industry.

The task is to pick the pearls from the hundreds of articles that appear each year.

If we look at the history since 1960, I think it looks like this: a women's movement arose within sociology too, and it changed who came into sociology and to some extent it changed the talked-about ideas in it. Looking back at the culture at large, certain aspects of the women's movement entered the mainstream of American life through a process aptly described by David Riesman as "resistance through incorporation." American culture incorporated what of feminism fit with capitalism and individualism and it marginalized the rest. The culture incorporated the idea that a woman has a right to a job and to equal pay. But it resisted a real change in the structure of work and in the social character of men. This social change "sandwich" is causing serious strains in American family life.

To understand the women's movement, I now feel we must understand the ideals of the movement itself (equality and the humanizing of a society we would be equal in), the cultural soil in which the ideas are received (individualist and capitalist culture) and the array of interest groups poised to see what they want in the new situation (business seeing a cheap skilled labor pool, men seeking a way out of commitments to children). At the time we were "seeing" through our ideals and not really understanding the messy way social movements work. We had some growing to do.

The Convergence of Personal and Professional: The Berkeley Sociology Department's Women's Caucus

In 1968, I was an instructor in the department, with a master's degree three years behind me. A series of women had come into my office in the fall of that year, each talking casually about dropping out of graduate school. When one highly able student, Alice Abarbinal, said she planned to drop out, I remember dropping what I was doing. "Why would Alice drop out?" I knew why X or Y might drop out, but Alice? She was doing so *well*. She seemed so at ease. It was one of those grains of sand that made me question the universe. A week later, after talking with friends, I invited women graduate students to my apartment on Virginia Street. Besides Alice—who did eventually drop out to become a psychotherapist—those who came included Judy Gavin, Dair Gillespie, Sue Greenwald, Suellen Huntington, Carol Joffe, Ann Lefler, Anita Micossi, Margaret (later Rivka) Polotnick, Marijean Suelzle, and Ann Swidler. The late Gertrude Jaeger, then a lecturer in the department, came to that first meeting, escorted to the door and later retrieved, amid much hilarity, by her husband, Philip Selznick.

That evening, we sat in a circle on the living room floor, drank coffee and beer, ate a lot of potato chips, and felt a certain excitement. I remember asking whether there was some problem we shared as women that is causing us to become discouraged. One by one we went around the circle: "No." "No." "No." One woman said, "No, I have an incomplete, but I had a hard time defining my topic." Another said, "I have been blocked too, but I have a difficult professor, nothing to do with his being a man." Someone else said, "I'm just not sure about this discipline—it's me." No one hinted that there might be a link between these hesitations, dropping out, and being a woman. I remember turning to a friend and confiding, "Never mind, we tried." But after adjourning the meeting, a curious thing happened: no one left. Two hours later, graduate students were huddled in animated groups, buzzing about professors, courses, housing, boyfriends. An invisible barrier had disappeared.

Apart from Gertrude Jaeger, no professors in our department were women. Yet a fifth of the graduate students were women, hoping one day to become professors. How was this to happen? That was the question our meeting allowed us to unbury. After that first meeting, we met periodically for several years. We were at our best in questioning the basic concepts in sociology, and in trying to picture what sociology would look like if women's experiences counted as much as men's. What are "social status" and "social mobility," concepts so central to our discipline? How do you measure a woman's status—by her husband's occupation (as it was done in the sixties) or by her own occupation? And if she's a homemaker, how do we appraise her status? Do we measure her occupational mobility by comparing her occupation with her father's? With her mother's? Or again, what are the stages of moral development? Are these the same for women and for men? Are nonverbal gestures understood through the same framework of meaning for men as for women? In those years there was some talk about race, ethnicity, and sexual choice, but these were topics whose centrality was yet to be fully understood.

In 1969, I was invited to edit an issue of *TransAction* magazine on the role of women, and various members of the caucus submitted articles. Anita Micossi wrote an article on women's liberation as a religious conversion. I suppose for some of us the movement had elements of that, but if so, we converted to a very talky intellectual religion—unitarianism, say—where the main point was to reinterpret the scriptures. Meanwhile, over the next few years we learned of similar small groups springing up in English, in History, in Anthropology departments. There is now a sex and gender section of the American Sociological Association with over a thousand members. Lucy Sells's dissertation data showed that the number of graduate women who dropped out of the sociology department decreased after the formation of our caucus.

If there had not been a social movement such as came along in the sixties, we would not have had that first meeting of the caucus, and probably would not have developed that intellectual world as deeply as we did. I think those questions are partly behind my book *The Managed Heart* (1983), and behind my essay, "The sociology of emotion and feeling: selected possibilities," in Marsha Millman and Rosabeth Kanter's 1975 edited collection, *Another Voice*. The idea of taking the world of emotions and feelings seriously went along with taking women's experience and public perceptions of that experience seriously. From there it was a small step to propose making the study of emotions more central to sociology. I think others drew inspiration from this collective consciousness in a similar way.

I have been deeply influenced by the writings of Erving Goffman, by his focus on the have-nots of dignity and by the poetry in his viewpoint. At the same time, the scrappy, politicking Hobbesian world in which characters such as Preedy (in *Presentation of Self in Everyday Life,* 1959) strut around almost seemed to describe a male world from the point of view of a highly sensitive and pained critic. But I began to think that such a vantage point left some things out. My direct contact with Goffman came after he had left Berkeley. He was teaching in the late sixties when I was a student, but it was his habit to brusquely shoo out auditors. Discouraged by his manner, I left along with the others. But I went home and carefully read everything he wrote. When he came back to UC Berkeley after accepting a position at the University of Pennsylvania, he visited a faculty study group that I had joined. (This was after I had my Ph.D., had taught at UC Santa Cruz and returned to Berkeley as an assistant professor). It was through this group that I got to know him. Once or twice I sent him articles, and he called me with wonderfully trenchant comments and warm human support. To me it was God himself calling. Years later, when he was sick with cancer, I called several times to see how he was doing, and humorously he turned the question around, "So how are your emotions?" After he died, his widow called to tell me that a paper of mine on "emotion work" was on his desk. That still means a lot.

So I had a foot in two worlds as I was working on *The Managed Heart.* If I had been only in the Goffman world or only in the world of the Berkeley Women's Caucus, the *Managed Heart* might never have been born. *The Second Shift* (1989) and, in some way, everything I have written since, is an extension of *The Managed Heart*.

During my graduate student years, my personal adviser and thesis adviser, Neil Smelser, responded to my struggling papers with insightful clarity and human care. He had more students than any other professor in the sixties, many different in approach and topic from him, but he nurtured us all. I found in him a pillar of support, for which I am extremely grateful to this day.

Current Concerns about Women and the Workplace

My next project is to follow up *The Second Shift* by looking at the workplace. The number of women doing industrial work worldwide has doubled since 1950. But they have done such work without the services they need, without changes in ideas about what was previously "men's work," and without altered ideas about a proper workday. So the price of women's entrance into the labor force has often been high: hurried childhoods, a scarcity of personal leisure, new emotional uncertainties. Given this new reality, the question is: How can we unstall a "stalled revolution"?

In addressing this question, I've begun to question what we mean by family, what we mean by work, and how we might create a healthy balance between the two. What gender strategies do women pursue to arrive at a balance? What emotional geography lies beneath these strategies and what emotional consequences follow from them? I have been focusing on women in the United States, but am beginning to look at other cultures in which the same revolution occurs with more or less of a "stall."

Let me end my essay in this book about women at Berkeley with a reflection about women of color. When I hear my graduate students struggling to de-center gender theories woven around white suburban homes, questioning the universality of Nancy Chodorow's theory of gender personality, or asking where black women are in Rosabeth Kanter's theory of corporate life, I am seized by a sense of déjà vu. In the sixties at our meetings on Virginia Street we were ferreting out the androcentrism in functionalism and Marxism. Now my graduate students are helping ferret out the ethnocentrism in feminist theory, itself derived through just such lines of questioning. Maybe that's what it's all about. Each generation cuts its intellectual teeth on the best social theory of the day, exploring every detail to see just how far it reaches when you ask whose experience it speaks to.

The clockwork of male careers has proved easier to join than to change. More women, including women of color, have careers. But careers themselves still fit into the same giant clock. The struggle to balance work and family is one we will have to continue into the next century.

But the challenge to this clockwork, and to the basic ideas and interests that sustain it, has inspired good ideas. I used to imagine that the sociologist got a brilliant idea sitting alone in the library, like the lone scientist concocting a potion in the garage. But behind any great idea, of course, is a great climate of opinion. It is the very culture of challenge that may well produce the enduring ideas of the future.

Chapter **11**

The Personal Is Political
and Professional

HARRIET B. PRESSER

The slogan "The personal is political" was a key insight fueling the resurgence of the feminist movement in the late sixties. Women increasingly came to understand that many of our day-to-day activities, such as our sexual and reproductive behavior and our work both within and outside the home, were not strictly private matters but also had political significance. Power can be subtle and if we, as women, want to expand our options and have greater control over our bodies and our lives, we need to raise our consciousness about the linkages between private and public and empower ourselves with this knowledge. In this way, we take charge of our lives and help other women.

When I was a woman in my early thirties, with a recent Ph.D. and a decade of being a single mother, the message rang loud and true—and I have identified as a feminist ever since. I understood, both theoretically as a sociologist and personally from experience, the strength of social constraints on one's behavior. But I did not anticipate at that time the extent to which my special interest in demography would generate a research agenda that reflected both my personal experiences and my political concerns. The potential to combine these domains as a demographer has undoubtedly enhanced my commitment to the field, and perhaps my perspective has helped broaden the field itself. For me, then, the personal is not only political but also professional.

Getting to Berkeley

Growing up in Miami Beach, Florida, my aspirations as an adolescent in the 1950s were to get married, have three or four children, and live happily ever after. In my senior year, I was head majorette of my high school, class vice-president, and selected by my class not only as "Best All Around" but—much to my surprise—also as "Brain Trust." (I felt uncomfortable with that title and would have much preferred "Most Popular.")

Going away to college was important to me mostly for social reasons, which included finding a good husband. I planned to major in education, so that if I managed to finish four years before getting married, I could have a better job than secretary.

I worked during high school as well as college to meet most of my college expenses. My mother and stepfather had little money and were not supportive of my college decision. They thought a high school degree was sufficient for me as a female, especially since I had a moderately active social life and thus was likely to marry soon. Both of them had had to drop out of high school because of the Depression, and they thus viewed a high school degree as a significant achievement in itself. My biological father's views were irrelevant, since we had not seen him in years; he had left the state of Florida to avoid paying mandated child support.

With my meager savings and little encouragement, I went off to the University of Florida at Gainesville in September 1954. I attribute my ability to override such constraints to my mother—an excellent role model in self-determination. After a bad first marriage, she raised three children essentially on her own (with some help from my stepfather) by working very hard and complaining very little. An astute business-woman, she borrowed money to lease small hotel concessions (a cocktail lounge and snack bars), and eventually became a hotel owner. I expect I was influenced more by watching her survive in the face of adversity than by her traditional role expectations for me.

At college, my first course in education was one of my worst. We sat in a circle and were expected to talk about child development. I was bored with what seemed like idle chatter. The professor gave me my only C and suggested that I change my major. The only alternative I could think of that would lead to an occupation after only four years of college (should I not marry) was social work or nursing. I thought only in terms of female occupations. Although I aced my math course and other "male" subjects as well, neither my professors nor I translated this ability to pursuing a "male-type" career. I decided on social work, and thus took my first sociology course.

My uncertainty over this decision was less a concern when, during my second year at college, I met the man I was soon to marry. He was to graduate in June 1956, and he elected to go to the navy's officer candidate school rather than be drafted. This meant we could afford to be married, as we were in December 1956. I was then twenty years old, the median age at marriage for my cohort. Our marriage was timed on the basis of his college completion, not mine—which seemed appropriate to both of us. (The common two-year age difference between brides and grooms undoubtedly had this effect for many women of my cohort.) He expected to be stationed near Emory University, where I would complete my education, but these plans did not work out. Instead, I followed my husband and his moving ship and became pregnant after seven months of marriage, again matching the national median: becoming a mother at age twenty-one. Soon after our daughter was born, my husband was stationed at the Pentagon in Arlington, Virginia, near Washington, D.C.

I decided, with my husband's encouragement, to go back to school. Although our daughter was but a few months old, returning to school was feasible because George Washington University (GWU) offered many courses at night, so I could take several courses a semester and still be home with our daughter during most days. My husband, who was working rotating shifts, could care for her some of the time, requiring only minimal baby-sitting expense. I was motivated by the fact that I was not happy with my marriage, we had no friends or family in the area, and school seemed one way of making my life more interesting. It was not career aspirations that led me to go back. I loved being a mother, wanted more children, and could envision being a full-time homemaker, as most mothers then were. I chose to major in sociology largely because that would pick up where I left off, and it minimized the number of additional courses needed for graduation.

While I was attending GWU, I decided to separate from my husband, forcing me to think hard about alternatives. In other words, it took a bad marital experience to jolt me into giving serious consideration to a career.

After receiving my B.A. from GWU in 1959, I had two job offers in the Washington area: one as a secretary and one as a statistician at the Census Bureau (for which my credentials had been stretched). The former paid more—but it would put me back in the job category I had before going to college. I chose the latter. While the job in the Field Methods Branch was interesting, I found I could not survive economically even working full-time because my low salary was not sufficient to cover child care plus basic living expenses. (I was receiving very little child support and no alimony.) Moreover, I felt I was not spending enough time with my daughter, who was only one year old. I decided to go home to Miami Beach and live with my mother, who was now separated from my stepfather.

It was not easy to cope financially in this arrangement either, and I soon took a job as a hostess in a restaurant, working from 5:00 to 9:00 P.M., while my mother, who operated both a day and a night business, cared for my daughter in the evening hours. My mother and I became very close at that time, but I was isolated from people my age and bored—experiencing the "feminine mystique" in the context of single motherhood. I then thought very seriously about going to graduate school. With a graduate assistantship, I could still spend much of the day with my daughter, be with people my age, and manage financially.

During my last year as an undergraduate, two of my sociology professors at GWU who had received their Ph.D.s from the University of North Carolina at Chapel Hill had encouraged me to apply there; indeed, Richard Stephens had nominated me for a Woodrow Wilson Award (which I did not receive—nor did most other female applicants in those years). The strongest attraction for me of Chapel Hill was that it had a child care center, which may have been unique at that time for a university.

I decided to apply to UNC and nowhere else. Since my grade point average was very good, I had every reason to expect that I would be admitted, and I was. I did not receive a graduate assistantship, however. Instead, I received an encouraging letter from the chair of the sociology department, leaving the possibility of funding open. The choice of sociology as a major, again, was a practical one; I was not sure what I could do in this field professionally, but I had liked some of the undergraduate courses, my sociology professors were willing to write letters of recommendation, and I had little sense of the alternatives.

When my daughter was two years old (and I, twenty-three), I left Miami Beach for Chapel Hill to earn a master's degree in sociology. The initial reception by the department chair was cold and very disappointing: the encouraging note I had received was a form letter not intended for a female divorcee with a young child; the chair, a family sociologist, explicitly told me that because of my family status, I was "a bad risk." Instead, he encouraged a wealthy female Mount Holyoke graduate who had *not* applied for support to take an unassigned assistantship. As he also had no reservations about providing support to married men with children, I was subjected to a very targeted form of sex discrimination.

The chair suggested that I consider secretarial work and apply for a loan. (I had only a few hundred dollars in savings and my child support payments covered only the cost of the child care center.) My loan application was rejected; the reason: my financial needs were "too great." I did not follow through on seeking secretarial work. Instead, I talked to other professors, and ultimately two arranged for some financial support: Richard Simpson gave me hourly work coding occupational data, which I did evenings at home, and Harry Crockett offered me a half-time teaching assistantship, which paid little but which carried a waiver of my tuition. For the spring semester and the subsequent year, I had a full research assistantship with Daniel Price, a sociologist-demographer. Price subsequently told me he had been impressed that I had chosen a graduate-level minor in mathematics (courageous, indeed, given that I had only one year of mathematics—and no calculus—as an undergraduate), and that I had done very well in my first semester there.

With Price as my adviser, I did my M.A. thesis on work I was preparing for his census monograph: racial differences in occupational experience between 1920 and 1950. (The thesis included a comparison of black and white occupational changes separately for men and women; it never occurred to me, nor was it suggested by my committee members—to include gender comparisons as well.) Although I had a wonderful working relationship with Price, I had no special course in demography and did not identify with any substantive specialization; my favorite courses were Price's social statistics and Ernest Campbell's research methods.

My two years in the sociology department at Chapel Hill were ideal in many ways for graduate study. Despite my initial chilly reception, it was a warm and supportive place for students (perhaps one-third in sociology were female). Faculty were invariably available, the students were helpful to one another, and I felt very much a part of student life even though I was a single mother, perhaps the only one in graduate school at the time.

I did, however, feel stigmatized as a divorcee outside the department, particularly by my female neighbors in graduate married housing (where I had to live because I had a child). These women were all working to put their husbands through school, and they had no qualms about making alternative child care arrangements for their children. Putting my daughter in child care so that *I* could go to school, however, was viewed more negatively. I felt so guilty about my daughter's being at the center that I would pick her up as early as I was free and take her with me to the library or wherever else I had to go. (In retrospect, she might have been better off had she spent full days at the center.)

When I received my M.A. degree in 1962, the department chair explicitly asked me to stay at UNC. Price offered me a research associate position at the Institute for Social Research (which he directed), at a salary that would exceed what most graduate students received. But I wanted to leave. Properly credentialed, I felt I could get a well-paying nonsecretarial job. Although I had an active social life in Chapel Hill, a small academic town felt very confining. I envied my friends in Manhattan and their seemingly more exciting lives in the big city. If I were to do further graduate work—a big "if"—it would be later. Social considerations now had primacy, including my hope of remarrying soon, giving my child a stepfather, and having more children.

Economic factors, however, were relevant in choosing a job. Price arranged two job interviews for me in New York City that generated offers: one from the Russell Sage Foundation and the other from the Institute of Life Insurance. I preferred the former, but the salary was too low relative to the cost of living in New York, including child care expenses, so I took the latter, which paid much more. The institute, a trade association, was interested in developing a social science program within their statistics division and I was to be their sole sociologist. Al Hermalin, then a statistician (who later became a sociologist-demographer) was my immediate supervisor. I had major responsibility for conducting a national survey.

Had I not had this job, I almost certainly would not have gone to Berkeley for my Ph.D. After one year, in 1963, the institute sent me to my first American Sociological Association meeting, held in Los Angeles. At the meeting, I accepted an offer to visit Berkeley and San Francisco and had a wonderful time sightseeing. I fell in love with the Bay area, deciding then and there that I would apply to Berkeley's graduate school. My daughter would soon be ready for first grade, which meant minimal child care costs.

I wrote to Price about my intentions and he contacted Kingsley Davis at Berkeley. While I had applied for admission in the fall of 1964, I received an offer to start in January of 1964 as a graduate assistant for Jacob Yerushalmy, a distinguished biostatistician in the School of Public Health. It was Kingsley Davis's wife, Judith Blake, who had an appointment in the school, who first knew of this opening. While working in the School of Public Health, I could be a graduate student in sociology.

Having successfully braved the unknown at Chapel Hill and now having been guaranteed an assistantship before moving to Berkeley, I decided to quit my job and make the move. As my daughter's father had not maintained contact since our divorce, I felt no reluctance to leave the East Coast.

The Berkeley Experience

While I knew of Berkeley's outstanding reputation as an academic institution, I was unaware of its reputation as a center for intense political activity, so this was not its attraction for me. My quiet politics were to the left, in support of civil rights, and I identified with the Free Speech Movement that erupted during my first year at Berkeley, but I was not an activist. I was, however, keenly interested in the ongoing heated debates at the coffee shop and on the radio; a major movement was underway and it was an exciting time.

Personally, however, what was most significant about Berkeley was that it took me, psychologically, totally out of the fifties. At Berkeley I became truly professionalized, with a strong commitment to the study of demography. Although I thought I might remarry if the right guy came along, this now became a back-burner issue. What helped keep the burner warm was my concern that my daughter was growing up without a father. Yet the men I found most interesting were not ones who would make good husbands or fathers. I spent most of my social time with three men who were friends: a mathematician, a physicist, and a professional bridge player. The intellectual discourse and social activities—chamber music sessions and gourmet dinner parties—made me feel I had come a long way from Miami Beach.

The Berkeley classroom, for me, was not a good way to make friends. In one of my first courses, the class had perhaps fifty students. Many were competing to be heard, to be noticed by the two professors who jointly taught the class. I remained silent in class and I consulted one of the professors about my term paper—that was the extent of interaction. It was an alienating early experience and quite a contrast to the warm, supportive Chapel Hill environment. The other sociology courses I took had fewer students, some fewer than ten, but even then I remained fairly quiet. I was awed that I was being taught by sociologists who had written the books and articles that were required reading at Chapel Hill, although disappointed with several who seemed more talented as writers than as teachers.

The two most important faculty members for me were Kingsley Davis and William Petersen, both excellent teachers and both demographers strongly rooted in the sociological tradition. They were accessible and supportive, and I greatly admired their intellect and scholarship. I audited two demography courses taught by Judith Blake in the School of Public Health, and admired her as well. That was my only exposure to a female professor as a graduate student.

The international perspective of demography opened the world for me, as my training in Chapel Hill had focused almost entirely on the United States. While we read about population growth and decline, mortality and migration, it was fertility that interested me most. Kingsley Davis continually stressed the connections between social structure and demographic change. The rapid population growth in developing countries, resulting from precipitous declines in infant mortality, was the major policy issue of the time and the focus of Davis's policy concerns. Both he and Judith Blake believed strongly that the expansion of family planning programs was not sufficient to counter this growth; that pronatalist aspects of these societies were important constraints. Although sympathetic to this view, the appeal of demography for me was that it dealt with the control of human reproduction in relation to women's lives. At that time, however, this linkage was not articulated from a feminist perspective. Even many years later, when Ruth Dixon (Mueller) and I participated in a session at the Population Association of America titled "The Roles and Status of Women: A Concern for Demographers?" this topic was considered radical. Demography also appealed to me because the phenomena that demographers were trying to measure and explain were concrete, not highly abstract.

Kingsley Davis was head of the International Population and Urban Research (IPUR) center at Berkeley. Although broadly interested in all regions of the world, his focus then was Latin America. Davis played an important role in helping me obtain a Population Council Fellowship for three years, 1964–67, which sealed my commitment to the field. There were not many women (or Americans) who were awarded these fellowships in the sixties. Although I received the same basic stipend as a man, as a woman I was not eligible for a dependent's allowance—even though the Internal Revenue Service recognized me as the "head of household" with a dependent child. Only men were entitled to the dependent's allowance, with an extra allowance for even an employed wife!

My fellowship did not require employment; thus I worked directly with Davis only in the summer, but Davis gave me a permanent desk at IPUR. This location had both positive and negative aspects. I had a "home" among the staff and students in demography at IPUR; on the other hand, it was far from the sociology department and I barely knew other sociology graduate students. Only when I was preparing for my oral comprehensive exams did I become friendly with some of them; we organized study groups in our overlapping areas.

I had some contact with graduate students in other disciplines (economics and history) who were interested in demography. A few took Davis's courses, but David Eversley, a visiting professor and economic historian from England, formed a larger group of students interested in demography to meet regularly in his home for informal seminars. (Only once was I invited to a Berkeley sociology professor's home, and only once in Chapel Hill.)

Overall, I did not feel discrimination either as a woman or as a single mother during my Berkeley days. Indeed, the fact that I had a young child might have kept Kingsley Davis from encouraging me to go to Puerto Rico for my dissertation research, but this was not the case. When we discussed my interest in studying sterilization in Puerto Rico, he suggested I go there and gave me names of Puerto Rican demographers to contact; he also helped me get supplemental funds for this trip from the Population Council. Davis encouraged other students to do demographic research outside the country as well; around this time, Robert Kennedy went to Ireland and Janet Salaff to Hong Kong.

Looking back, it is hard for me to understand how I was able to leave for that distant island with my eight-year-old daughter, having little knowledge of Spanish, only a vague dissertation plan, and the names of a few people to contact. I was more frightened than when I had left for Chapel Hill or Berkeley, but perhaps I was strengthened by the success of these experiences. I knew I did not want to do a boring library-based dissertation, based on published data, which is my view of my M.A. thesis.

In Puerto Rico, I was given access to the data from a recent island-wide health survey, and found—much to everyone's surprise—that over one-third of Puerto Rican women had been sterilized. How this unprecedented widespread phenomenon came about and the social and demographic correlates of its practice were the subject of my dissertation. This was my first taste of the thrill of discovery—rare in sociology—and has influenced my research approach ever since.

By the time I returned to Berkeley after six months in Puerto Rico, in the midst of data analysis, I had two job offers: one from the University of Texas, where Price had moved, and one from the University of Sussex, where Eversley was on the faculty. The fact that these offers were instigated by professors who had already worked with me undoubtedly overrode the prevailing discrimination against women that existed at that time. I received letters of inquiry from other places where former costudents from Chapel Hill were then placed. I think I would have had difficulty finding a good job at a university where I had no personal contact, as suggested by my experience with one job possibility I was not particularly interested in, at Brown University. The Berkeley professor who had encouraged me to apply to Brown later told me he had learned, much to his dismay, that they had not been interested because I was a single female; they were concerned that I might marry and resign.

I accepted the tenured position of lecturer in demography at the University of Sussex, with the understanding that I would probably stay for only a year or two. I remember feeling that if I did not go to England at that point, with travel expenses paid by Sussex, I probably would never have another chance to travel abroad. (As I have since traveled throughout the world, this was an incredibly poor prediction.) My daughter and I left Berkeley in September 1967 for Brighton, England.

Life after Berkeley

The University of Sussex, the recently opened "red brick" equivalent of Oxford and Cambridge, was an excellent introduction to the academic world of a professor. The students were very good, I team-taught in small classes and lectured in large ones, and I was given some research assistance in completing the data analyses for my dissertation. My daughter and I lived in the charming village of Piddinghoe, she went to an excellent private school, and we both experienced a deep immersion in British culture.

Toward the end of the academic year, however, I was ready to come back to the States. I reopened an earlier job possibility as staff associate at the Population Council in New York City, a foundation committed to population research and technical assistance. Negotiations were conducted by mail, and I accepted the job. The council was an excellent introduction into the international family planning arena. As the first woman Ph.D. in their New York office, I also experienced an introduction to sexism at the entry level as a professional. The most significant overt demonstration came seven months after I arrived, when the Demography Division reallocated job titles. My job title was changed from staff associate to research associate. The other research associates were two women with master's degrees. All the men were made staff associates, even a former research associate with a B.A. degree. This change, which came across my desk as a memo without explanation, offended me greatly. I went to see the head of the division, but he was out of town, so I immediately wrote a memo offering my resignation (despite my lack of immediate alternatives).

A special meeting was called and it was explained that the changes in title were simply a means of distinguishing staff who did work-related travel from those who did not. Division policy excluded women from work-related travel, but this practice was not viewed as discrimination! Why this criterion and not others was used for assigning titles was never satisfactorily explained. However, the council promptly decided to drop the research associate title altogether and to designate all professionals within the division as staff associates.

About four months later I left the council—not because of the job title incident, but because of the general nature of my job. I was about to complete a worldwide assessment of voluntary sterilization for the council, and I did not want to continue doing such integrative review-of-literature research.

My new position at Columbia University in 1969 offered an opportunity to do original research as well as some teaching. I was an assistant professor in sociomedical sciences at the School of Public Health, but my salary came from my joint appointment with the International Institute for the Study of Human Reproduction, located in the Medical School. Ford Foundation had given the institute a multimillion-dollar grant, which enabled me to hire a full-time research assistant and secretary. I was asked to write a proposal for a fertility study in New York City, to help demonstrate Columbia's commitment to the community, but otherwise had no substantive constraints. The perspective I took— a focus on the determinants and early consequences of the mother's age at first birth—marked the beginning of research projects that merged my personal experience with political and professional interests.

Fertility research in the late 1960s generally focused on family size; the issue of teenage fertility was not yet of central concern to demographers. The study at Columbia, which was externally funded, was distinctive in considering the significance of the timing of first births for women's nonfamilial achievements (as well as for subsequent childbearing), offering a life course perspective also rare then among demographers. My own experience as a young mother undoubtedly influenced this perspective, but the reemergence of the feminist movement in the late sixties was also relevant.

At the Population Council (1968–69), I had become interested in the feminist activities of Emily Moore, a friend and colleague who was involved in several new women's organizations. New York State was then considering legalizing abortion. Emily organized a protest at City Hall in New York City because no women had been asked to testify at a hearing on the proposed legislation and the only woman on the hearings panel was a nun, added after an earlier protest against an all-male panel. It is hard to imagine now, but at the time Emily had great difficulty finding women to join the protest. Ruth Dixon (Mueller), a fellow graduate student at Berkeley, had arrived in New York City for a job interview and was willing to join our group of no more than fifteen women. We picketed outside City Hall before the hearing began, then went inside and staged a walk-out during the hearing to gain media attention. That was the beginning of my political education as a feminist. Only a year or two later, there was a huge march down Fifth Avenue in support of the women's movement and reproductive rights; it was no longer difficult to find women (and men) to demonstrate.

The New York fertility survey became longitudinal, and dominated my research interests for the seven years I was at Columbia University, although I also continued to do research on sterilization, documenting its widespread practice in the United States. To help finance my daughter's private school (to which Columbia made a small contribution), I also taught at Rutgers University, commuting one day a week to New Jersey. (We lived at the edge of Harlem: issues of safety as well as quality led to the choice of private school.)

In 1976, when my daughter was about to graduate from high school, I accepted a job offer at the University of Maryland as a tenured full professor in a traditional sociology department. This was a contrast to my untenured position at Columbia, an associate professor on soft money in the School of Public Health. The location of the University of Maryland, in College Park, a suburb of Washington, D.C., was an important factor in my decision; it was part of an attractive, large metropolitan area with an extensive nonacademic demographic community. (Brown University had asked that I come there for a job interview—despite its earlier rejection—but living in Providence, Rhode Island, was not appealing.)

At the University of Maryland, I was the first female full professor in the Department of Sociology. I was insistent on this rank, and believe they agreed because of a then-active lawsuit that had been brought by Margaret Cussler, a tenured associate professor of sociology. She had sued the university for promotion to full professor on the grounds of sex discrimination. (She lost, but in my view she deserved the promotion.) I was the only female full professor in the department for about twelve years.

At Maryland, after completing my New York City study and publishing many articles on the timing of motherhood and its consequences for women, I moved to other research areas that continued to show strong linkages with my personal experiences. Some of these topics, such as child care problems as a constraint on women's employment, are now central to the study of gender, work, and family, but they were not areas of sociological or demographic concern then. Other topics, such as shift work and more generally the work schedules of parents, both men and women, remain peripheral both to sociology and demography— but perhaps not for long. The high prevalence of nondaytime employment in the United States and my finding that one-third of American dual-earner couples with young children include spouses who work different shifts (one during the day and the other during the evening, night, or on a rotating schedule) adds an important temporal dimension to family life, with implications not only for the well-being of parents but also for children.

It startles me as I reflect on how closely my personal experience relates to these topics. Child care constraints were highly relevant to my educational as well as employment decisions. When I was married, my husband worked a rotating shift, facilitating my return to college. After our separation, my mother and I shared child care by working different hours. (My research has shown that one-third of all grandmothers who provide child care in the United States when the mothers are employed have such an arrangement, and the proportion is even higher when employed mothers are single.) The fact that my mother worked nights and at times had two jobs not only bears on my own moonlighting at Rutgers, but also on my interest in work schedules and the rearing of children. I am currently writing about "gendered time," and our need to know more about the meaning of children's time with fathers as well as mothers. Studying gender equity issues resulting from gender differences in parental time in child rearing has strong personal resonance. My current research on gender differences in work-related travel bears directly on my experience at the Population Council.

Whereas personal experiences stimulated interest in certain research areas, political events affected the availability of data to do this research. At first my research progress was threatened by the politics of others, but later I learned how to be political if I was to obtain needed data.

On the threatened side, soon after I was awarded the federal contract to do the longitudinal survey on mothers' timing of first births, tensions arose between Columbia University and the federal government concerning provision of data on gender and race for university personnel. Because the university was deemed noncompliant with affirmative action regulations, the government stopped all contract research funding; ironically, funds for my study on women, directed by a woman, were the first to be impeded. After this issue was resolved, clearance of my questionnaire was delayed by the U.S. Office of Management and Budget because of a general edict to postpone sensitive surveys until after the presidential campaign that brought Richard Nixon's reelection.

On the proactive side, my location in the Washington area some years later helped me to generate government interest in collecting data on certain topics. For example, I worked with the U.S. Bureau of the Census and the National Institute for Child Health and Human Development to get child care data included in the Current Population Surveys. Subsequently, in 1985 and 1991, I worked with the U.S. Bureau of Labor Statistics to resume and expand their data collection on work schedules. Having national parameters that challenge preconceptions of the way Americans engage in their work and family life has helped convince others to collect data on these topics that permit more indepth analyses. Knowledge of these national parameters can also lead to political change.

An important example in this regard is the work of the group Social Scientists in Population Research, which I organized soon after coming to Maryland. Comprised mostly of women in the Washington, D.C., area, and influenced greatly by Barbara Bergmann (an economist then at the University of Maryland), we lobbied successfully to remove the ambiguous and hierarchical concept of "head of household" from the U.S. Census (starting in 1980). Our next effort, again successful, was to get the Census Bureau to collect data on child support. These data revealed a shocking number of American fathers who provided no child support whatsoever, information that played a critically important role in gaining support for the passage of federal legislation to enforce child support. My interest in this effort was fueled by my own father's failure to pay any child support, and the small amount of child support mandated from (and paid by) my ex-husband despite his growing prosperity over the years.

The merging of the professional, political, and personal was collectively validated by the Women's Caucus of the Population Association of America (PAA); many caucus members identified with the merger. It was with great pleasure that I gave my 1989 PAA presidential address

on the topic of work schedules and child care, regarding this as an important platform in which to help legitimate the study of child rearing—and not just child bearing—by demographers. The new Center on Population, Gender, and Social Inequality, which I helped establish at the University of Maryland in 1988 and where I am the first director, is the only demography center in the world to focus specifically on gender issues.

It is extremely satisfying to be spending one's professional time on topics of such central social importance. The disciplines of sociology and demography make this possible. It is also satisfying to have exceeded the career expectations that I as well as others have had for me. This experience is probably less likely among men than women (since career expectations are generally higher for men), and less likely among younger than older women. It is a poor reflection on our society, however, that the choices for women of my cohort were so limited and that it took an unhappy marriage and an early divorce to route me toward my career. Should I be grateful for my bad marriage? Grateful for being a young mother so that additional schooling seemed the best way to generate income and manage child care?

Clearly, we are always making trade-offs, consciously or unconsciously. Seemingly small events (such as my sightseeing trip to the Bay Area in 1961) can direct one's future in unexpected ways. For the past twelve years, I have had the good fortune of having a loving, support-ive man as my partner, as well as wonderful women friends, including three from childhood, who continue to be a vital part of my life. My daughter, now a lawyer, remains very dear to me. A major concern I now have is that the future seems much too predictable.

After writing this chapter, I was offered (and declined) an opportunity to return to Chapel Hill as director of the Carolina Population Cen-ter—an explicit affirmation that I was no longer considered a bad risk. Perhaps the future offers more surprises than I anticipate.

Acknowledgment: This chapter was written while I was a fellow at the Center for Advanced Study in the Behavioral Sciences at Stanford, Cali-fornia. For a more detailed oral history of my career as a demographer, provided as past president of the Population Association of America, see Jean van der Tak, ed., *Demographic Destinies,* vol. 2 (Washington, D.C.: Population Association of America, 1991).—H.B.P.

Chapter 12

On the Way to the Forum

METTA SPENCER

Once upon a time, all the people on earth took off their life stories and hung them on a tree. Then they walked around the tree inspecting lives and chose the one they liked best, to keep as their own. In the end they all picked the life that had been theirs originally. This is a true story. Try it. You'll find it's true for you.

What I prize most about my life is the excellence of my problems. I got them all at UC Berkeley. However, their lingering influence on me cannot be attributed so much to the sociology department there as to the utopian zeitgeist of California in the sixties. Berkeley culture fostered an openness to change, not only among the identifiable crowd of astrologers, orators, and vendors, but also in academe. Only mainstream businesspeople and professionals were unaffected. No doubt that is why I still feel ambivalent toward professionals, though most of my colleagues identify themselves as such. For myself, I prefer to be an intellectual—to orient my work toward civic issues and public discourse.[1]

Russell Jacoby has argued that intellectuals have been in decline in North America since universities expanded after World War II and created professorships that measure performance by publications for academic peers. Productive work for the educated lay audience does not count. Jacoby laments the demise of the "little magazine." In Britain and on the Continent academics are still recognized for contributions to public discourse, but the trend in North America is toward professionalism.[2]

My career has been shaped mostly by two factors: the Berkeley culture, which prized breadth of intellectual vision and activism, and my gender. Berkeley taught me to integrate my work with my personal life, and to direct both toward social reform. Being a woman taught me to choose projects that serve real human beings, and not to be aggressive. These traits have combined in a career in which research and writing constitute praxis, chiefly addressing problems of security and peace.

I have rarely experienced sexist discrimination. Academic men treat me no better and no worse than they treat male students and male colleagues. However, as a woman I rarely fight or negotiate as strongly as a man might for what I want, so I end up with less. On the other hand, I have been able to live by my own values without extreme sacrifice, and I ask for no more than that. Indeed, this is my chosen life story, the one I picked off the tree.

My earliest memories are of an Oklahoma town during the Great Depression: hoboes eating in our back yard; summer evenings at an outdoor revival; winters in Granddaddy's drugstore, where old men sat around the coal stove, spitting and listening to President Roosevelt's fireside chats and, on one scary afternoon, to the news of Pearl Harbor. That changed our lives. Our family moved to Southern California and turned into Republicans.

When I reached eighteen, I left for Berkeley and moved into an interracial co-op for radicals of both sexes. It was 1949, the year of the loyalty oath, and I joined in the defense of professors who refused to sign the anti-Communist pledge. We lost, and some of the most principled professors departed. Our mood was defensive, not daring, as the Free Speech Movement (FSM) would be fifteen years later. I was committed to free speech, not to socialism. That winter, after Norman Thomas finished a lecture in Wheeler Auditorium, I stood up and asked him how socialists proposed to control bureaucracy. I didn't like his answer (which belittled the problem) and I was right.

When I was nineteen, I married a psychology graduate student and left academic life for ten years. I worked at several jobs—some I liked, some I did not—but I lacked a sense of direction and was susceptible to depressions. If there had been a feminist movement at the time, I would not have joined it, but I did learn in therapy what many other women later discovered in consciousness-raising groups: that the dark side of our nurturing trait is a compulsion to respond to all demands.

Even this insight would not have impelled me to take charge of my life if I had remained responsible only for myself. Pregnancy pushed me into making decisions for the sake of my child. Thus, at the age of thirty, I left my marriage, and five months later, in 1960, gave birth to a son. I had three hundred dollars and felt ready for anything.

Alimony was due to be paid for three years, while I earned a B.A. and a teaching credential. The first baby-sitting scheme was the hardest. I pushed the stroller two miles from Oakland to Berkeley to share child care with a history student. She left her class five minutes early and ran to her apartment, where I was ready to run to my class, arriving five minutes late. After several such relay sprints each day, I pushed the stroller home.

I was fortunate that Karl Popper visited Berkeley, as his social philosophy class was the most valuable course I ever took. I learned from it not to measure the effects of teaching by students' immediate responses. At first, his class filled a large hall. Within weeks, it had dwindled to fill only the front row. Now I realize why: Popper made everything so clear that it seemed self-evident. But he was giving us the answers to questions we would understand only later. Whenever I got into a muddle writing a paper, I reviewed Popper's notes, and there his answers were for me, like money in the bank. Another thing I learned from Popper was the value of good intellectual fighting. When a truculent Maoist visited class to hassle the great anti-Marxist philosopher, Popper decided the spatial arrangements did not facilitate fair debate. He placed two chairs face to face on the dais and beckoned the young radical to join him. "Now," he said with a smile, "we can talk." Marx was defeated in the encounter, but his protagonist went away feeling good, beaming and winking at Popper.

I took two courses from Dennis Wrong, who said he was visiting Berkeley because it was Mecca for sociologists; I hadn't realized the department was special, but I was loving sociology and dreaded the education courses. When a friend suggested that I take a master's in sociology and teach in a junior college instead of elementary school, I thought it a brilliant idea.

And so I joyfully began graduate school. In my memory, it is a continuation of the undergraduate period, as I studied with some of the same professors (Herbert Blumer, Neil Smelser, Wolfram Eberhard, Kenneth Bock, and Jerome Skolnick). The other graduate students were headed toward the Ph.D. and assumed that I was too. I made no real decision to go for a doctorate but was swept along by the crowd. (In this case, it carried me in the right direction.)

Graduate work was no harder than the jobs for which I was qualified. The hitch occurred after the first term in 1964, when my alimony and child support unexpectedly stopped and I had to earn additional income. Herbert Blumer genially referred me to a Catholic women's college. The Sister there reasonably judged that I was not yet qualified to teach, but Blumer refused to send her anyone else so I got the job. For the next few years, I worked half-time as a research assistant, taught one course a term at Holy Names, and took a full load.

There was a day care center near home, but my child was barely two and he hated it. I shared his opinion of total institutions for babies and liberated him quickly. He went most places with me; when he was old enough for Montessori school, I scheduled my teaching and errands during his school hours. Many things were sacrificed for my Ph.D.; regrettably, that sometimes included the quality of my son's parenting.

I became a sociologist not through coursework but through my work as a research assistant. At Berkeley's Survey Research Center, social science students of my generation developed a sentimental regard for counter-sorters, machines equivalent to the village well or community quilting frame. Card sorting required long hours of attention, but not careful attention, so each occasion was an opportunity for stimulating talk or for poking into interesting projects. One day I came across a box of cards from India—a political survey of university students. Seymour Martin Lipset was running a major project comparing student politics around the world. I asked for, and was given, the job of analyzing those blessed cards. Blessed because, first, I was paid to do the work and got course credit for it. Blessed because I turned the study into an M.A. thesis. And most blessed because, just before the thesis was complete, that requirement for a master's degree was abolished. By 1969 I had completed a Ph.D. dissertation: "The Politics of University Students in India."

My graduate study, as such, lasted only five years; I could not have kept going longer. Lipset, who surely knew that, was generous all along, one year getting me a fellowship so I did not have to work; he pulled me through. I worked for Marty for about five years. The best possible way to study a text is to edit it, and I had a chance to edit some pieces for him that are still at work in my thinking.

While Lipset was comparing abstract student politics around the world, the real thing began to happen in Berkeley in 1964, when the

Free Speech Movement exploded. I did not participate in the FSM, though I felt its attraction. Watching others sitting on the pavement around the legendary police car, with the captive student inside, I had to remind myself to pick up my four-year-old and fix his supper. Political sociologist Bill Kornhauser, who was standing there too, said thinly to no one in particular, "You don't turn the police on your own students."

The movements of the sixties have run together in my memory like the tie-dyed colors of the period, but at the time my responses to them were differentiated. I was ambivalent about the FSM, which I couldn't help seeing as displaced affect—a substitute for something else that was never articulated, perhaps a Weberian disenchantment with bureaucracy. Lipset came to represent a dark figure in the collective myth. He was a friend of Clark Kerr, president of UC Berkeley, but that cannot explain the image he acquired. Perhaps the explanation was the view of him as a liberal who had once been more radical. In any case, the next term he left Berkeley for Harvard.

My fervor was strongest for the antiwar movement. I passed out leaflets for Robert Scheer, the anti-Vietnam candidate, and marched with thousands on San Francisco's Market Street, carrying my son piggyback. I wrote letters to politicians every night. One day I watched on TV a seventeen-year-old soldier die in Vietnam and, weeping, picked up a felt-tipped pen, scrawled "Murder!" and mailed the word to Lyndon Johnson, complete with my return address. Soon two Secret Service agents appeared at my door in University Village, flashing badges and my letter, now in a transparent folder.

"What did you mean by this?" one asked.

"That Johnson is a murderer!" I replied.

"Oh," said the other, with evident relief. "We thought you were threatening to kill the President."

Before the conversation was over, one of the men said he agreed that Johnson was a murderer. Nevertheless, the event made me feel helpless. I gave up. No more letter writing. No more marching. My activism lay dormant for sixteen years.

Every Sunday night a group of graduate students met at my apartment to prepare for the oral exam. One of us critiqued the book assigned for the week, while the others played examiners. Harriet Presser had started the group by recruiting Janet Salaff and me. The group's emphasis shifted from demography to politics when Harriet moved on. Dick Roman, Arlie Hochschild, Steve Warner, Randy Collins, Dave Makowski, Jean-Guy Vaillancourt, Hal Jacobs, and Barbara Ballis were the longest-running players. Today, Dick and Janet are my colleagues in

Toronto, and Jean-Guy is a treasured ally in the Canadian peace movement and peace research. Arlie is still a best friend. As for Randy, I cited him sixteen times in the last edition of my textbook,[3] compared with twelve times for Durkheim and nineteen for Weber. In the new edition, the gap will close further, especially since Randy alone predicted the decline of the Russian Empire.[4]

In 1967, after my oral exam (not a barrel of laughs), I left for Harvard, where I spent two years. Lipset gave Ann Swidler, another research assistant (now a professor at Berkeley), and me one of his three offices, where we snooped on the John Birch Society for his book written with Earl Raab, *The Politics of Unreason* (1970). The office was a grand room in the Center for International Affairs, whose acronym dropped a hint about a source of its funding, according to the radicals who later blew up the center's library. Henry Kissinger and his staff occupied the offices around us, and Erving Goffman had one across the lounge, where sherry was served to the fellows before lunch. Goffman came in only at night. He was working on *Strategic Interaction* (1969); its title was the only thing linking his work to that hawkish institute.

Harvard differed from Berkeley in ways that meant I had some adjusting to do. In the fall of 1987, Ann Swidler went off to graduate school in sociology at Berkeley, and we used to phone each other and complain. A Radcliffe graduate, she regarded Berkeley people as rude. Whenever she joined a meeting, nobody rose to shake hands; people remained sprawled on the floor, acting as if she had been there all along. She could drift in or drift out; everything seemed to happen in public, where anyone could attend. My complaints about Harvard were the reverse. Harvard was closed doors, closed discussions, and professional demeanor. Once at a cafeteria table, I overheard an interesting conversation and chimed in, as I would have done in Berkeley. I sensed immediately that this was considered rude: nobody had introduced me, so I should have remained invisible. I made my best friends in the India lunch group, intellectuals who met once a week and were not exclusive; Indians are culturally used to socializing in big groups without boundaries.

After a year, Lipset's money ran out and I had to find another job. I taught two courses each term at the University of Massachusetts in Boston and worked on Alex Inkeles's comparative modernization project.[5] Alex, a Harvard professor, had edited a series of short books, *Foundations of Modern Sociology,* that Prentice-Hall wanted to turn into a textbook. Recalling that I loved editing, he invited me to collaborate with him. I said yes, since I was homesick for Berkeley, but I couldn't hunt from Cambridge for research work in California, and the editing project was portable. Little did I expect the book to become a main occupation for the rest of my life.

Back in Berkeley in the spring of 1969 with a brand-new Ph.D., I found myself in a newly competitive job market. I rented a house on Albany Hill, where the schools were still good places for eight-year-olds. As an undergraduate, I had coded data for a study of anti-Semitism and race prejudice among adolescents. Since a book based on the study had never been published, Charles Glock, head of the Survey Research Center, asked if I would like to take the original tapes out for a road test. Yes, indeed.

In the tables, I saw a compelling new story line emerging—one that made us uneasy. The conclusion seemed inescapable that anti-Semitism reflected hurt feelings that became more frequent as the students approached dating age. Under increasing pressure from their parents to socialize only with members of their own religious community, Jewish students evidently withdrew from friendships with lower-status white Christians and formed separate social cliques. The most anti-Semitic white Christian pupils seemed to be those whose previous friendships with Jewish students no longer existed, although their former Jewish friends had not left the school. The Jewish students were likely to win the highest marks and school leadership roles, achievements that exacerbated the resentment. The tables showed powerful percentage differences, but how could such findings be reported without seeming to blame anti-Semitism on Jewish parents?

The dilemma for me became moot. I was hired at the University of Toronto in 1971 and had to move there before the controversial report was written. To my astonishment, Glock told me he would hire someone else to write up my analysis, assuring me that I would be credited as a coauthor. The book that finally appeared bore little resemblance to my research.[6] With ladylike grace, I had let Glock's decision pass without objecting. He suggested that I write a monograph of my own, analyzing the far less promising data on prejudice against blacks. I regret not having insisted on reporting the awkward but important discoveries that I had made.

My other project, the textbook, was more successful, though Inkeles's original plan was not feasible. Not a single book in the series could be turned into a chapter merely by editing. I wrote most of the text, which became an authored book of my own. The first two editions of the textbook sold 52,000 copies during the first year, second place among U.S. textbooks for number of sales. I have now completed eight editions—

four in the United States and four in Canada. Normally, it takes one year to prepare a revision and another to interact with the publisher during production. Then I get a year off before starting over again. I enjoy the work and believe it worth doing. The introductory course is probably sociologists' best way to influence the wider culture.

In 1971, the University of Toronto was still expanding, and I realized I had made a good move. Toronto is a civilized, sophisticated city, hospitable to anyone willing to put down roots. However, Canadian sociology is not exciting. Its orientation is local, not cosmopolitan; professional, not intellectual. Apart from a strong component of nationalism (which I reject on principle), critical social commentary and experiential reflection are rare. (Such a statement shows how deeply my opinions continue to be influenced by West Coast culture.)

My depressions recurred several times, although they were neither conspicuous nor debilitating. I tried a variety of therapies, meditative disciplines, and seminars. I had a long-term interest in Eastern religion, and I found its teachings pervasive in the new therapies. I began to classify various subcultures of therapy and to look for their connections to Eastern religions. During the late seventies I experienced three epiphanies that clarified the origin of my own depressions, and I became sure I would never have another. I decided to write about therapy, not in a way that would rack up points on my curriculum vitae but in a way that would convey insights to other depressed people. I spent a sabbatical year (1979–80) working on the project in California and Asia, interviewing monks and teachers. A huge manuscript resulted— part philosophy, part fiction, part social analysis. I stopped writing after failing to help depressed friends when I attempted to communicate the crucial insights. Some say that people have to find their own solutions through their own efforts. (I don't quite believe that, and may some day resume the project.)

Soon after I ceased working on the cultures of therapy, an inner toggle-switch flipped from introspection to praxis. I regretted giving up activism and advocacy during the Vietnam War. In a stirring film, Helen Caldicott told us, "You must change the priorities of your life if you love this planet." In 1982, like millions of others, I did. I joined a remarkable organization, Science for Peace, and found "hard" scientists more active than social scientists in working for disarmament.[7]

Sociologists have an acquired distaste for advocacy, whereas scientists generally acknowledge a duty to ensure the ethical use of the knowledge they generate. My friends in Toronto are mainly mathematicians and physicists, not sociologists. Throughout the mid-eighties and again before the Gulf war, some of us in Science for Peace lectured or appeared on television at least once a week. And at my suburban college, the peace research resource center adjoining my office was filled with students, endlessly discussing events and planning teach-ins.

In Canada, the party in power consults citizens more than do American administrations. Policy commissions travel the country continually and Ottawa pays attention when groups write policy papers. One consequence of this concern is the creation of remarkable networks. For example, I was for some years a consultant to the Canadian ambassador for disarmament,[8] meeting military advisers and peace activists several times a year, either in a retreat in Canada or at the United Nations. As a result, I know many other Canadian activists well. The government also indirectly funds other peace movement projects, such as my beloved *Peace Magazine*. In 1982–83, the peace movement coalesced in opposing the testing of air-launched cruise missiles in Alberta. The academic community had not yet been mobilized on that question, so I phoned several members of Science for Peace and the chancellor of the University of Toronto, George Ignatieff. We drafted a letter to Prime Minister Trudeau. One of Trudeau's assistants, David Crenna, called and proposed to fly to Toronto to meet us for dinner that very evening.[9] He implied that Trudeau did not want to test the cruise missiles but that Washington's requests could be denied only under strong domestic pressure. Masses of protesters were not in the streets, as Trudeau had hoped they would be. I began to consider how to use my writing and editing skills in mobilizing protest.

In 1982, the disarmament movement needed an information center, so I invited activists to a meeting. We organized the Canadian Disarmament Information Service and began printing a calendar of events. With my son's full-time assistance, this became a tabloid and later *Peace Magazine,* which appears on newsstands across Canada six times a year. I am the editor, my home is the editorial office, and for years I did all the production work. Since I was the first person in Toronto to produce a magazine with desktop publishing, there was no one to teach me and no one to help out. I loved the work, but it absorbed more hours than a full-time job.

Soon I had contributed more to the magazine than I could afford to lose, which gave me a new understanding of the nature of commitment. As Howard Becker once noted,[10] commitment is not a free psychological decision, but an objective predicament—a trap. One finds oneself constrained by the consequences of one's own previous actions, such as painting oneself into a corner, or having to throw good money after bad to protect an investment.

Still, a trap is sometimes an excellent place to be. I had to persevere with *Peace Magazine* because I had foregone other career opportunities and had invested such a large chunk of my savings that I could not turn back. I found myself trapped into doing work of more value, I now believe, than I would otherwise have done.

Peace research has become the liveliest academic area; it is broad enough in scope to suit intellectuals, while creating enough technical problems to attract professionals as well. There are now more than two hundred peace studies programs in American universities, several excellent publications, and some academic organizations, such as the International Peace Research Association (IPRA), the Consortium on Peace Research, Education, and Development (COPRED), and, especially, the War and Peace Section of the American Sociological Association, where one can hear the most stimulating papers of the whole annual convention. (I have served on the boards of these groups.)

The key debate within the Canadian peace movement in the eighties concerned nonalignment. Initially, I focused strictly on convincing people in the West to reverse the nuclear arms race. To concentrate our forces, I believed that related issues must be deferred. We could not progress by including campaigns for democracy or human rights. I recall with chagrin a dinner with historian Edward P. Thompson, prominent member of the British disarmament movement. I spoke so vociferously along these lines that he observed, "You are a very aggressive woman." Thompson, from a nonaligned position, recommended standing by democratic values, supporting independent peace activists in the East, and criticizing NATO and the Warsaw Treaty Organization equally for the arms race. By 1983, I came around to his position, but it was not the predominant view in the Canadian peace movement until the Soviet Union began to fall apart.

The pre-eighties movement had been disproportionately influenced by the Canadian Peace Congress, an affiliate of the World Peace Council, which was funded by Moscow.[11] The old taint of communism impeded the effectiveness of activists in Canada. It had to be eliminated, but the attempt always provoked fights that many non-Communist activists preferred to avoid. By never placating anyone, our magazine made many enemies. Peace activists and researchers are often expected to be so spiritual that they have no conflicts, but that is not the case. The only people who never get into fights are those who are not seriously engaged in anything they care about. In fact, movement activists are conflict-prone; for one thing, all movements require sacrifice and there are too few rewards (such as fame and leadership roles) to go around.

While avoiding Canadian Communists, I took every occasion to meet the Communists who ran the Soviet Union and the other states in the Eastern bloc. Such opportunities arose often; indeed, Western peaceniks found Soviet officials more accessible than policymakers in their own countries. I usually attend conferences about twice a year in Europe and (the former) Soviet Union. During the early eighties, this was often at the invitation of the rich, publicly funded Soviet Peace Committee. I always augmented my itinerary by quietly visiting our true counterparts, the Moscow Group for Trust, a daring group of intellectuals who discussed peace issues and built bridges to the West. They suffered extraordinary abuses, including frequent jailings, beatings, loss of jobs, and incarceration in mental hospitals, where their drug "treatments" caused intense pain. One of these amazing friends, Olga Medvedkova, then pregnant, was arrested in 1984 on a trumped-up charge, for which a three-year imprisonment was expected. Her many friends in the West tried to help. I spoke on talk shows, organized a rally—and phoned David Crenna. Along with other activists, I was invited to lunch in Ottawa with Trudeau; the Canadian government sent an observer from the embassy to Olga's trial. After such pressures, the authorities released her, although other members of the group went to prison. Her release was one of the first signs that the Gorbachev regime might become more tolerant than previous ones.

In conferences with Soviets, I usually spoke about how their repression of independent activists impeded our peace work in the West. Their "on-stage" responses were fabricated, but I knew they were paying serious attention to what we said. On one occasion in 1985 I had arranged to go from Montreal to attend a conference in Moscow, then to Stockholm for two weeks for another conference, return to Moscow overnight, then fly back to Canada. The transatlantic flight was at Moscow's expense; I would pay the rest.

At the Moscow conference, I had just made an intervention about a mathematical model on the probability of mistaken launches of nuclear war under varying conditions when I was summoned by two low-level officials, Slava and Leonid, to discuss my bad behavior. (I had distributed copies of *Peace* containing a story about the Group for Trust.) Our "discussion" lasted three hours. Hearing my Moscow friends vilified, I dug deep into my psychic resources to practice conflict management—but failed. Leonid handed me a ticket on a flight leaving for Montreal the next day. I reminded him of my agreement with the Soviet Consul in Canada, and showed my pricey ticket to Scandinavia. Nyet! Eventually, I was officially deported. Except for the Gorbachev reforms, I would still be excluded from the country. (For a few years I kept running into Slava and Leonid at peace conferences outside the USSR. The KGB always accompanied Soviet delegations traveling abroad.)

However, as perestroika gathered momentum, the quality of the officials improved visibly. When a delegation entered a room I could pick them out: that's a New One, that's an Old One. I particularly liked Alexander Likhotal, whom I got to know in Austria. Jean-Guy Vaillancourt and I were sent by UNESCO Canada in 1988 to work on a charter and curriculum for a graduate center for peace studies in a renovated castle outside Vienna. Likhotal, the new pro-rector of the Soviet Diplomatic Academy, was a New One. Democratic and nonideological, he had been appointed to implement Gorbachev's foreign policy. On a long excursion, he and I talked about how to put Europe back together. My idea involved getting rid of NATO; his did not. He would remove Soviet troops from Eastern Europe and eventually NATO would become irrelevant. I thought his plan risky; the people would revolt. He thought not: everybody loved Gorby. We were both half right.

In the summer of 1991, I was in Moscow interviewing people about Soviet policy changes, doing research for a book with Olga Medvedkova and Tair Tairov about the East-West dialogue of the eighties and how it grew. After I interviewed Likhotal, who had been promoted to research director for the Central Committee, he invited me to write for a new magazine he was starting. Inwardly I chortled, imagining the reactions of Canadian Communists to an article written by me in such a publication. But it was not to be. The coup in the Soviet Union took place three days later and, back at home, I watched TV for Likhotal's face among Central Committee employees locked out in the street. He was not there, but I did see him later. He was Gorbachev's spokesperson during the Soviet Union's last weeks and remains his spokesperson today. He is one of my best informants in the Gorbachev Foundation about the period that I am studying.

My current work is immensely enjoyable. We are receiving wonderful submissions to *Peace*. I have completed about 150 interviews of peace activists and Soviet officials for my study of the East-West peace dialogue. Few people recognize how much the conversations with peace researchers and activists influenced Soviet "new political thinking"; my coauthors and I are documenting this intellectual history with a network analysis. I spent the summer of 1992 in Moscow again, tracing the changes in military doctrine and foreign policy. I am also working on separatist nationalism, and am organizing a session for the American Sociological Association meeting in Miami (1993) on the partition of states.[12] At the University of Toronto, I coordinate a degree program in Peace and Conflict Studies with seventeen students.

Organizationally, my primary commitment is to the Helsinki Citizens Assembly (HCA). Based in Prague, it facilitates activism in peace, human rights, environment, economics, women, media, culture, and ecology in all nations belonging to the Conference on Security and Cooperation in Europe—the organization that we hope would become the main regional government of post–Cold War Europe. HCA resulted from contacts throughout the eighties between Eastern dissidents and Western peace activists who supported nonalignment. I am chairing a committee to write the structure document for the HCA, an organization that unfortunately has been divided since its founding meeting in 1990, both because of the war in Yugoslavia and more generally because of the rise of xenophobic nationalism. Despite these difficulties, the HCA is the most promising social change organization in the Northern Hemisphere.

At age sixty-one, I must address two questions about my career. Which are more apparent in my work: the continuities or the discontinuities with my Berkeley experiences? And what is my advice for young women whose interests resemble my own?

The main discontinuity is that I see my career as my primary spiritual and moral project, whereas people did not talk in those terms in my Berkeley classes. The main continuity is that the Berkeley faculty members whom I knew best viewed their work as connected to their politics, and they took politics seriously, as I do. At the top of their discipline, there was not a single opportunist or a careerist among them. I am grateful to them all.

What shall I say to young women? I must both warn and encourage them. My career is not a huge success in "professional" terms. I am satisfied, but my situation is unusual. Because of the royalties I receive from publishing, I can usually afford to do what I believe in, but others may find such choices more difficult. Female professors are more likely than males to contribute time to public education projects (lecturing on foreign affairs, editing a general magazine) and public service (committee work in voluntary organizations). These activities are not rewarded by academia. In fact, they are a sure way of stalling a career as measured by income and rank. But success can be measured in many ways. It was nice to receive, as I did recently, a medal for public service from the governor general of Canada. It was even nicer to hear Gorbachev acknowledge the impact of the peace movement in ending the cold war. It is as a peace educator and activist that I measure my work.

However measured, there are no guarantees for success or satisfaction. I often question the worth of what I do. Too often, I let others set my agenda and my limits. That goes with being female, and it is bad, bad, bad. Still, I am satisfied. After all, this is the life story I picked off the tree. It's mine and I wouldn't trade with anyone.

Notes

1. This orientation came early for me. In one of my first published articles, "Professional, Scientific, and Intellectual Students in India," in *Comparative Education Review,* June 1965, I compared the political orientations of Indian students whose self-identification was professional, scientific, or intellectual. The intellectuals regarded public affairs as integrally part of their role, while professionals limited the scope of their activities to concerns defined internally by their discipline or even to a narrow specialty within it. I knew I belonged to the first group.

2. Russell Jacoby, *The Last Intellectuals* (New York: Basic Books, 1987).

3. Metta Spencer, *Foundations of Modern Sociology,* Canadian 6th ed. (Scarborough, Ont.: Prentice-Hall, 1993).

4. Randall Collins, *Weberian Sociological Theory* (Cambridge, Mass.: Cambridge University Press, 1986).

5. Alex Inkeles and David Horton Smith, *Becoming Modern* (Cambridge: Harvard University Press, 1974).

6. Charles Y. Glock, Robert Wuthnow, Jane Allyn Piliavin, and Metta Spencer, *Adolescent Prejudice* (New York: Harper and Row, 1975).

7. Anatol Rapoport is a notable exception. A psychologist as well as game theorist and mathematician, he is author of *The Origins of Violence* (New York: Paragon, 1989), which has been a text for my course on peace and war.

8. I have worked with two such ambassadors, Douglas Roche and the incumbent, Peggy Mason. See Roche's book, *Building Global Security* (Toronto: NC Press, 1989).

9. This promptness reflects the prestige of the late George Ignatieff, who served as Canadian ambassador to Yugoslavia, to NATO, to the United Nations, and briefly as disarmament ambassador, and who would become president of Science for Peace after stepping down as chancellor. See the memoir of this remarkable man, *The Making of a Peacemonger* (Toronto: University of Toronto Press, 1985).

10. Howard Becker, "Notes on the Concept of Commitment," *American Journal of Sociology* 66 (1960): 32–40.

11. For a brief summary of this relationship, see Alan Silverman, "Where Have All the Peace Activists Gone?" in *Research in Social Movements, Conflicts and Change,* vol. 13, ed. Metta Spencer (Greenwich, Conn.: JAI Press, 1991).

12. "Politics Beyond Turf: Grassroots Democracy in the Helsinki Process," *Bulletin of Peace Proposals* 22 (4 December 1991).

Chapter 13

A Sociological Venture

AUDREY WIPPER

For me, learning to be a scholar took place at three institutions: McGill University, UC Berkeley, and Makerere University, Uganda. They stand as ideals of what academic life can be like. One was challenged to excel among supportive colleagues and to have fun while doing it. Along with my experiences in these places, my background of early interests and influences also had lasting effects on my career.

My Family

Mine was a sporting family—my father an avid fan, my brother a superb athlete. (His name is found in Canada's Lacrosse Hall of Fame). Dad liked to go hunting and fishing and I decided early on that his interests were more intriguing than mother's. Later I came to appreciate her talents and qualities. Of Anglo-Irish ancestry, she had a no-nonsense approach to life that emphasized the Protestant ethic. Her life demonstrated hard work, excellence in everything she tackled, and a sympathetic understanding of others. An accomplished gardener, she kept a large English-style flower garden that was a showplace. Even in her dying days she insisted that the roses be sprayed. She canned a winter-long supply of fruits and vegetables, fertilized by her compost heap. I well remember trying to sneak vegetable peels into the garbage pail rather than trudge twenty yards through the snow to deposit them. A talented weaver, she blended softly colored yarns into complex patterns. My father was proud to wear a jacket made from cloth she had woven.

My parents' disdain for sham over substance, for social climbers who judged people by wealth rather than achievement, fitted well with the egalitarian values I encountered later in sociology. My parents joked about pretentious neighbors who sacrificed in order to send their children to private schools, where they could meet the "right" people.

My passion for horses dates back to early childhood. Our backyard bordered on a riding club where, every year, a glittering show attracted some of the best horses on the North American continent. I was enthralled with their beauty and animation, and with the skill of the people who handled these magnificent creatures. When the fence-line was patrolled, we kids climbed the poplars at the foot of our lot for an aerial view of the show ring. One of the games we played with our cousins was horse show. As the eldest of six, I, as ringmaster and judge, would announce the class and the "jumpers" or the "hackneys" would prance into the ring, sometimes pulling "carriages" with the youngest as passengers. (A home movie of these performances never fails to elicit gales of laughter at family gatherings.)

My family could not afford a horse for me, so I earned rides by mucking out stalls and cleaning tack. One learned to ride high-strung horses with a light hand, to discipline the headstrong, and to activate the sluggish. As my skills improved, I was permitted to ride the more difficult horses and eventually showed horses for owners who did not ride competitively. This was an excellent way to hone equestrian skills, to gauge a horse's mood from body language, and, in time, to "think like a horse." These early experiences gave me an enduring respect for and interest in the grooms, trainers, and riders whose hard-won skills outshine those of the merely affluent, who purchase horses they may be unable to ride.

The McGill Years

My family assumed that I would go to university. Mother always said, "It's important to get an education. Then you can do whatever you want and be financially independent." I chose McGill mainly because it had a physical education program and was some distance from home. I liked the idea of living in a residence with other students.

In the forties, Montreal was Canada's only cosmopolitan city. Hemmed by hills and the St. Lawrence River, it was an exciting mix of Francophones and Anglophones, of English and French traditions.

Situated in downtown Montreal, McGill benefited from this ambience. Students could dine at an inexpensive French restaurant, then drop into the Alberta Lounge to hear jazz pianist Oscar Peterson (now chancellor at York University), or they could hike or ski in the Laurentians.

After my freshman year, I took a job as swimming instructor at a summer camp on Vancouver Island, where I broke my neck while diving. I returned to McGill in a body cast from my waist to the top of my head. Unable to play the sports required for a physical education major, I shifted to sociology. I had liked the introductory course because it dealt with the nature of race relations and the family, providing tools for understanding social institutions.

Almost all the sociologists in the Department of Sociology and Anthropology were graduates of the University of Chicago. They shared the fieldwork tradition and considerable consensus about the nature of the discipline. Oswald Hall, Fred Elkin, Bill Westley, Aileen Ross, and David Solomon were students and colleagues of Everett C. Hughes, who taught at McGill from 1927 to 1938 and who, with his Canadian wife, Helen, visited Aileen Ross's farm house every summer. (Many years later, on my return to Canada, I was included in the Hughes's annual visit.)

Students were exposed to the classical literature and vigorously encouraged to gather raw data as part of the sociological enterprise. An empirically based dissertation was required for a master's degree. This emphasis on close contact with one's subjects contributed to the department's reputation for excellence. Thus I developed the view that recording direct observations of social groups in field notes was the definitive sociological method.

This emphasis fitted my inclinations. My interest in horses was a laboratory tailor-made for someone who enjoyed studying society "on the hoof." After graduating with a B.A., I worked as a groom in two stables, one a small family enterprise, the other a top show stable of jumpers. I collected data on horsepeople, returning to McGill the next year to work on my master's. Oswald Hall, who had been a farm boy in Saskatchewan, had a sympathetic understanding of animal-people relationships. He provided a framework for my simple observations that made them more significant. I always left his office with the feeling that my data were truly exciting.

By the time McGill students of sociology reached their senior year, they had become part of a warm, cohesive group of teachers and students, sometimes forming lifelong friendships. Oswald's 1991 Christmas card displayed a "rocking-horse" deer complete with bridle and saddle. He wrote, "I couldn't find a card that reflects your avocation; this one is an effort to call you my 'rocking deer.'" (Oswald celebrated his eighty-sixth birthday in 1994.) The small sociology department at McGill gave me a sense of being special and encouraged me to believe that I could produce good research. The faculty's enthusiasm was contagious, although few of us will ever match Aileen Ross in that respect. At age ninety, living in a retirement home, she wrote: "I keep busy with my research" (on older people). Close relationships with these pioneers provided a sturdy sense of being an authentic sociologist, useful in later confrontations with clashing sociological perspectives.

After completing my M.A. thesis, I was invited to join a Defence Research Board team of five sociology and anthropology graduate students studying the socialization of infantry recruits in the early fifties, during the Korean War. My role was that of the proverbial typist. We were outfitted in army uniforms and spent three months in an isolated training camp in northern Alberta, where I distinguished myself by easily running the obstacle course set up to test tough infantrymen. According to Oswald Hall, the army completely rebuilt the course as a result.

Later, David Solomon offered me a job in the Psychological and Sociological Section of the Defence Research Medical Laboratory in Toronto. I studied the influx into the city of refugees from the aborted 1957 Hungarian revolt, participated in Fred Elkin's study of army recruiting, and worked on Jacques Brazeau's study of integrating Francophones into the English-speaking air force.

During my introduction to sociology, I met people I admired and was introduced to a subject matter and methodology that had definite appeal. Employment doors were opened; I could do what I liked to do and actually got paid for doing it. Though the next career step took me to one of the world's greatest sociology departments, I had no feeling of being disadvantaged. Although I had difficulties arguing positions in front of people, I felt that, given my master's degree cum laude, I could hold my own in written papers.

Berkeley: At the Hub of the Sociology Universe

After three years at the research laboratory in Toronto, I began to think about doing further graduate work. My inclination was to go to the University of Chicago, but Kaspar Naegele, the brilliant dean of arts at the University of British Columbia, suggested Berkeley. Herbert Blumer had recently become chair and the department was fast becoming the continent's most luminous. Since I admired Blumer's work and liked the idea of living in the San Francisco Bay area, I enrolled there in January 1958, the first Canadian student.

Berkeley's department, with long lines outside professors' doors and short time allotted to students even by their thesis directors, contrasted sharply with McGill's close-knit one, where graduate students and faculty often met both formally and informally. Many Berkeley students, discouraged by lack of professorial attention, dropped out. I was more fortunate.

Professor Blumer welcomed me graciously and said I must meet his wife, Marcia, who shared my horsey interests; she owned several jumpers, trained and shown by professionals. Meeting Marcia was a happy coincidence since I got to accompany her to horse shows and talk about my favorite subject. One day, driving out of their lane on our way to a show, I looked back and saw Blumer hauling a bale of straw to the stable. I thought, What a good sport! (Horses didn't interest him in the least.

At Berkeley, I was introduced to the world of politics. The posters and recruiting desks at the Sather Gate entrance to the campus advertised a spectrum of causes, an education in themselves. I joined the collective protests against the Hearst newspapers in San Francisco and the university administration on the steps of Sproul Hall.

My previous experience had not prepared me for Berkeley's intellectual and left-wing political climate. I had barely heard of Karl Marx, let alone the Wobblies (for all I knew, they were a team in some minor hockey league). I was humiliated after one intense political discussion, to which I had contributed nothing, when someone turned to me and said, "Audrey, do tell us about the horse world." Remarks such as that goaded me into learning about social systems larger than occupational and sporting subcultures. Seminars at times were painful because the reading assignments never readied me for the wide-ranging discussions that took place while I sat silently marveling at the self-confidence, knowledge, and verbal fluency of students and professors. My diffident Canadian self was astonished at the students' aggressive challenges of professors whose names I revered.

Erving Goffman greeted me as a fellow Canadian and often alluded, in his conspiratorial style, to "our Canadian-ness." I was a teaching assistant for the social psychology course he taught. During one class, two students decided to test his presentation of self with a Goffmanesque prank. When he arrived at Wheeler Hall, he found them seated on the stage playing cards. As his bemused TAs watched to see how this master of interpersonal interaction would handle a public invasion of his territory, he strode over and spoke quietly to the cardplayers. Whatever he said, they immediately left the stage. Goffman began his lecture as if nothing had happened.

Although graduate life involved hard work and little money, it was also enjoyable. At one marking session, several TAs gathered at my flat. We drank beer (supplied by Goffman), and marked papers all day and into the night. Eventually, all went home except Irwin Sperber, known affectionately as the Kid, since he was at least a decade younger than the rest of us. I went to bed exhausted, waking up the next morning to find him still marking papers. When Goffman heard about Irwin's overnight work session, he asked in mock Victorian shock, "Doesn't he realize he has compromised you?" Although he could be infuriatingly inconsiderate, Goffman could also be endearingly helpful. Mindful of a graduate student's perpetual need for a job, he had called me to say that I could count on him if I needed a TA-ship. I spent several summers house-sitting his home high in the Berkeley hills, with decks and panoramic views of the Bay area, while he was collecting data in Las Vegas as a blackjack dealer.

During 1962–63, my last year in Berkeley, I took a seminar on new African nations from political scientist David Apter. Americans were converging on Africa to study the changeover of regimes and to test their development hypotheses. This was an era of enormous optimism as one after another colonial state became free. Hopes were high among Western social scientists for progressive development and the growth of democracy.

I worked as a research assistant for Apter, who sponsored my successful application for a Canada Council fellowship to do a thesis in Africa. The fellowship provided an opportunity to pursue a longtime interest, but it forced me to make a hard choice: stay in Berkeley and do a thesis under Goffman and Blumer or go to Africa and study institutions in the making? I opted for Africa. Goffman treated me like a pariah for a while, but I didn't see that my going to Africa was different from his going to the Shetland Islands for *his* dissertation research. He was wiser than I. Doing research in Africa was indeed a crucial career decision. Once embarked on research in a particular area, investments accrue and disengagement becomes complicated and difficult.

In retrospect, my five years at Berkeley were among the most rewarding of my life. Berkeley had a special ambience. Every time I walked through Sather Gate onto the beautiful campus with its age-old trees and eucalyptus groves, I felt exhilarated. We students felt we were at the hub of the sociological universe, among the best and the brightest in the country's number one sociology department. As a foreigner I was privileged indeed to receive at low cost a degree from one of America's great universities. Those giants of sociology were among the most unpretentious and warmest people I had known. I was sad to say goodbye.

East Africa: Years of Optimism

I arrived in Kenya on the eve of independence in 1963, in time to see the Union Jack formally lowered and Kenya's red, green, and black flag raised for the first time. I stayed until 1966, collecting dissertation data, and returned to Africa in 1969 and again in 1973–74. In the early years, researchers could go anywhere and talk to anyone. District commissioners (trained in European or U.S. universities) were hungry for conversation and welcomed visitors in their remote areas. With authority over wide regions, they could open doors, suggest informants, and even provide lodging at administrative headquarters. One commissioner invited me to accompany him in making the rounds of his Mt. Elgon area. We traveled over territory in his Landrover that I could not have reached in my Volkswagen, climbing to the lake revered by a protest movement I was studying and exploring rocky crevices where the faithful went to worship and or to hide out from the police.

My research focused on religious-political movements, which I called protest movements. A massive breakaway from Roman Catholicism occurred shortly after I arrived in Kenya, creating an opportunity to study an indigenous movement among the rural people who comprised more than 85 per cent of the population. My fieldwork consisted of attending church services and the rituals of casting out devil spirits, as well as talking to the leaders, followers, local people, and authorities. Sometimes my informants spoke English; at other times I used a translator. I traveled alone except for a teenager and was completely dependent upon the willingness of the residents to talk to me. Since I lived locally, they became used to me. I didn't fit the usual categories of foreign women, so curiosity worked in my favor. One elder, who had tired of my "tedious" questions, complained to my sponsor, another elder. My sponsor asked him to be patient and help me out: "She's only a schoolgirl."

When James S. Coleman, head of African Studies at the University of California, Los Angeles, arrived at Makerere University in Kampala, Uganda, in 1965, his need for a research assistant gave me a way of prolonging my stay in Africa. Graduate students and academics from various countries and diverse backgrounds soon became a community of scholars. An easy exchange of ideas took place among Westerners and Africans at seminars, at a tiny on-campus bar, and at dinner parties hosted by Jim and others. These were settings in which energetic, enthusiastic, talented people worked hard and played hard.

In Kenya, I had become interested in the contradictions evidenced in gender roles. Women's formal education lagged far behind men's, their contributions to the economy were grossly undervalued, and men could beat their wives publicly with impunity. Yet the Kenyan women were among the most outspoken, strong, and independent I have known, nonchalantly handling multiple roles, especially those combining mother of many children and major economic provider. (In the late sixties and the seventies my research focused on the nascent women's movement spearheaded by women's voluntary associations.)

If Berkeley had aroused my interest in the larger political scene, East Africa was to provide an array of extraordinary events—coups, riots, assassinations and downfalls of ancient regimes—that freed me from many taken-for-granted assumptions about political processes and that furnished absorbing topics of conversation. Part of my African research on protest movements was published in 1977 by Oxford University Press as *Rural Rebels*. Since it was published in Nairobi, it received little publicity in Canada or the United States, a disappointment for me.

Waterloo: Working as a Sociologist

My teaching career began during the sixties, a time of immense expansion of higher education in Canada. Universities that had formerly catered to a small minority who could finance their own schooling were changing to mass institutions that educated middle-class and working-class students. New universities were competing for faculty and even those lacking a dissertation were sought for job openings. I received offers, sight unseen, from a couple of now major Canadian universities. I wanted to stay in Africa but I needed funds, so I accepted the University of Waterloo's offer, not even sure exactly where it was located (seventy-five miles west of Toronto).

To my credit at that point, a few articles I had written had been published, but my easy access to employment at a university is a stark contrast to the difficulties of today's graduates. Nor was I subjected to the stringent tenure regulations that open one's teaching, research, and service contributions to scrutiny by committees at all levels. The small print of my contract, which I didn't read until years later when a colleague pointed out its meaning, specified that I would be granted tenure after completion of my thesis, provided I didn't commit some heinous crime.

In recent years at the University of Waterloo, I have been trying to complete my African research but, as Goffman foresaw, leaving an area is not easy. The decision to do so was complex. The excitement over Afri-

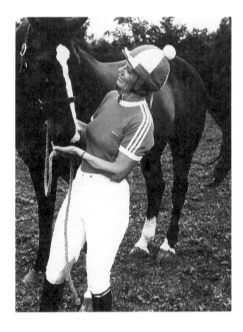

can independence has died out and the monotonous reign of one-party states, military regimes, brutal dictatorships, tribal fighting, corruption, and declining economies has taken its toll. Young blacks with political agendas and anti-Western ideologies can see maternalism, paternalism, and racism in almost anything a Westerner does. There thus comes a time in a country's evolution when it is best for the indigenous peoples to study themselves. Furthermore, a peripatetic lifestyle prohibits owning animals who, like children, need constant care. For an animal-lover like myself, that is quite a sacrifice.

A field researcher at heart, I am returning to what I enjoy most, participant observation research. For the past decade I have been collecting data on the horse world. The project started in 1981, when I was scouring the country for a good horse, a four-month search. Since there is a great deal of lore about horse dealers, and horse trading is pervaded by the advice caveat emptor, this first-hand experience was a great research opportunity. I'm particularly interested in occupations and avocations that become a way of life when people work at what they love.

Participant observation has been facilitated by my ownership of a superb jumper, Happy Fella, who has his adoring fans. A judge who placed him first in several classes at a hunter trials competition admonished me: "Take good care of him. He's a jewel."

The lack of collegiality at Waterloo has been offset by my involvement with people who never tire of discussing horses. Friendships and loyalties among those who love horses go back many years, and people greet one another with hugs and kisses. Even though horse-people live miles apart, many on farms, word of personal triumphs and tragedies quickly goes round. Congratulations and sympathy are freely expressed, for this is a community of caring people.

My sociological venture has come full circle, beginning with and returning to the world of horses. Although the countries in which I learned to be a sociologist differed greatly from each other, contrasting the world's most advanced industrialized nation against a tiny agrarian state, they were exciting intellectual environments, characterized by an active flow of new ideas, supportive fellow students, and dedicated teachers who enjoyed each other's company. Perhaps most rewarding of all my experiences have been the happy and durable contacts with academics and those in a soul-satisfying avocation who have shared the journey.

Editors' Note: Because of space limitations, it was necessary to shorten Dr. Wipper's original paper, completed after other chapters had been edited.

Chapter 14

New Perspectives,
New Freedoms

JACQUELINE P. WISEMAN

Going to UC Berkeley changed my life in a way that has been permanent. While I enrolled with certain limited goals, the ultimate payoff was much broader and richer than I had ever envisioned.

Growing up in a Nebraska town of 3,000, I knew I had to have a college education if I were to escape to an interesting life. My parents thought I would make a good hairdresser, but reluctantly acquiesced to my plans after listening to my high school salutatorian address extolling higher education for women. With a scholarship, I majored in chemistry at the University of Denver until my junior year, when I switched to sociology after learning that women chemists could expect only to become lab technicians.

In seeking a summer job, my ability to read the "Openings" list upside down across the student placement adviser's desk took me to the National Opinion Research Center, with headquarters on the university campus, to apply for a position as research assistant. Claiming to be sent by the placement office, I was hired. My sociology career was launched. NORC (and, later, its branch, Opinion Research Center) sponsored my master's degree.

After receiving my M.A., I obtained a position at Stanford Research Institute in Palo Alto, where I handled all phases of survey research, including creating questionnaires, hiring and training interviewers and coders, and writing reports. SRI would grant me "second authorship" of reports of which I was sole author, telling me that no client would accept a report by a woman. I actually thanked them for this credit, since other women received no recognition. I started to consider getting a doctorate when I noticed that male names listed above mine had "Ph.D." affixed.

It also seemed to me that teaching in a college or university would be an ideal way to have a professional life and still spend summers with my two small children. A Ph.D. was needed for such a plan. My husband was incredibly supportive and understanding of my hopes, and in those days (not so long ago) that encouragement made the difference between trying for a Ph.D. and deciding to forget it.

Selecting UC Berkeley: The Start

When I decided to get a Ph.D., I first applied to Stanford because I lived only fifteen minutes from Palo Alto. As a backup, I applied to UC Berkeley, which was a one-hour commute across the Bay Bridge. I was accepted by Stanford, but before registration I met some knowledgeable people from the East Coast who said, "What are you thinking of? Berkeley has the best sociology department in the country!" They urged me to call Berkeley sociology professor Seymour Martin Lipset (whom they knew) about the status of my application. With much trepidation I did so. He was most gracious, saying he had read my application, was impressed with my survey research background, and was recommending my admission.

During my admission interviews at Berkeley in 1958, one junior professor told me that many are admitted to the department but few are chosen to remain. Thus, if I didn't cut the mustard in one year, I would be out. Wolfram Eberhard, a senior professor, had a different message. He took my hand in his two and said, "I see you have two children. Going to graduate school may be very demanding for you. If you find you are having a hard time, don't hesitate to see me about cutting your course load."

Erving Goffman, assigned as my adviser, had a unique but equally useful message:

> You are older than many of the graduate students, but you have a track record in the field. Therefore, I'm going to pay some attention to you. You work your ass off here the first year. Then, if you don't do so well the second year, people will say, "Why, Mrs. Wiseman, what happened? Have you been ill?" On the other hand, if you don't do well the first year, it will take you a long time to overcome a bad reputation.

I took Erving Goffman's advice and thus did not need Wolfram Eberhard's assistance. However, working hard on sociology was time-consuming and I was trying to be the good wife and mother as well. I was concerned also that my advanced education should not be a drain on the household finances, so I devised ways of saving time for my husband and children and making money to pay for afternoon child care and gasoline.

Time-creating Strategies

Because of the hour-long commute each way, I wanted to get as much as possible out of a day in Berkeley. Thus, for several years, instead of creating a master plan of study for myself, I took as many sociology courses as I could handle on Monday, Wednesday, Friday, in one semester and then selected from those offered Tuesday and Thursday the following semester. (This bothered my adviser, Erving Goffman, who sometimes recommended a course that I declined because of my travel schedule.)

I strictly prioritized my life. Husband, children, and sociology had first claim. All efforts and pretense at a social life were dropped. I never played bridge again; in the eight years that followed my enrollment at Berkeley, I never looked at a fashion magazine or any other popular publication. I read sociology only. I always carried a book in case I had to sit in a doctor's or dentist's waiting room. Inasmuch as I started Berkeley before husbands were expected to help with the housework, I did the next best thing about any task that cut into my precious time: I let it go and taught myself not to care. Once my kitchen floor was so dirty that the pattern could not be discerned. A neighbor remarked on this and I answered, "Well, my tombstone won't say, 'She kept her kitchen floor clean.'"

To study uninterruptedly, I made a thermos of coffee at night and put it in my study area with a sweet roll. When my alarm sounded at 3:00 A.M., I studied until the family got up. I pretended I had just risen, as well. At Berkeley, I sometimes slept for an hour in my car between classes. I managed on five hours of sleep or fewer per day for several years.

To spend some weekend time with my children at the same time as studying, I often took them to Berkeley with me on Sunday afternoon. In good weather, we picnicked along the creek behind the science building and I read while they made mud pies or floated boats. In bad weather, we went to the library. They played or colored under a table while I studied. (This did not go over well with some of the librarians.)

I attended church services (mandatory if my children were to attend Sunday school) with a sociology book inside the prayer book. I also put sociology material on a tape recorder and played it while I cooked or did anything else not requiring full concentration.

Handling the Money Problem

I was unaware of the existence of scholarships for graduate students, so never applied. Rather, I fashioned my approach to paying for my education by simultaneously earning money while maintaining my children's best interests as paramount. Inasmuch as all graduate classes were offered late afternoons and evenings, I decided to start a morning nursery school for four children the ages of mine that would include crafts projects and a hot lunch. The money earned covered both the cost of a sitter in the afternoon while my children napped, and my commute to Berkeley.

After receiving a nursery school license, I advertised. The initial result was encouraging. My clients were a doctor's wife, who wanted some time to work in his office, and a professor's wife, who wanted to be free for the League of Women Voters and the American Association of University Women. But there was an unexpected repercussion. The women in our neighborhood were outraged, claiming that I was "starting a business in a residential area," and, even worse, bringing in "strange children with strange germs." Although my husband and I went from door to door to explain that there would be only four children in the nursery school and that they were from good homes (actually a higher social class than our neighborhood), the neighbors were adamant. As long as my children were playing with "strange children," their children could no longer play with mine.

Though I worried about the effect of the ban on my children's feelings, I couldn't afford to abandon my nursery school plan. I "solved" the problem by taking the initiative from the neighborhood wives. I forbade my children to play with their children, giving as the reason that the families were of a lower class with less education than ours. Fortunately, my children enjoyed the four newcomers each morning.

A year or so later, when my children entered school, I changed to another approach to earning money. I started a free-lance market research business, soliciting clients who were too small for large firms. Stanford Research Institute and Field Research Company sent me referrals. Among my projects were studies of salad dressing preferences, packaging tests, plant fertilizer, pasta, and voters' opinions on bond issues.

Meanwhile, Back at Berkeley

The first year in the Berkeley sociology department was a mixture of pure bliss and gradual awareness of my inadequacies. The positive aspects of being a Berkeley graduate student came initially from the courses and the outstanding professors. Later the riches flowed from the friends I made during those years. Hanan Selvin and Martin Trow's course in research methods, primarily concerned with survey methodology, was superb. (Seymour Martin Lipset's excellent seminar in stratification helped me understand my problems in a working-class neighborhood.)

After my first six weeks at Berkeley, Erving Goffman asked me to drop by his office. When I arrived, he asked if I was getting to know any of the other graduate students in sociology. He wanted the names of persons with whom I might be eating lunch or meeting for coffee. He mentioned names of students he thought I should get to know. I told him I had two children, operated a nursery school in the morning, and commuted an hour each way from my home. My time at Berkeley was for classes, study, and the library. Making friends, drinking coffee, and having hour-long lunches were out of the question. He advised me that I was making a great mistake:

> Don't you realize that these other students will be your peer group after you get your doctorate? They are the ones who will read your papers and give you criticisms on them before you send them out; they are the ones who will nominate you for offices in the ASA; they are the ones who will get you on programs to give scholarly papers. They will refer their promising students to you and you will refer yours to them. Now don't miss this opportunity. Go make some friends.

My first friends were Marcia Aron (with whom I later wrote a text on sociological research methods), the late Patricia Richmond (who taught at Long Beach State University), and Audrey Wipper (who now teaches at University of Waterloo, Canada). I studied and ate with these women; we traded class notes and term papers and tried to help each other. Knowing them offered an unexpected bonus: I was freed from worrying about my neighbors because I had new, more interesting friends. Goffman had been more right than he knew.

Another time, Goffman told me I spoke in class and interacted with professors "like a well-brought up suburban housewife." (That really hurt, considering my experiences in suburbia.) He said that my ideas were often good ones, and I should speak up more boldly.

What he didn't know was that my hesitancy came from a growing awareness of my weakness in sociological theory. I excelled in research methods, however, and this skill eventually saved me. First of all, I told Hanan Selvin that while I knew how to analyze research data, a theory paper seemed ethereal by comparison. He invited me to lunch at the faculty club and tried (with some success) to show me the parallels between thinking about the analysis of data and thinking about the application of concepts and comparison of theoretical frameworks. I still have the notes from that meeting. But I needed more help than that.

My rescue came in the form of a proposal from another graduate student, Marvin Scott. Hearing that I was doing well in research methods, he asked if I would tutor him in that subject in exchange for being tutored by him in theory during the next semester. Without hesitation, I accepted.

I worked intensively with Marv, going over lectures, epistemology, and the logic of multivariate analysis, as well as giving him advice on the secondary analysis assigned as a term paper. I had never tutored before, however, and was afraid I couldn't help enough. I remember waiting in the Student Union to find out what grade he received in the research methods class, my hands sweaty from worry. I was thrilled to learn he had done well.

Then Marv addressed, with enthusiasm, the task of my remedial education in sociological theory. He gave me extra assignments. He scolded me if he suspected I had not read them all. He lectured to me (I remember his striding up and down as he talked about Marx—a born teacher). He gave me guidance on my paper. Thanks to him, I managed the theory course.

Marv became a good friend who spanned several cohorts over the years. Popular at Berkeley, he made a point of including me with his coffee-drinking friends. I, in turn, gave him rides home after evening seminars. Often we alternated buying ice cream and taking it to share with his wife, Joyce, at their apartment while talking about sociology and the department. We did this on a regular basis for about six years. During our conversations, Marv tried to convert me to qualitative research and even to ethnomethodology, in which he was dabbling. He would say, "Survey research is too 'wooden.'" I resisted conversion at the time, but later I finally saw the truth of his arguments.

After I survived the first year in sociology at Berkeley, a hot fudge sundae was my way to celebrate the grades on my papers. Then I awaited the letter from the department that would inform me of this triumph. When the letter arrived, I was somewhat disappointed in its low-key message: the faculty had reviewed my progress thus far and invited me to register for the next year. Later, in talking with Reinhard Bendix, I mentioned that the department's letter was the coldest letter I had ever received. "What did you expect?" he asked. "Well," I replied, "I had an A average. At least it could have said, 'Congratulations on your good work thus far.'" (I felt that Goffman would have been proud of my bold pronouncement to Bendix, whom I scarcely knew at the time.) The next year, when I received my letter suggesting I continue in the program, there was a handwritten P.S. from Reinhard Bendix: "Congratulations on your good work to date."

Other good things happened. In 1961 we moved our family to a wonderful big, old house in Redwood City. My mother, Editha, came to live with us, providing child care when I was in Berkeley. Martin Trow hired me to work on a longitudinal attitude survey involving students at four colleges or universities that he and Burton Clark (now at the University of California, Los Angeles) had undertaken. It was a wonderful opportunity, and I learned a great deal. Later, Charlie Glock's invitation to work at the UC Survey Research Center (SRC) meant I could stop freelancing in market research. I worked on several projects while at the center, but the most memorable was the Wilderness Study, conceived to aid in the settlement of a disagreement between the U.S. Department of Agriculture and the U.S. Department of the Interior about the multiple uses of wilderness areas.

Our research mission was to interview backpackers who camped in the wilderness about having some logging and mining in hiking areas. I helped construct the questionnaire, and King's Canyon was selected as the site of the study. I was to be a part of a team that rode horseback in this area to interview hikers. Other researchers included a professor of economics. For this project, I bought a piece of foam rubber to put inside my jeans. I was assigned an assistant—Ann Neel, a sociology graduate student and a good friend ever since.

We collected some interesting data on this trip, although by definition wilderness users are few and far between. Our packers made breakfast and dinner; researchers were to make sandwiches for lunch. On the first day out, Ann and I discovered the other researchers' assumption that, as the only women on the research team, we would make lunch for everyone. We quickly set them straight on that. After ten days of living and interviewing in the wilderness, Ann and I walked into a rest room at the edge of King's Canyon. Suddenly we saw two very dark-complected, somewhat dirty-looking women coming toward us. Actually, we were looking in a mirror at two people returning to civilization after living in a pup-tent, bathing in ice-cold lakes, and spending ten hours a day on horseback.

Another shock came with my paycheck from SRC—smaller than usual—quite a surprise considering overtime wilderness interviewing. I was told, "You girls had a free horseback vacation in a scenic area, complete with packers." I replied firmly that our understanding had been that it was a job assignment. We were paid.

I worked part-time at the Survey Research Center for several years and enrolled in or audited almost every class offered by the sociology department. I also took several courses in the psychology department because I wanted to be a social psychologist. Marvin Scott, in his continuing role as friend and mentor, advised me to sit in on Herbert Blumer's class in sociological theory, and I did so. Blumer's class, combined with one on George Herbert Mead I had taken from Tamotsu Shibutani—topped off by my arguments with Marv—resulted in a permanent change in my perspective on both sociology and social psychology.

Through Blumer's lectures, the true import of symbolic interaction theory and the shortcomings of attitude surveys became clear. Further, I realized that the opportunities for serendipitous findings were far greater through the gathering of qualitative data. From then on, symbolic interaction would be my major research and theoretical framework, and qualitative data gathering my method of choice.

At that time, the sociology department at Berkeley offered no courses explicitly concerned with gathering and analyzing qualitative data. Erving Goffman had given a guest lecture in the Selvin-Trow methodology course, but at the time I had failed to grasp its import. Herbert Blumer's paper "Sociological Analysis and the Variable" was published in the *American Sociological Review* in 1956, but for some reason had not been on any reading list that I received (even Blumer's own). Many of us interested in qualitative sociology and symbolic interaction analysis pieced together a methodological agenda. Marv Scott suggested I review Howard Becker's discussion of his methodology for *Boys in White*. Hanan Selvin suggested a closer look at Merton and Kendall's "The Focused Interview." Later, while I was working on my dissertation, another student suggested I read an article in *The Behavioral Scientist* explaining Glaser and Strauss's grounded theory.

During this time, the Free Speech Movement (FSM) gained increasing momentum. From its inception, it tore the campus apart. Every day there were demonstrations. Some professors stopped teaching to show support; others continued to teach as a way of indicating their disapproval. A graduate student friend of Audrey Wipper's carried a sign during the protests: Less Analysis; More Action. Erving Goffman voiced disapproval of any participation: "Sociologists *study* social movements; they don't take part in them." (Years later, however, he joined other professors in a New Orleans restaurant sit-in to protest the refusal of service to women members of the American Sociological Association.)

The FSM did prove good practice for my academic future. I taught through the San Francisco State University strike in the late sixties and was a visiting professor during the strike at Yale in 1970 and the one that erupted at the University of Helsinki in 1973.

But the FSM brought new problems to my life. My suburban neighbors across the Bay began to fear I might be a dangerous Berkeley radical. At the same time, many of the students at Berkeley felt I was probably a conservative housewife. I donated money to the movement and continued classes. The urgency of attending lectures was too ingrained for me to give them up. Besides, I was discovering the joys of social demography from Kingsley Davis and William Petersen. Analyses of births, deaths, migration and the related social factors were like looking down from a high hill as social life swirled in discernible patterns. I loved it.

One prerequisite for taking the oral examinations at Berkeley was a demonstrated reading ability in two foreign languages. (Erving Goffman noted that unless a student already had this skill, the required study would take two years out of her life. He was right.) I attempted French first, driving to Berkeley weekly to study with Marvin Scott and Carl Werthman. We compared translations, talked about grammar problems, and tested each other. Despite this teamwork, only Carl passed the first time, when there was a typographical error in the exam that confused many students, including me. The department was adamant in its refusal to reconsider the grades: "If you really knew the language, you would have recognized the typo." In the month that elapsed before the exams were graded, one had to refresh the memory constantly on vocabulary, in case retesting, at six-week intervals, was necessary. I remember sitting under a tree, watching my son and his friend swim, going through my vocabulary cards. "What is your mother doing?" the friend asked. "I don't know," my son replied, "but she's been like that ever since I've known her."

Three years had elapsed by the time I learned French (and then Italian) well enough to read sociological literature. During that period I was teaching full-time at Foothill College, a community college in the hills behind Stanford. It was good experience for me and paid much better than being a teaching assistant at Berkeley. Foothill was architecturally stunning and I loved my colleagues there. At the same time, I continued to take graduate seminars at Berkeley. With an eighteen-hour teaching load, this was not easy.

Somewhere during my language-studying years (or before) I met a new cohort of wonderful friends at Berkeley: Shirley Hartley, Kay Meadow, and Ruth Wallace. Both Shirley and Kay had children about the ages of mine and we began to socialize outside the university since our husbands liked each other as well. When I first met Ruth Wallace, she was Sister John Baptist. An Episcopalian, I was a little in awe of people of the cloth and did not relax with her until she started wearing street clothes. John Irwin also belonged to this cohort. We met a bit later in Dave Matza's seminar on deviant behavior and became close friends when we both obtained positions at San Francisco State University. He taught me tricks for breaking a writing block that I still use.

Studying for the Orals

Many Berkeley students postponed the oral examination as long as possible—taking or sitting in on course after course "just in case they ask something about that area." I was one of those perpetual students, as I loved what I was learning. After my first cohort of friends, then the second, took the orals and passed, however, the handwriting was on the wall: I had to do it too.

My first move was to take a year's leave of absence from my teaching post at Foothill. I felt, rightly or wrongly, that I needed that much preparation time. I also had to select a committee, a decision that graduate students discussed constantly, weighing the pros and cons of every professor as an examiner. Finally, I went to Erving Goffman for advice. He said, "Don't get anyone sociologically young." He elaborated by saying that assistant professors were likely to be more concerned with impressing their peers than with testing the candidate, and thus a student could be destroyed while the examiner triumphed with highly sophisticated questions. He also suggested I take courses or get a reading list from anyone I was considering for the committee. Goffman especially recommended I audit a class in deviant behavior (one of my declared areas) from David Matza. When I protested that I had already taken a seminar on that subject from Goffman himself, he said, "You will get something valuable from Matza, too." And he was right, as usual. I learned a lot.

When Goffman asked how the studying was going, I complained that the typing room in the library had been converted to computer use and typewriter space was no longer available to students. He reached into his pocket and took out some keys. Detaching one, he tossed it across the desk. "This is my key to this office. Have it duplicated. Put your typewriter and books here. You may be here at any time except Tuesday afternoons, when I hold office hours. I work at home on other days." I had the use of his office for a year. But there was a catch. When I asked him to serve on my oral examination committee, he declined, saying: "Since I have loaned you my office, it might look as though you had a biased person on your committee."

Ultimately, Herbert Blumer was my chair and John Clausen, David Matza, and Dorothy Smith were my departmental members. Joseph Lohman of the School of Criminology was the outside person. I had been afraid that Blumer would refuse to serve because I had never taken a course of his, although I had audited several. When I explained this in asking him to serve on the committee, he half-rose from his chair and said, "Madam, it is my loss." I was speechless at this gallantry.

Blumer then recommended that I take a tutorial from him. It was extremely valuable for me in developing a comparative theoretical viewpoint and a symbolic interactionist stance. John Clausen not only gave me a reading list to discuss with him, but also did me the favor of suggesting that Dorothy Smith, one of his students and then a lecturer at Berkeley, give me a tutorial in the sociology of health and illness. That year of concentrated work helped me to see the interrelationship between the sociological subdisciplines I had been studying, making me aware of sociology's unity and scope in both theory and research.

A few days before the orals, Goffman wished me luck. I told him I was worried. "The faculty want their students to pass, you know," he responded. This was a new concept for me. I didn't think the faculty cared, one way or the other. I assumed that if you passed, they were pleased that you had learned what they were trying to teach, and if you failed—well, that was the way it was.

Goffman then asked me to call him after the examination to tell him how I had done. I replied, "I'll call you if I pass." Then I reconsidered and said, "I guess I can be mature enough to call you in either case."

I passed. (I later heard from Charlie Glock that I had done very well.) Dorothy Smith invited me for a drink to celebrate. I called Erving Goffman to give him the good news. I shall never forget his reply:

> One of the pleasures of teaching is shepherding talented and promising students through their graduate training. And now I may call you Jacqueline and you may call me Erving.

He didn't know I was crying at the other end of the line.

After passing, I didn't have the slightest idea what I would do for my dissertation. I turned to Erving Goffman again and received advice that I often pass on to my students:

> Whatever you do, don't work on someone else's project just because you might finish sooner. Follow your heart. Work on something that truly interests you. It may be the last time you have such complete freedom.

The Dissertation

While I had been studying deviant behavior with both Erving and David Matza, I was struck with what appeared to be "the mystery of alcoholism." Why could some people drink socially while others became addicted? I decided I wanted to solve this puzzle. Goffman discouraged such a lofty goal: "Millions of dollars have already been spent on that quest. If you want to study alcoholism, investigate some smaller aspect."

My next thought was to study how middle-class adults are socialized to the role of an alcoholic; however, I had formulated no plan as to how to go about such a study. Then fortune intervened. I met Maurice Rogers of the San Francisco Department of Public Health at a party and shared my idea with him. He suggested it would be extremely difficult to identify an alcoholic in the middle class, because alcoholics lie a great deal. He suggested I study Skid Row alcoholics because I would be more certain of the validity of my sample. That made sense.

When I wrote my father and told him what I planned to do for my dissertation, he called from Nebraska and shouted, "Can't you find anything else to do except study Skid Row?" My husband, Stan, was also concerned about the dangers I might face. John Irwin told me later that he laughed when he heard I was going to study Skid Row because he thought I was too lady-like and not hip enough or brave enough to carry it off. David Matza, who chaired the dissertation, also told me later that he had had doubts about the project. Erving Goffman suggested I go to Skid Row in drag so as not to look like a woman. When I balked at this proposal, he recommended that I dress as a "nonperson." So I went to the Salvation Army and bought a gray dress a few sizes too big that I wore with a raincoat and flat shoes. With the aid of graduate student Max Heirich, I found a man who lived on Skid Row and was willing to walk around with me for a small salary. (When I walked in Skid Row alone, I attracted police attention. "Ma'am, do you know where you are? This is not a good area for women to be walking in.")

Goffman also sponsored me for a grant from the Scientific Advisory Council of the Licensed Beverage Industries Inc. to pay for my respondents' time, for coding assistance, and for costs of driving to and staying near various mental hospitals and other institutions where Skid Row alcoholics were committed. He arranged for aid from the departmental staff in writing my grant proposal, and made me promise to provide them with a picnic of champagne and cake when the money came through. We all had a good celebration. After asking me to send him some copies of chapters as I wrote them, Erving went off to Harvard as a visiting professor.

Dissertation committees could include some, but not all, orals examiners. There was also to be a person from a related field who could offer a different perspective on the subject matter of the research. In addition to Matza, my dissertation committee members were John Clausen and Herbert Blumer, plus Scott Briar from the Department of Social Welfare.

John Clausen invited me to join a select group of graduate students supported by a newly funded training grant, Behavioral Sciences in Public Health. We were given a monthly stipend for living expenses and provided with an office, typewriter, telephone, secretarial aid, and, most important, colleagues with whom to discuss findings and analyses. As explained by Andie Knutsen, of the UC Berkeley Department of Public Health, who managed the project:

> There will be two sociologists, two anthropologists, two psychologists, and two public health researchers. You will all be in the same suite of offices and you can have intellectual intercourse.

I laughed involuntarily and said, "Well, I certainly wouldn't want to miss that." Knutsen frowned a bit.

I extended my leave from Foothill College. The new group held one or two seminars a week throughout the year, and it helped immensely to have feedback from the others. Andie Knutsen also read parts of my dissertation and offered advice.

David Matza arranged a small grant from the UC Berkeley Center for the Study of Law and Society because of the legal implications of my study. Along with that grant came Sheldon Messenger of the Criminology Department, who gave me more feedback on my dissertation. He was a tough critic, but gave me advice I also pass on to my students:

> Remember, people can find things to criticize in Durkheim and Weber, if they wish. In the end, you should listen politely to the criticism, thank the critic for taking the time, *and then use what you agree with in your own way and ignore what you disagree with.*

Since I planned to study how a person became socialized to the role of an alcoholic, my first research goal was to find out how men survived on Skid Row and kept on drinking, as well as whether they had significant friends who aided this process. I started my interviewing in Skid Row hotel lobbies and one of the questions I asked, after discovering that the men moved around a great deal, was how they kept track of their friends. The reply shaped the study:

We never worry when one of our friends is missing. We know he's out making the loop.

When I asked what the loop was, the man explained that it was going from Skid Row to city jail, to county jail, to the state mental hospital, to a halfway house or a mission, and then back to Skid Row again. He further made it clear that the movements were not necessarily in that order and that some were legal commitments, while others were self-commitments. Combined with Andie Knutsen's suggestion that I interview the persons who work with Skid Row alcoholics, this insight resulted in another break. I had noticed a chart created by the City Department of Public Health showing the orderly progress of an alcoholic through treatment institutions. I asked some of my Skid Row respondents to draw a chart of their experiences through the same institutions. Their rendition was totally different, indicating that they went back and forth between the institutions almost at random. This discrepancy alerted me to the very different perspectives on the same phenomena. I was off and running.

With the aid of Scott Briar and Maurice Rogers, I gained access to various public institutions that treated Skid Row alcoholics: welfare homes, the county jail, the state mental hospital. I also talked my way into private charities that worked with alcoholics. When I interviewed in the county jail, I wore my "Skid Row uniform" because the sheriff felt that a well-dressed woman might "upset the men." (On my last day of interviewing there, I dressed as I do at home or on the campus, and an inmate volunteered, "Hey, you aren't so bad when you fix yourself up a little.")

One interesting phenomenon concerned the problem of institutional access. At first, no one wanted me to interview either clients or staff; later in the research, I was actually getting calls from treatment institutions inviting me to include them in the study!

I lost my first guide to the streets when he became involved with drug dealers and had to hole up in his hotel room to avoid them. He telephoned to say it would be dangerous for me to be seen with him. I asked how dangerous, and he replied, "Like with guns."

I obtained my next escort through Prisoner's Aid. He was on parole for murdering an unfaithful wife. In addition to paying him, I agreed to write a job recommendation he could use to get more permanent employment. I mollified my husband and other relatives by showing them statistics indicating that crimes of passion were almost never repeated. So much for the aggregated data. This case was an exception. One day, after he had worked for me for several weeks, I read that he had walked in on his new girlfriend—a prostitute—and found her with a sailor. Angered, he bought a gun and killed them both. I sent his last check to San Quentin.

My final escort was a young man also located through Prisoner's Aid. Unfortunately, he was involved with a married nurse, and thinking he had been caught by her husband, fired through a wooden door, aiming high, to scare the man off. A policeman was on the other side, and my escort went back to jail. Luckily, by that time, I had completed my work on Skid Row.

I hired an anthropology graduate student to live with alcoholics sheltered by a group I called the Christian Missionaries. He was to observe and report on the treatment of alcoholics at their shelters. (Erving Goffman again had suggested I do this myself, disguised as a man, but I didn't take the suggestion seriously.)

In all, I worked for two years on the dissertation, gathering data at jails, from policemen, from Skid Row men inside institutions and after their release. Following Blumer's suggestion, I always carried a notebook to jot down theoretical insights on my data. I found that writing chapters as my interest was kindled, rather than in the ultimate order of the study, helped with writer's block. The final dissertation was over five hundred pages long. (The book manuscript was pruned to about 350 pages.)

I walked in the 1969 graduation with Shirley Hartley, who had finished shortly before me. Our proud and ever-supportive husbands sat together in the audience. Graduation was highlighted by Margaret Mead's speech and a peaceful demonstration concerned with "People's Park," a controversy about the proper use of some university-owned land. I thought about what Marvin Scott and I had called Berkeley during our years there—Nirvana.

Writing about my experiences at Berkeley brought a flood of memories:

- Ann Neel giving me my first cat, Pyewacket, and bringing a friend to Redwood City to play guitar and sing for my husband, Stan, in the hospital.
- sitting in my car in a heavy downpour waiting to help Pat Richmond

move her stereo set from a boyfriend's apartment after their breakup. (Following an hour's wait, I went in to find them making up.)

- Kingsley Davis arranging a scholarship in social demography for me just when I had decided to be a microsociologist.
- John Clausen coming to campus on a Saturday in the heavy rain to meet me, his hat dripping with moisture. (All my professors were considerate about making appointments to fit my schedule.)
- going out after a lengthy session with Erving Goffman concerning an early term paper and buying two Heath Bars, which I immediately ate.
- Pat Richmond and I watching stricken (but silent) while plumbers labored over clogged pipes at the Survey Research Center, where we often made gourmet meals on a hot plate brought from home, washing our dishes in the women's room sink.
- a campus policeman checking on my safety in Goffman's office late at night and arranging nearby (nonstudent) parking for my car.
- sharing the loneliness of dissertation research with Kay Meadow, as well as her ideas for not losing work that had been done (keep one copy in refrigerator in case of fire, another in the car trunk in case of theft).

My Berkeley experience armed me with new freedoms and new perspectives. My neighborhood problems taught me not to let petty persons dissuade me from my chosen path. I found that complete and intense immersion in a topic aids learning more than small and more comfortable increments. I gained theoretical and methodological perspectives that help me locate and analyze pertinent data. I am convinced that my studies taught me how to think, categorize, and then link conceptually disparate facts. I made many lifetime friends. Most important for my future as a teacher, I learned how much professors can facilitate the progress of their students. In fact, I was once a randomly selected respondent in a survey of graduate students' opinions of their Berkeley departments, and I remember saying, "I feel surrounded by friendly geniuses."

Once I told Dave Matza that I felt I had been at Berkeley during the golden years, thinking in terms of the professors. "But I suppose everyone thinks theirs were the golden years." He answered:

> I'll tell you something. They *were* the golden years. We have never had a class quite like yours. (And then he named many of my friends.)

I once asked Erving Goffman how I could possibly repay all the favors of my professors at Berkeley. He said:

That's simple. Don't disgrace us with bad work and pass on the help you received by aiding promising graduate students when you spot them.

I have tried to live up to that advice, too.

Chapter 15

Accidental Tourist

RUTH DIXON-MUELLER

Students gazing at what seems to be a successful woman professional are prone to assume that she has led a linear life. If she is now at point B, she must have known that she wanted to be there, and she must have proceeded there by a straight line from point A. "When did you know that you wanted to be a sociologist?" they ask. "Did you always intend to be a professor?" "Why aren't my own goals so clear?" they wonder, unfairly blaming themselves for a lack of vision. When I say that I did not decide to attend university until I had been out of high school for six years and that I don't remember having ever decided to become a university professor (quite the contrary),

they seem relieved. Perhaps there is room for ambiguity, for changing one's mind. Perhaps there is more than one way to get there from here.

It is interesting to look back on a life and see the markers that caused it to change direction. Often the markers are chance events—a passing comment, a class taken at random, a book perused, a person casually met. One becomes an accidental tourist in one's own life, stopping occasionally to look around and wonder how we got to be who and where we are. How did things turn out this way, when they could have turned out a thousand different ways? I might have mothered a large family, yet I have no children. I might have been a veterinarian, a secretary, an artist, yet I am a sociologist. I might have lived almost anywhere, yet I am here. Who is this person I am married to, and how did he come into my life? Who is this person I have become, in professional disguise with a résumé that might belong to someone else? What happened to the person I was? One scrutinizes old photographs trying to discern in a beaming teenage face a sense of common self. One reaches out to family and old friends. They seem reassuringly the same; how could we be so different from what we were?

Students also assume that we at UC Berkeley in the sixties were at the forefront of feminism, battling against all odds to fulfill our ambitions. Our male professors must have made it difficult for us; we must have taken risks. Yet, that assumption isn't quite right either. Sometimes we were our own worst enemies, refusing to take advantage of the opportunities that were there. Sometimes we willingly subverted our own career plans. I look back in some amazement at my own reluctance to stake a claim and go for it. My ambitions rose in incremental steps. After many pauses, each step was a toe in the water, a testing of possibilities, a decision (often encouraged by others) to go forward. I was the quintessential fifties girl. Going back to school would be fun, I thought, and might lead to more interesting jobs. But I was married when I first arrived in Berkeley at the end of the fifties. My husband was the student, and our future depended on what *he* decided to do.

The Cocoon Years

For a girl who had spent her teenage years in saddle shoes and a pony tail in a Toronto suburb, listening to records of the Four Lads and Johnnie Ray, California was a magical place. In the fifties, Toronto the Good was still living up to its name. Insistently Anglophile among the upper crust and pervasively WASP in its dominant middle class, the city closed down at midnight on Saturday with the last round of nightclub drinks. There were no Sunday movies, and the introduction of baseball on the Lord's Day marked a significant decline in moral standards. Although an infusion of refugees from Hungary and Czechoslovakia was beginning to add coffeehouses, ethnic restaurants, and foreign film clubs to the city's amenities, for a Willowdale teenager the idea of escape was irresistible. In September 1959, newly married to my high school sweetheart (our parents would not let us leave without the formality), I joined the great migration of young adults determined to leave home. Ruben had been accepted as an undergraduate at UC Berkeley. We were not just leaving our friends, families, and "boring" Toronto behind. We were leaving the fifties.

Berkeley was enchanting. The brown shingle homes with their leaded glass windows and redwood beams were only slowly being demolished to make room for concrete block apartments. The elegant shops and bookstores gave Telegraph Avenue an almost genteel quality. The Cinema Guild, now long gone, showed a remarkable array of foreign films and Hollywood classics with program notes by critic Pauline Kael. Coffeehouses were filled with folk music. San Francisco's jazz and comedy clubs were bursting with vitality, the beat poets were making the scene, and the Pacific coast drive beckoned from Mendocino to Big Sur. This was nothing like Toronto, and there was no looking back.

Typical of my generation, I had no particular plans. Although my mother, father, and sister were all college graduates, the idea didn't interest me. My best friend in Toronto went into "Soc and Phil at U of T." But what was "Soc" to me, let alone "Phil"? My favorite subject in high school had been art. By the fall of 1959, arriving in Berkeley as a high school graduate and art school dropout with a few odd jobs under my belt, my skills were slim. "Gal Friday" jobs were my specialty, first as a temporary Kelly Girl, then on the payroll of a shop in Oakland that made draperies, installed carpets, and cleaned venetian blinds. I kept the books, answered the phone, looked after my bosses, Joe and Lou, and felt pleased with myself. The pay was $325 a month, including Saturday mornings. With an extra $75 each month from Ruben's mother, we were doing fine.

Ruben was, I thought, a real intellectual. At the university he was learning a language of discourse that sounded exotic, exalted, and impossibly inaccessible. He spent hours over coffee with his friends debating the fine points of Marx, Freud, and Dostoevsky. I was doing what any young wife would do: Putting Hubby Through. My parents' career advice had come in handy: learn to type, and you will always be able to find a job if you have to. I had already ignored their educational advice: if you want to be a good wife, then go to college. I had also ignored their sexual advice—"don't play with fire"—and had found myself as an art student searching for an abortion in Toronto when it was illegal, expensive, and underground. The innocence of the fifties had some rough edges. We had not yet learned that the personal is political; we were struggling with these embarrassments on our own.

These were the cocoon years: from the cocoon of a WASP family with New England roots and a firm authoritarian hand, to the cocoon of mild rebellion in refusing to go to college, studying art, and living in a rented room, to the cocoon of an early marriage and a view of the world that was filtered through the haze of romantic fantasies. The cocoon was political as well as personal. During the fifties, Canada had its own Eisenhower years. Canadians were smug, self-satisfied, anti-American but lapping up American popular culture. Only the Korean War interrupted the national preoccupation with searching for our uniquely Canadian identity.

In California, the demonstrations against Senator Joseph McCarthy's House Un-American Activities Committee hearings in San Francisco and the civil rights sit-ins on automobile row were a distant backdrop. It would be several years before the Berkeley campus was torn apart with antiwar and free speech demonstrations, before tear gas floated down in clouds from a helicopter hovering over Sproul Hall, before one had to take a stand. Meanwhile, there were songs to be sung and letters to be written home extolling the pleasures of California living. And there were other parts of the country to see. We moved to New Orleans, where Ruben entered graduate school at Tulane University. After six more months as a Gal Friday, I decided it was time to get a higher education. The classes at Sophie Newcomb College (the undergraduate school for women at Tulane) were small and the students preoccupied with debutante balls and sorority events. My classmates were eager to graduate and get on with their "real lives." But what was *my* real life? I was eager, but frightened, to be back in school. Ruben and I were a self-sufficient couple living in the French Quarter and feeling adventurous. The cocoon years continued amidst the Dixieland clubs and refurbished slave quarters of the Old South.

It is not easy to raise the aspirations of a Willowdale girl. Looking back, I realize now that I was pushed, not pulled, into each succeeding step of my academic career. Back in Berkeley after the New Orleans interlude, graduating with a B.A. and a Phi Beta Kappa key in hand, I was "finished" with school. At a time when many talented women were being discouraged, my senior honors professor urged me to apply for a Woodrow Wilson graduate fellowship for students interested in an academic career. But nothing was further from my mind. Despite my interest in school—sociology had been a congenial major, triggered accidentally with an eye-opening class at Newcomb—I was still living vicariously. My husband would become a psychology professor at a small liberal arts college (I thought) and I would be the professor's wife and helpmeet, research assistant, and (yes) editor and typist. I would be Deborah Kerr, dispensing tea and sympathy to Ruben's troubled students in our lovely home on a leafy campus somewhere in . . . fantasyland.

Awakening to the Possibilities

After working for six months as a research assistant in the Institute of Governmental Studies on the Berkeley campus, going back to school seemed like a good idea. I thought I could do what my boss was doing, and it looked as if Ruben might be in graduate school forever. The marriage was beginning to unravel, a victim of disillusion, hurt feelings, misplaced sexual liberation, and the social chaos of the sixties, in which everything was possible and nothing was required. Ruben was a free spirit; far from thinking about an academic career or starting a family, he was dreaming about sailing around the world. I was beginning to realize that I could have my own career. It would take two more years before the marriage was completely undone. Meanwhile, we sailed with friends on San Francisco Bay, danced to the Beatles and the Mamas and Papas, daringly smoked marijuana. Life as a graduate student was pleasant and the classes were stimulating. There were papers to write and exams to take, but those were part of the game. Being a graduate student was a lifestyle, not a plan, for both of us.

In 1966, with an M.A. degree and thoughts of finding a job in city planning, I was ready once again to leave school. The turnaround time on this occasion was very fast, however. Scrutinizing my application, the campus career placement officer wanted to give me a typing test and announced that my salary expectations were too high. I heard a prefeminist "click" and decided to stay in school after all.

It was Harriet Presser who first suggested I take a population course from Kingsley Davis. Harriet and I had gossiped and dozed through a year-long statistics seminar on factor analysis and had become thoroughly bonded by the experience. The other students working with Davis included Janet Salaff, now a professor at the University of Toronto; Shirley Hartley; Nadia Youssef, who went on to the International Center for Research on Women in Washington, D.C., and to UNICEF; and June Sklar, who would die in 1977 of a brain tumor after a promising professional start. Each of us was doing research on some aspect of women's lives. Harriet was documenting the grassroots demand for sterilization among women in Puerto Rico, Janet investigating the work and childbearing roles of women in Chinese collectives, Shirley analyzing international trends in illegitimacy, Nadia contrasting women's economic and family roles in Latin America and the Middle East, and June tracing historical changes in marriage patterns in Eastern Europe. I was to write a dissertation on social factors influencing the timing

Ruth Dixon-Mueller

205

of first marriage among women in Europe and Asia and proportions of those who never married. That first graduate course on population was another turning point resulting from a casual conversation: I had found my metier.

Kingsley Davis was a difficult man, but he had an exciting way of using demographic data to analyze social institutions. The field of demography in those days was far more sociological than it is now, since it has been captured by neoclassical economists and other dubious types. The work of Davis and his wife then, Judith Blake, had a deep influence both on those of us who were their students and on the field as a whole. Their classic article "Social structure and fertility: an analytic framework" identified the biological and behavioral paths through which economic, social, and cultural forces influence birth rates. Davis's paper "The theory of change and response in modern demographic history" challenged prevailing theories of fertility decline just as his article in *Science,* "Population policy: will current programs succeed?" challenged the international family planning establishment in a highly publicized debate. Meanwhile, Blake was confronting the establishment with her challenge to economists ("Are babies consumer durables?") and to the U.S. family planning establishment ("Population policy for Americans: is the government being misled?"). Davis and Blake were arguing in their policy pieces that offering family planning services was not sufficient to influence birth rates substantially. More fundamental structural changes were needed to undermine what Blake called the "coercive pronatalism" of social and economic life in developing countries and even in the United States. In the heady atmosphere of the late sixties, when the global population explosion was a topic of intense public debate, these were our texts.

I see now that there was a lot of feminism in those early papers. Blake and Davis both emphasized the need to steer women away from inevitable marriage and childbearing by offering independent alternatives such as higher education, rewarding employment, and equal pay. But feminism was not its name. Indeed, successful women professionals like Judith Blake were still insisting that "I am not a feminist, but. . . ." Blake and Davis were outspoken critics of conventional wisdom, however, and offered important role models in that respect. Judith Blake, who became chair of the new department of demography, was a terrifying but brilliant teacher. And, although Kingsley Davis had the reputation of being a womanizer and told sexist jokes in class, he was ultimately a strong mentor for his female students. He had the capacity to make us feel that we could do demography. Unlike some professors whose intellectual reputations thrived on mystification, Davis gave us the analytical tools with which to work, and most of us thrived.

Stumbling over Feminism

The late sixties were intensely political years in the sociology department and on the Berkeley campus. The sociology faculty was ripped apart and lifelong friendships were destroyed. Several key faculty left the department. Classes were disrupted every semester by strikes and demonstrations. Antiwar protests focused on the escalation of the war in Vietnam, the U.S. bombing of Cambodia, trying to get the ROTC military presence and Dow Chemical recruiters off campus, the killings at Kent State. Third World protests focused on the demand for an ethnic studies department and for classes taught by Angela Davis and Eldridge Cleaver. Free speech protests, black power, the student movement, gay rights, women's liberation: they were all there, persistent, insistent, demanding attention, commitment, and change. In the midst of the political turmoil we were trying to take our oral exams and write our dissertations.

The sixties were also intensely personal years. In the spirit of the times, I moved in with a professor in the department who had recently divorced his wife. Several faculty marriages were breaking up, and some of the female graduate students (especially those of us who were newly divorced ourselves) were willing accomplices. The thought that a "famous" professor might find us attractive and interesting was thrilling. Fifteen years later, some of us would be chairing campus committees on sexual harassment and drawing up guidelines that would prohibit such relationships. We had learned some lessons, and they were not all good.

In the late sixties the women students in the department were taking their first hard look at feminism. Betty Friedan had stirred us up with *The Feminine Mystique* and the launching of the National Organization for Women (NOW) in 1967. Women's consciousness-raising groups were blooming all over the country and radical feminist collectives such as Redstockings were issuing manifestos. Sisterhood was powerful! Some of us had our consciousness raised sooner than others. For me, it was later, and—as usual—I stumbled over feminism more or less by chance.

Being divorced and out of the cocoon encouraged me to make friends with women (at first, rather awkwardly) for the first time since high school. There were a lot of women students in the sociology department in the late sixties but classes were large and most of us did not know one another. It came as a surprise to realize that there were no tenure-track women faculty in sociology and had not been for many years. Like many students at Berkeley I had only two classes taught by women professors during my undergraduate and graduate career. Yet when the female graduate students, urged on by visiting lecturer and radical feminist Pauline Bart, mobilized around the demand that the department hire a woman, I found myself in the position of confronting a resistant faculty committee that included my lover. The situation did not make for good politics; the conflicting emotions were just too strong.

By 1970, with an almost completed dissertation, I was thinking about working in the international population field. A tentative inquiry to the Population Council in New York City led the interviewer to wonder who I might have lunch with there, since the professional researchers were all men and I would have to lunch with the secretaries. (Definitely a feminist "click.") The Ford Foundation was more forthcoming: they offered me a job in New York in their population program.

The Ford Foundation interview was exciting not only for the business-class air ticket and the glamour of the foundation's office, but also because Harriet Presser took me to one of the first street demonstrations to liberalize the abortion law in the State of New York. It was my first encounter with Emily Moore, an abortion activist who went on to a career in family planning and international development. We picketed and disrupted hearings. It was a heady introduction to the politics of abortion and feminist agitation. Yet, despite the temptation of the Ford Foundation offer, the Willowdale girl decided not to move to New York. Deciding that she was "in love" with the aforementioned professor, she would stay in the Bay Area (the relationship lasted one more year). I found an opening in the sociology department at the Davis campus of the University of California, under pressure to hire its first woman. I would teach there, commuting from the Bay Area, for the next 18 years.

Finishing the Ph.D. in 1970 was symbolic. The sixties were over. Fresh out of graduate school, our cohort transformed itself into would-be professionals. We bought new clothes. We formed a women's faculty research group to discuss research in progress that was to continue for twenty years. Anxious about achieving in a male world, we were determined to transform that world. On the one hand, we would learn how to publish, but on the other we would insist that research on women was a legitimate endeavor. We would get academic positions and benefit from affirmative action, but we would challenge those same institutions for their sexist ideologies and practices. Eventually we did publish, we were appointed to committees, we got tenure. We had arrived.

The early years as a professional were active ones. At UC Davis, the newly hired women formed a committee to investigate the status of women students and faculty. Like women at other campuses, we tracked hiring and promotion rates of female and male faculty, sent questionnaires to the faculty about their attitudes toward women, and scrutinized admissions and retention records for male and female graduate students in different departments. We demanded a standing committee on the Status of Women and took turns as chair; we demanded a Women's Center. On the basis of the findings of our report, Lenore Weitzman, newly hired in sociology, filed a class action sex discrimination complaint with the U.S. Department of Labor. At a rally complete with TV coverage we announced the results of the study and publicized the complaint. Our consciousness had been raised, and we were feeling feisty.

In the Population Association of America (PAA), a vocal cohort of young women professionals with a few older allies organized a Women's Caucus similar to those in other professional associations. We organized a restaurant sit-in at the meetings in New Orleans where women were not permitted at the businessmen's lunch, demanded more representation of women in PAA paper sessions, wrote in successful women candidates for the board of directors to challenge an all-male slate, and organized sessions on the status of women and feminist demography for the first time. The PAA as an association has been transformed since those early days. Women presidents have been elected, the board of directors includes many women, and women give papers in every session. In essence, however, the field of demography—its proponents preoccupied with the mathematical modeling of population processes— has remained almost untouched by the feminist movement despite our best efforts.

Beyond Academia: Discovering the World of Women

The faint sounds of a gamelin orchestra wafted into the darkened room from the hotel courtyard; the scent of spices filled the air. Was someone really paying me to be here? The year was 1973; the place, the Ambarukmo Palace Hotel in Yogyakarta, Indonesia. A group of women from throughout Asia and the Pacific was passionately debating the effects of Islamic law on women's status at a two-week seminar on the status of women and family planning sponsored by the United Nations. As a consultant to the UN on a one-year assignment in New York, I had been sent to Indonesia with several colleagues to participate in the seminar and act as rapporteur. The Indonesia assignment was to be the first of many professional visits to Asia—to India, Nepal, Pakistan, Bangladesh, Thailand, Indonesia, and Malaysia—and I was smitten.

The Section on the Status of Women at the United Nations, now located in Vienna, was then (1973) part of the Division of Human Rights in New York. Much activity was being generated around the planned celebration of World Population Year in 1974 and International Women's Year in 1975. The Commission on the Status of Women wanted a study on the relationship between population and women's status, with a strong focus on human rights. A "right to family planning" had been established in international declarations. The question was how women's exercise of this right might be influenced by—or might influence—the exercise of their rights in education, employment, the family, and the community. My job was to analyze the questionnaires that had been sent to governments and international organizations, review the research literature, participate in regional seminars, and write the report.

The year at the United Nations pulled me into a world of feminists who were pioneers in their own countries—in Morocco and India, Venezuela and the Dominican Republic, Great Britain, and what was then the Soviet Union. We discussed women's liberation over espresso in the delegates' lounge, slipped into the back seats at General Assembly debates to catch a glimpse of world affairs, and worried about whether our work could have any impact on women's condition. More broadly, the UN assignment pulled me irretrievably into the world itself. One could no longer remain comfortably parochial. The world of women beyond national borders began to take on real geographical, political, and personal meaning. The idea of discovering that sisterhood is global sounds hopelessly naive, yet across the great divides of power, privilege, and wealth, there was a sense of immediacy, of sharing, of empathy, of sisterhood, that transcended divisions. The women were real. They had faces, families, life stories that infused our work with passion and purpose.

The UN assignment also pulled together the intellectual threads of demography, development, and feminism in ways that would not come undone. All of my subsequent work would focus on the lives of women as they intersect with population trends and development processes. Almost miraculously, it seemed, the tools of social demography could be put to good use in the service of global feminism. Statistical data could describe, identify, probe, analyze, and question what was happening in women's lives. Births and deaths, marriage and divorce, contraception and abortion, family size and composition, education and illiteracy, employment and unpaid labor at home: these were the materials of demography, and they were the measurable components of how women were faring in comparison with men and with women of other classes, other places, other times. Most important, our analyses had policy implications. One could try to influence how governments made decisions about health, family planning, agriculture, employment, education. One could try to influence the research and funding decisions of bilateral donors such as the U.S. Agency for International Development, the foundations, nongovernmental organizations, and the UN agencies themselves. We would stick like thorns in the side of the entrenched male bureaucracies. And, despite the resistance, some progress would be made.

Imagine that there is now a field of study called Women in Development (WID) that simply did not exist in 1970. Imagine that some of us started our research with a single file of articles labeled "Women," which grew to two files: "Women, U.S." and "Women, international." The publication in 1970 of Ester Boserup's classic book *Woman's Role in Economic Development* was to the WID field what Friedan's book had been to the women's movement. It started a revolution. An annotated bibliography by Mayra Buvinic on *Women and World Development* published in 1976 lists 444 books, bibliographies, journals, and articles, many of the latter being unpublished mimeographed papers given at conferences. Only twelve of these works appeared before 1970. The celebration of the United Nations Decade for Women, beginning with the international women's conference in Mexico City in 1975, provided a vital stimulus to research and policy as well as to the growth of the international women's movement. There is now a thriving interdisciplinary body of work on women in international development, drawing on economics, sociology, anthropology, history, feminist studies, and other disciplines. Books number in the hundreds; articles in the thousands. Students are writing theses and dissertations on the topic. What began as a process of learning about the situation of women in different countries and the "negative impact of development on women" by experts such as Ester Boserup and Irene Tinker has evolved into a full-fledged program of teaching and research. And what began as a few tentative efforts to influence public policy has evolved into an integrated assault on the major institutions. International agencies have adopted policies to integrate or "mainstream" women in all aspects of development and decision making, with mixed results. The five-year plans of developing countries often include sections promoting women's education, employment, legal status, property rights, and participation in economic and social life. In 1991, the sixth meeting of the Association for Women in Development in Washington, D.C., attracted more than 1,100 participants from North America, Europe, Africa, Asia, and Latin America to engage in a North–South dialog on what we have learned.

The excitement generated by this explosion of feminist research fueled my own work on the relationship between women's productive and reproductive roles, the measurement of women's work in agriculture and the nonformal sector, marriage and divorce, reproductive health and rights, and population and development policies. Some of my work is theoretical, some applied. Some is qualitative, some quantitative; some based on arm-chair conceptualizing, some on investigations in the field. The most fulfilling involved four months of travel along the back roads and village paths of Bangladesh, India, Nepal, and Pakistan in the mid-seventies in search of the women's producer cooperatives described in *Rural Women at Work* (1978).

Traveling alone, often with no clear idea of where I was going or what I was doing, was accidental tourism at its best and worst. In Bangladesh, my first experience with a totally sex-segregated society, the village women often ran away to hide when they saw me coming. Only the men and little boys were brave. Gradually, the women would slip out of their doorways to take a closer look. Was I a woman or a man? It was difficult to decide about a tall foreigner in a shirt, trousers, short hair, and an appalling scarcity of gold jewelry. The most daring of the women would finally approach, touch my clothing, and giggle with the others as they decided that I must be female after all. But what a strange specimen I was! "Where is your husband?" they demanded. "Where is your mother, your father? Where are your children?" How could one explain to these women that one was happily single and childless? That would be a disaster in their culture.

One of the recurrent themes of my research is the question How does becoming literate, or earning money, or forming a group affect the ability of girls and women to take more control over their sexual and reproductive lives? Bangladesh, the quintessential patriarchal society, offers glimpses into the possibilities of change. "Since we started the credit program for women in this village, three women have divorced their husbands!" crowed Muhammed Yunus. As founder of the renowned Grameen Bank rural credit scheme, he was rightly proud of its accomplishments. More than 80 percent of the borrowers at that time were women, all of them in poor households. Having formed credit groups of five borrowers each, most were earning money for the first time from their investments: a milk goat, rice hulling equipment, a supply of jute for weaving mats. The women rushed excitedly forward in Yunus's familiar presence to meet the foreign woman. The pencil stubs tied to their saris proved they could write their names, a skill trium-phantly acquired as a condition of becoming a borrower. One woman's husband had secretly tried to sell her cow; when he was discovered in the market, the entire borrowers group went to confront him and the "barefoot banker" in charge of the loan accompanied them. The hus-band was humiliated into returning the cow, forced to recognize that it belonged to his wife, not to him. Simple stories such as these are the lifeblood of change. Learning to write, earning an independent income for the first time, forming a woman's group: they seem so elemental to us. Yet, in a Bangladeshi village, they are revolutionary achievements.

More recently, visiting women's health clinics there as a consultant for the International Women's Health Coalition in New York, I have been struck by the changes that have occurred. One sees more girls and women on the village paths and city sidewalks. Women who were once cloistered are increasingly "coming out" to attend a meeting of a women's group, go to a health clinic, and even to earn a living. In the clinics, such as those run by the feminist Bangladesh Women's Health Coalition, women emerge from their identities as the "wife of" or the "mother of" to speak their own name. They seek, sometimes eagerly and sometimes fearfully, for a method to postpone or avoid the next preg-nancy or to terminate the one they have. Many visit the clinic without their husband's permission, having somehow found the independence to take this step on their own. With their saris pulled up and their feet in the stirrups, the women assume the universal female position: on their backs, first for sex, then childbirth, now for a pelvic examination, an IUD insertion, or an early abortion. The low moaning of the women and the reassuring voices of the paramedics who assist them provide a backdrop for this panorama. There is blood. Yes, sisterhood is global.

Second Thoughts on Academia: Is This All There Is?

On the UC Davis campus in the mid-eighties, an important adminis-trative meeting of dean and department chairs is taking place. The men had occupied all the chairs around the long conference table by the time I arrived, so I sat along the wall with a few secretaries. As a fully fledged grownup, I was by now a full professor and for two years would be department chair. This was my first meeting with my esteemed peers.

Sometimes we look around at a meeting and wonder why we are there, an inevitable question when the meeting is a waste of time. But the feeling I had about this meeting was something different: this was accidental tourism in one's own back yard. "Where *am* I? What club is this, of which I now seem to be a member?" These were not my people! The director of personnel was taking the group to task for failing to stop the clerical staff from becoming unionized. Now the teaching assistants and research associates were organizing, he warned, and it was time to take a firm stand. The longer he spoke, the more agitated I became. Was this a corporate seminar on union busting? I had been president of the campus chapter of the American Federation of Teachers in the early 1970s and had enjoyed handling faculty grievance procedures. Snapping at the heels of the administration and making nonnegotiable demands (a skill learned in the sixties) was our specialty. This was another scene entirely. Flushed and emotional, I protested. It was shocking to listen to an antiunion speech, I charged, when many of us had worked hard over the years to organize the faculty, and for good reason, too (a list of examples followed). The silence settling over my heroic intervention was palpable. After a long pause the personnel representative gave a silky response, the vice-chancellor of academic affairs said a conciliatory word or two, and my erstwhile colleagues remained silent. When the meeting broke up I began to understand the Amish art of shunning.

Planning programs, thinking about the role of social sciences in the university and the role of the university itself, hiring faculty: some aspects of chairing a department were rewarding. But being in charge—however temporarily—changed personal relationships with colleagues, some of whom were good friends. Just as in friendships with graduate students whose futures are then determined by our decisions on an exam or our comments on a paper, the same awkwardness pervades the relationship with a friend and colleague who is up for promotion, who isn't publishing, who is ineffective in the classroom.

Are women "in power" more likely to have difficulty with these feelings than men? Are we too socialized in being nice, in wanting to be liked by our peers? Do we want too much to be liked by our students, too, suffering real pangs from a nasty evaluation of our teaching even when most students thought we were doing just fine? Are women more likely than men to say to themselves, "I'm a fraud! I was never meant to be a university professor, a department chair. I've overstepped the bounds and someone is going to expose me." The occasion may be a student's rising in class to demand, "What do *you* know, anyway?" It may be a renowned sociologist rising at a professional meeting to challenge the assumptions of a paper just delivered. I have talked about these fears with other women, and many admit to them. I have not talked about these fears with men, which means that (1) I don't know whether men are as likely to have such feelings and (2) I apparently fear what men will think if I admit these fears. The issue is one of feelings of entitlement. There appear to be major differences between women and men in their sense of entitlement to power, privilege, and professional success. The Willowdale girl had a respectable résumé, but she was not "entitled." Although she secretly knew that she was as smart as most of her colleagues and smarter than some, being on top was not a middle-class, WASP, Canadian thing to do.

Being married was. After ten years of living the single life, part of it on a houseboat in Alameda with a canoe and a cat, I had married again. I was fascinated with Martin's multilingual background and his work as an international exporter; he was fascinated to meet a professional woman with a Ph.D. My decision to marry was a surprise to my friends who had heard me denounce the institution of marriage at every opportunity and in no uncertain terms. Once again, the decision calls for some reflection. Why does a feminist living an independent life do such a conventional thing? In particular, why does she choose to marry an older man raised in a patriarchal family in the Swiss mountains, a widower with three teenage sons, a businessman, and (well, yes) a Republican to boot?

Perhaps it is because the Willowdale girl was turning forty, had just received tenure, and thought that it was time to leave the single life. Moving into a ready-made family, she could attend high school and college graduations as she "should have" been doing all along. After all, her sister was in a stable marriage with five teenage children. The prospect certainly made her mother happy. After the marriage, the first letter arrived addressed to "Mrs. Martin Mueller" rather than to the usual "Dr. Ruth Dixon." I had lost my first name, my last name, and my title. My mother wanted to know if Martin would "allow" me to keep working.

The 1980s were establishment years. Living first in suburban Marin County and then in a Berkeley brown shingle exactly like those I had loved from a distance in the late fifties; housing a series of Swiss au-pairs here to learn English; commuting to Davis; having a secure job with retirement benefits; being a professor and department chair; acquiring a list of publications and a professional reputation; traveling to meetings and assignments overseas. The die was cast. Or was it? On a glorious fall weekend in 1987 while I was grading midterms instead of hiking at Point Reyes National Seashore, a light went on in my head. I didn't need to do this any more! I didn't need to do the respectable, responsible thing and wait until I was sixty-five years old—or even fifty-five—

to retire. Life was becoming much too predictable. I could quit my job right then, at (almost) fifty. Martin was supportive (he thought I would stay home and cook). Four days later my resignation was announced to the Davis sociology department. The response was immediate. "How can you resign a full professorship? What will you do? How will you make a living? How can you leave the university with all of its perquisites and status? Why not take a leave, go part-time, wait until early retirement?" "Don't do it!" they cried, except the two or three who said "Good for you!" or confided "I would love to do what you're doing, but I can't."

Future Unknown

The impulse to leave the university was a good one. The combination of demographic skills and interests in women, population, and development offers consulting possibilities and travel. The work on women has been sustaining; that is not what I left. As an "independent scholar" I have continued to write, struggling as before with articles, a book manuscript, and thoughts about other projects. The book in progress— on population policies and women's rights in developing countries— is a challenge. Reflecting years of agitation by feminist friends and colleagues within the population establishment, it argues that a population policy should protect the reproductive rights of women from threats by both the pronatalist and the antinatalist forces, that is, from patriarchal family systems and the international right-to-life movement, on the one hand, and from population control advocates and overzealous family planning providers on the other. The need to undermine the "coercive pronatalism" of social and economic institutions harks back to the work of Davis and Blake in the sixties; the focus on women's rights and family planning to my work at the United Nations in the seventies. The eighties are reflected in the broadened concept of reproductive rights and quality of reproductive health care articulated by feminists in the international women's health movement.

The department of demography at Berkeley provides some academic sustenance, collegiality, and a courtesy appointment as a research associate. I work with students, attend professional meetings, and insist to colleagues that I have not retired, merely resigned. I am working full time, I announce, except for numerous cappuccino breaks at Cody's Bookstore or Caffé Meditteraneum (two fine old institutions on Telegraph Avenue). An off-campus office in an old house provides a congenial working place. I had bought the house in 1983 as a joint workspace for four of us who were close friends and colleagues of long standing:

Judith Tendler, a development economist working for USAID and the World Bank who is now at the Massachusetts Institute of Technology; Karen Paige Ericksen, a psychologist at UC Davis; and Norma Wikler, a Berkeley sociologist teaching at UC Santa Cruz. Adrienne Germain of the International Women's Health Coalition holes up there occasionally to absorb the Berkeley ambience and to write. A group of Berkeley women—offshoots of our long-standing faculty research group—offers additional sustenance along with good-humored reminders that we are all growing older. Calling ourselves "old feminist farts" (OFF), we meet occasionally over Thai food to discuss the pros and cons of estrogen replacement therapy, the illness of aged parents, and the latest *New York Times* review of someone's book. The group includes Lillian Rubin; Arlene Skolnick, who writes on the family; Judy Stacey, on feminist theory; Nancy Chodorow, on feminism and psychoanalysis; Kristin Luker, on the politics of abortion; and Norma Wikler, who works with judges and lawyers on gender bias in the courts.

In 1989, Norma Wikler also took matters into her own hands by resigning from UC Santa Cruz. We had been friends since graduate school days. Faced with an open future, the two of us conjure wild plans—aided by Canadian Club whiskey on my part and Kentucky bourbon on hers—of a nonsociological life as farmers, feminist activists, and subversives in some other country. The fantasy of *Thelma and Louise* has replaced the fantasy of *Tea and Sympathy*. Not surprisingly, Martin finds it difficult to understand this surge of restlessness in his wife despite his own history of moving from Switzerland to Germany to Argentina to California as a young man. For my cohort, however, the fifties as a time of life have replaced the fifties as an era. This fact is truly alarming. Precisely when is it that we started counting backward, trying to estimate the number of good years we have *left?* Is it too late to try something else? Do we have another twenty years of being temporarily able-bodied? If so, that is a healthy chunk of time. One could pull on some jeans and boots, trade in the Volvo for a pickup truck, turn up the country music, and head south across several borders. One could start over somewhere else. One could still be an accidental tourist in one's own life, waking up in the morning to the sounds of a gecko's chirp, a parrot's screech, or a language not yet understood, to wonder, Who am I? Where am I? And what am I doing *here?*

Chapter 16

Running between the Raindrops: From the Margin to the Mainstream

MARY HAYWOOD METZ

Madison, Wisconsin: The View from the Chair, 1991–92

I became chair of the Department of Educational Policy Studies at the University of Wisconsin, Madison, in August 1991. The office is the best reward for the chair's difficult, invisible work. Large windows on two sides present a wonderful view of Bascom Mall, the symbolic heart of the campus. Working here, I recognize that I play a significant role in this university; I am in the mainstream of contemporary academia. Yet in another sense I am still marginal. Belonging to the Department of Educational Policy Studies makes me marginal to sociology. That marginality has much to do with the theme of this book—the careers of *women* with sociology doctorates.

I have reached this place from my days in Berkeley by running between the raindrops. Looking out my window, I am always startled when I see Peter Hansen among the passing students. I have seen Peter several times a week since he was four, but never here. Peter, a close friend of my younger son, is part of my other life in Milwaukee, more than eighty miles from Bascom Mall. There I wear jeans and sneakers and am called "Mom." Here I wear skirts and heels and am called "Professor Metz." The integration of Professor Metz and Mom required both social and personal change after my Berkeley student days.

The Early Years

My education was unusual. I was taught at home until, at the age of almost eight, I entered the fourth grade at the first of a series of private schools. Forever after, I was a year or more younger than my classmates. Since my family had very little money, I had to win and keep scholarships at all these institutions and could not join expensive extracurricular activities. After high school I entered Radcliffe College. With one woman for every five Harvard men, we were on the periphery of the university. Thus, throughout school and college, I was always marginal—different because of age, social class, or gender.

Radcliffe: Discovering Social Science

In my junior year, I was assigned to David Riesman, author of *The Lonely Crowd,* as adviser for independent study and thesis. I was amazed to find this renowned professor personable, relaxed, and friendly. He asked me about my interests, listened to my comments, encouraged me with badly needed praise. This mentoring relationship was the only one I ever had.

I was accepted for graduate school in sociology or sociology-psychology programs at Chicago, Michigan, Stanford and Berkeley. Riesman advised Berkeley because the faculty was strong, diverse, and not orthodox. There would be room to develop and then to follow my own interests. That advice was sound. After a year on a German Academic Exchange Commission Fellowship in Freiburg and West Berlin, I entered Berkeley's sociology department in the fall of 1961.

Berkeley 1961–69: "It's a Shame to Waste a Berkeley Training"

At Berkeley there was intellectual freedom, diversity of opinion, and a willingness to let graduate students develop their own paths. Some classes were extraordinarily well taught. The introductory course in methods was especially strong, with Hanan Selvin and Martin Trow cooperating and sparring, comparing quantitative and qualitative methods. The work required of students was superb training.

The most intensive education took place outside the classroom, when students had assistantships for working on professors' research projects. To a lesser extent, teaching assistantships could also be opportunities for learning. In my second year, I was a research assistant for Burton Clark in a study that became *The Distinctive College* (1970). He taught me much that was valuable about qualitative research and gave me a window into the life a sociologist might lead after getting the degree.

My teaching assistantships brought little contact with the professors, although Bob Blauner made some effort to develop assistants' abilities and make us a cohesive group.

Much of the apparent intellectual freedom in the department was the product of social indifference. The faculty appeared to agree to pursue separate paths that would not intersect with others. With large entering cohorts of graduate students, they simply taught their classes and let students accept or reject the offerings. Available only during office hours, when students often lined the hall outside their offices, faculty expected large numbers of dropouts, even among those who passed the preliminary examination. The only route to serious attention was to become a research assistant. The faculty dismissed other students as a drain on their time; they made early judgments about students' promise and thus about their opportunities.

The informal student leaders set a tone that either reflected faculty perspectives or was an unconscious parody of them. The students regarded by others as successful appeared to me to be tough, cynical, and manipulative: self-centered careerists. Moreover, those students seemed to place themselves outside society, never participating but only studying it. This attitude was best exemplified for me in the fall of 1963 after John F. Kennedy was assassinated. That weekend, while most citizens were numb with shock, I got a call from another graduate student asking me to join a group doing a telephone survey on attitudes about the assassination.

Even before I came to Berkeley, I was experiencing a conflict between "warmth" and "intellect," two sides of myself that seemed hard to maintain simultaneously, paralleling the tension between woman and scholar. In the late fifties and early sixties, my male peers at Harvard and Berkeley (and the popular culture) expected a "real" woman to be interested in the affective side of life, to be on her way to becoming a good Parsonian wife-mother. To take my intellect seriously, to do what the men around me were doing, was to be a nonwoman, at best a disembodied intellect. There were few persons or ideas abroad to suggest that synthesis was possible. There were no women on the faculty to show what a woman scholar might be like.

With two exceptions, the women students that I knew well dropped out. Like me, they were young, single, and heterosexual. Most of the women in this book, the survivors, went through graduate school bearing family responsibilities that made it impossible for them to participate fully in the social and intellectual life of the department. To them, the freedom of the young single women must have seemed enviable. It was less evident that their family responsibilities proclaimed the solidity of their gender identities. It was more difficult to call their womanhood into question—though just as easy to question their ability to be serious students.

I did well during my first semester, but confided to my adviser that I was not certain that sociology was the right place for me. His reply was immediate: "Why don't you get a job in San Francisco? You're a pretty girl. You'll get married." I was surprised, disconcerted, taken aback, but—not yet—angry. The raindrops were falling, but I did not get wet. It was not until five or six years later, after the start of the women's movement, that I replayed that comment, which I vividly remembered, and felt consciously angry.

After my second year, doubts about merely studying society led me to a summer project run by the American Friends Service Committee. I spent the summer of 1963 in the ghetto of Memphis, Tennessee, exposed to racial separation and oppression from the perspective of the black community. I returned to Berkeley with more confidence, with mind and heart closer together. The values of the Quaker project were ones I could embrace.

The following fall, I was a teaching assistant in Martin Trow's undergraduate course on research methods, along with Don Metz, whom I had not previously met. As our conversations expanded beyond the course, we found common interests and values. In the spring of 1965, we both were awarded Kent Fellowships from the Danforth Foundation. With its promise of support through the dissertation, we informed the foundation that we would be members of a single family; we were married in July 1965.

My Berkeley education began to come alive as I was preparing for orals, the preliminary examination for the Ph.D. I discovered that organizational literature that had previously appeared dull contained intriguing controversies and observations. After the prelim, I chose to write a dissertation on authority, drawing on a theoretical paper that had been my most sustained work to date. I decided that junior high schools would be a fertile setting for observing conceptions of, and conflicts about, authority. Armed with my theoretical paper, my training from David Riesman, and my knowledge of qualitative research from Selvin and Trow's methods course, I entered the field.

I was thrilled with what I found. In the teachers' lounge, alternative models of authority were the subject of passionate factionalism, and teachers and students took one another to the mat in classroom conflicts that also reflected discrepant conceptions of authority. I was enthralled, a detective on the trail of understanding; a lifetime commitment to scholarship was born.

My adviser yawned. He saw me every few months and made a few unfocused, though helpful, comments. I was in the field for more than a year, collected tons of data, but had difficulty ordering it. During a year of analysis and writing, my adviser saw me infrequently, only during office hours, often leaving other students waiting. When I produced a draft, he was surprised; he had thought I would never be able to bring the material together.

I left Berkeley in August 1969 with all but my concluding chapter written. The next summer, I sent the completed dissertation to my committee. Philip Selznick, the second reader, wrote that it was a contribution to the theory of authority. My major professor did not respond. When I finally called after several months, he said he had not yet read it, but would sign off "since Phil liked it."

The last year we were in Berkeley, Don and I were looking for two jobs in sociology, rare in those days. My major professor's contribution consisted of asking where Don was looking. When we decided to take a position and a half at Earlham College, a Quaker liberal arts college in Indiana, he remarked, "It's a shame to waste a Berkeley training on Earlham."

Earlham College 1969–75: Half-Time on the Tenure Track

Earlham offered Don a full position and me a half-time one. Since we wanted to start a family, I thought working half time would be a wonderful compromise. I expected to follow Don and for my career to be secondary to his.

Life at Earlham was hardly idyllic. In the first two years I taught three courses a year, six different preparations, for half salary. Don taught six courses a year and had nine different preparations in two years. He was department chair for two quarters while the long-term chair was on leave. It was a scalding introduction to teaching, but we learned sociology in both depth and breadth. As members of the same department, we became a collective entity called the Metzes. (I was the minor half.) At the end of two years, in our chair's formal evaluation of our work, he wrote only a single account of "the Metzes'" teaching!

It was important to me to spend a lot of time with our children, born during our Earlham years. Working half time was in practice a difficult compromise, though one I would make were I to choose again. With a colleague and friend, a mother who held a parallel position in the philosophy department, I worked out formal parameters for half-time tenure-track positions. When I left the college, my legacy was a clear definition of such positions for parents of either sex.

After our second son arrived in 1973, the pressures on family life of two jobs and two very small children became searing—even though we had an excellent long-term baby-sitter. In 1975, Don moved to a position at Marquette University in Milwaukee. I went there without a job, hoping to hold onto my career by writing until our children were older.

Interim 1975–79: What Is Commitment?

In our last year at Earlham, I was funded by the newly formed National Institute of Education (NIE) to rewrite my dissertation as a book and to do some parallel research in schools serving a different population. During our first fall in Milwaukee, 1975, I faced revisions requested by a publisher. Our four-year-old attended afternoon nursery three days a week. On those days I walked him, and our two-year-old, five blocks to nursery school; on returning home, I put the younger one down for a nap and went to my attic study to work on the book. I sent the manuscript to the press in January 1976.

For the next year, my career swung precariously in the balance, held in the hands of an editor so indifferent he did not send the manuscript out for review for three months. After many delays and my serious request to withdraw the work, he accepted it. In the spring of 1978, *Classrooms and Corridors* appeared, published by the University of California Press.

After a year in Milwaukee, I got a job as a lecturer at Mount Mary, a Catholic college for women. I taught first one and then two courses a semester, with little prospect of a long-term appointment. My pay barely covered baby-sitting, housecleaning, and purchase of professional clothes.

In 1977, I was interviewed by the sociology department at the University of Wisconsin, Milwaukee. They declared themselves ready to make an offer, but then the funding disappeared. I learned that my appointment had been controversial; some faculty thought I showed a "lack of commitment" to the field because I had worked only half time. I was outraged. Revising the manuscript for *Classrooms and Corridors* while my preschooler slept, with no academic position in sight, persisting though no one else cared whether the book was completed, I had shown an intensity of commitment that few can match.

I was feeling the effects of a stunning social change. Women in the Earlham community had raised their eyebrows because I worked at all, even half time. Five years later, I was criticized because I worked no more than half time. I had forged my compromise, living with one foot in traditional family life and one in the new world of career women; the consequence was disapproval from every side. The rainstorm rarely let up, and it blew from all directions.

With Mount Mary as my institutional base, I submitted a proposal to NIE to study a set of urban magnet schools. NIE funded that project, which became the book *Different by Design* (1986).

In 1978, the Department of Educational Policy Studies at the University of Wisconsin in Madison called to ask if I would be interested in a position as assistant professor. The eighty-mile commute seemed daunting, but Don pointed out that two tenure-track jobs are better than one. When I interviewed for the position, I realized that I had missed the excitement of a university, where others were doing research; I was delighted to be offered the job.

Teaching at the University of Wisconsin: From Home to Work via Clark Kent's Telephone Booth

In the fall of 1979, ten years after leaving Berkeley, as I turned forty and our younger son entered first grade, I began my first full-time appointment. Having taught only in very different contexts, I was terrified. Department members were pleased; looking at the newly published *Classrooms and Corridors* and at my NIE research grant, they believed they had hired an established researcher at the assistant professor level.

For the first two years, my research grant provided some space for transition. I worked in Milwaukee most of the time, either doing fieldwork or writing. I went to Madison once a week to teach a broadly defined course in the sociology of education, much of which I learned along with the students. When there, I was constantly alert, constantly learning. Despite the impostor syndrome, it was challenging, exhilarating, satisfying—and exhausting.

Not only was I returning to the world of the research university, I was also starting a new career in the field of education. I had studied education through the lens of organizational research. In a school of education, I needed a more comprehensive knowledge of the sociology of education, as well as familiarity with policy and practice.

I also needed to make some subtle shifts in my orientation to knowledge. Most students wanted to use theory to increase their understanding of the real world of education rather than using the real world to build elegant theory. Through my work with students, especially in directing theses and dissertations, I gradually learned to help them use theory as a tool for practical understanding. In the process, I learned to join my intellectual and moral commitments. I could speak more plainly about the urgent dilemmas facing both teachers and children in urban schools.

In my early years at Wisconsin, I felt like Clark Kent. The 7:00 A.M. bus from Milwaukee to Madison became my phone booth: I climbed out near Bascom Mall clothed as Superwoman. At the end of a long day, I was glad to be back on the bus, with a little transitional time to shed my identity as Professor Metz and become Mom again.

While our children were in elementary school, Don and I were under pressure to establish a tenurable publication record. I was often eighty miles from home fourteen hours a day; sometimes I was gone overnight for three days a week. The demands were high; those were extremely difficult years. Don did a lot of parenting. Flexible schedules allowed us to teach on different days, to work at home, to come home early, to be available for emergencies. Don shared almost equally in the burdens of being a working mother. Fortunately, our children adjusted cheerfully and in fact became contributing family members earlier than some of their friends.

The tension between work and home subsided as I became more comfortable with being Professor Metz and as the demands of mothering decreased. I could bring my two roles together in my teaching by illustrating general arguments with stories from my sons' experiences in the public schools. I worried about the homey, anecdotal quality of these tales about my children. However, I relaxed after a sophisticated sociology graduate student, floundering in an explanation to another student, turned to me in frustration and said, "Tell him about your kids." We both knew which story would make his theoretical point understandable.

My colleagues in the Department of Educational Policy Studies were helpful, sharing a humane outlook and collegial civility. From the beginning, I found real pleasure in work with graduate students, intelligent, curious, eager to embrace intellectual life. For several, I was able to supply the modeling and mentoring that I never had. To some women students, my dual life was testimony that their ambitions could be realized without sacrificing marriage and motherhood. Spontaneous and generous, my early students cheered me on. Some are now valued colleagues. We exchange papers and participate together at professional meetings.

These final paragraphs have skimmed thirteen years that were not easy but that have been satisfying. They were productive years of moving toward an integration of my work with my gender identity and roles

as wife and mother. I know that my congenial part of the university is not the whole, and that many problems exist at Wisconsin. Still, universities today are more hospitable to women than they were in the sixties. By dodging raindrops long enough, it was possible for me to get inside a dry house. I hope that my work makes it less necessary for children and teachers in schools, and for women in universities, to weather rainstorms if they are to find a respected place.

Editors' note: Because of space limitations, it was necessary to shorten Dr. Metz's original paper, completed after other chapters had been edited.

Chapter 17

An Unanticipated Life

LILLIAN B. RUBIN

"You don't have to go to college; you'll get married and your husband will take care of you," my mother declared every time the subject of my future arose. It seemed so reasonable that neither she nor I noticed how absurd her certainty was. Absurd because her own husband, my father, had died when I was five years old and my brother six, leaving her a twenty-six-year-old widow with two small children to support. Having emigrated to the United States from a shtetl in Eastern Europe only a few years earlier, she was virtually penniless, barely able to speak English, with neither family nor marketable skills. The Great Depression had just struck.

The rich were leaping from windows as fortunes fell away. The poor, accustomed to privation, plodded on stoically, a little poorer, a little hungrier, a little colder, a little more forlorn. It was more than two years before my mother finally found her way into New York City's garment industry, where she was laboring as a pieceworker at the very time she spoke with such certainly about my own secure future.

It was assumed that I'd work, of course. In a family like mine—a family periodically cast onto the welfare rolls during the "slack season," when there was no work—my brother and I were expected to work and to contribute our wages to the family economy. For him, however, college was also on the agenda. "How else will he support a family?" my mother would demand when I complained about the inequity of her plans for us. But my protest was a feeble one, born as much of sibling rivalry and my anger at having to support my brother through school as of any serious discontent with the gender expectations of the time.

It would be many years before women would make it to my list of the oppressed. In the difficult years of my childhood, it wasn't my gender that seemed so suffocating, that defined me as outsider. It was the grinding poverty, the struggle to survive; it was living in a fatherless family in a world of families with fathers; it was living with the fear that my mother would die as suddenly as my father had died; it was being called an orphan and feeling like one; it was moving ten times in as many years so that we could take advantage of the rent concessions that Depression-strapped landlords offered; it was the three of us stuck together in one small room; it was sleeping in the same bed with my mother until I got married.

It was all these, not my gender, that were so oppressive, that made me feel different, that said I didn't belong. Yes, I saw that my brother had some advantages that I didn't. Yes, I even knew that my mother valued him more than me, just because he was a son. These things angered me, made me ready to fight, but they didn't sear my soul.

I knew, of course, that women had a hard road to walk; I had only to look at my mother's life to understand just how cruel the path could be. And lest I should forget, she would remind me regularly. "Girls shouldn't be born; life is too hard for women" was her constant refrain, the background music of my young life.

Talk about mixed messages. This was the same woman who assured me that I'd marry some good man who would take care of me forever and with whom I'd live happily ever after.

It wasn't that my mother was without aspirations for me. I was expected to marry well, which meant a professional man who would provide me with all that my mother never could. Until that happy day arrived, I would work in an office. "I do dirty work; you'll do clean work" was the mandate with which I grew up. But so powerful was the ideology about women, men, and family life that, despite her own experience, my mother took for granted that for me work would be temporary, only until my real life as a wife and mother would begin.

In 1939, when I was fifteen years old, I graduated from high school and did what was expected. I got a "clean" job and was soon working my way up from the stenographic pool to a secretary's desk.

Four years later, when I was nineteen, I fulfilled my mother's dream for me. I married up—a young man headed for middle-class professional life. I didn't know it then but my father-in-law, a self-educated European Marxist, was to have a more lasting impact on my life than my husband.

Politics in the home I grew up in was simple and narrow: Is it good or bad for the Jews? Unions counted, too, since my mother knew from personal experience the benefits they could bring. But in her heart, the only real question was: Is it good or bad for the Jews? A concern I could understand, given her experience with anti-Semitism in Russia, but a vision that was too cramped for her assimilated, Americanized daughter.

For me, the unions afforded my first political lesson when, as a small child, I saw the difference they made in my mother's life and, therefore, in my own. Before the organizing drive of the ILGWU, the garment workers' union, my mother worked fifty-five hours a week. No overtime pay, no benefits, no one with whom to register a grievance, even if she'd allowed herself to have one. From Monday to Friday she left our apartment in the Bronx for her job in Long Island City at six in the morning and didn't get home until six in the evening. On Saturday she worked half a day, arriving home at about one in the afternoon. Her wages, barely enough to pay the rent and put food on the table, were never sufficient to accumulate the savings that would have tided us over the inevitable slack season. After the union won recognition in the industry, the five-day, forty-hour week (later to drop to thirty-five hours) became the standard; the pay scale, while never generous, was considerably improved; and grievance procedures were established to protect workers from unfettered exploitation. It was a lesson in the power of collective action I would never forget.

But I had no framework within which to fit that lesson. I hungered for some larger vision of the world, for something to explain my unformed but deeply felt sense of the world's injustices. My father-in-law gave me that. I listened avidly when he talked about politics, and felt the gnawing hunger inside me abate as I came to view the world from a Marxist and socialist perspective. This was the beginning of my years as a political activist.

At first my involvement was tentative, modest—committed but inexperienced. By the time I moved from New York to Los Angeles at the end of 1951, I had gotten my political feet wet and knew what I was doing. In my ten-year residence in Los Angeles, I was active in the struggle against the McCarthy attack on civil liberties in the fifties; I was an organizer of one of the pioneer women's political organizations in the state; I was deeply involved in the early civil rights struggles and instrumental in organizing the first district to elect a black congressman in California; I managed the political campaigns of liberal Democratic congressional candidates in 1960 and 1962.

My first marriage, whose most lasting gift was my daughter, ended in divorce in 1960. Two years later I married again and moved to the San Francisco Bay Area, where I was happy to leave my work in politics behind me for a while. But pleasure in my new life was soon diminished by an old restlessness. I had resolved my personal and family life, but it wasn't enough. My fourteen-year-old daughter was busy with her teenage activities, my husband with his career. And I was left to wonder how I would fill my days.

I had dreamed for years about becoming a lawyer—a dream that began during the fifties, when I knew some brave men of the law who gave up financial success and social and professional respectability to represent the victims of the witch hunt of the McCarthy era. (I say "men" because there were no visible women in the law at the time, at least none who were practicing constitutional law in Los Angeles, where I was living then.) Those men became my heroes, a model of what was possible with training in the law. I wanted to become one of them, to put myself and my knowledge into the service of those whom our society had abandoned. But it was only a dream then.

After some months of thrashing about, of seemingly endless conversations with my husband, with my friends, and with myself, I began to think it might not be an impossible dream. But first I had to get the college education I had missed in my youth. I spent hours trudging over the UC Berkeley campus thinking: What will I do on a college campus with eighteen-year-olds? One minute I was excited about the possibilities, the next it seemed like a ridiculous idea. Finally, half convinced I wouldn't be accepted anyhow, I applied and waited, anxiously but also ambivalently.

On a Saturday morning a few months later, my husband handed me a letter from the university. "Open it," he demanded, hovering anxiously over my shoulder. "What if it says I haven't been admitted, then what?" I asked. "Open it," he said more gently. In it was a small, formal notice of admission, a document too insignificant looking for me to imagine, in that moment, that it heralded the beginning of the rest of my life.

At thirty-nine I became a college freshman—a lone grown woman among several thousand fresh-faced entering students only a few years older than my daughter. As I walked through the main gate of the

Berkeley campus on that warm, sunny day in January 1963, fear dogged my steps and clutched at my heart. I was half certain that the admissions people would realize they'd made a mistake and would move to rectify it as soon as I arrived. Even if that didn't happen, I knew I'd never be able to compete with the bright eighteen-year-olds who would be my classmates. True, I had by then undertaken and mastered other challenges. I had already known success in the world, and I savored it. But I remained uncertain about my intellectual capacities, often feeling like a sham, waiting in some part of myself for others to find it out. So it didn't surprise me to hear my inner voice warning: *This time you really are in over your head; this time you'll surely be found wanting.*

I've never worked harder than I did that first year in college. Partly I was driven by a crisis in self-confidence that left me filled with anxiety about failure. But I had more than my internal issues to overcome. It was nearly twenty-five years since I had last sat in a classroom as a student. I had to reclaim lost skills and learn new ones. Never having been to college, I knew nothing of how to write a term paper. My first attempts in freshman English earned me Cs and Ds—enough to validate my worst fears, nearly enough to convince me that the whole enterprise was a gigantic mistake.

In my sophomore year, I enrolled in a political sociology class, assuming it would be a snap. Politics in the academy, I quickly came to see, had nothing to do with politics in the real world. Therefore, I, who had years of experience in the political trenches, spent most of the semester trying to figure out what the professor was talking about. A task at which I wasn't wholly successful. It was the only sociology course in my undergraduate career in which I got less than an A.

That same year, 1964, I saw another example of the isolation and insularity that so often afflicts professors in the academy. I was taking a course in social movements in which we were studying theories of collective behavior and learning about some of the social movements of times gone by. As I left that class one bright fall day, I noticed a buzz in the air, a kind of high-pitched, almost feverish energy that was like a physical vibration in the atmosphere. I moved toward Sproul Plaza, where a crowd had gathered. At its center stood a police car, held captive by hundreds of students who listened with rapt attention as speakers leaped to its roof to give voice to their collective grievances. The Free Speech Movement, the opening shot in a revolution that would soon reverberate on every college campus in the country, had begun.

As the days passed and it became clear that we were witness to the birth of a social movement, I couldn't understand why we never talked about it in our social movements class. The Anabaptists were fascinating, all right. But one of the important social movements of our time was in progress right outside our window, and it was never mentioned, let along analyzed. Exasperated, I finally asked if we could discuss the FSM, which by then not only had a name but an acronym. He didn't think so, the professor replied with a smile; it wasn't really a movement, just students suffering from unseasonal spring fever.

It was a wonderful, exciting time to be a Berkeley student. For me, it was a dream come true: I could be both political activist and student. Until FSM came along, I had assumed I would have to put my former self in cold storage, at least until I'd completed my mission, which was to get my bachelor's degree and go to law school. But with the rise of the student movement, I no longer needed to maintain the separation between politics and intellectual life that, from the beginning, I had found so difficult.

Every biography is colored by the element of chance, the unexpected encounter, the unforeseen event. Instead of becoming a lawyer, I became a sociologist. Chance intervened. I was entering my junior year, waiting with hundreds of other sociology majors for the ritual, obligatory meeting with the undergraduate adviser. "Undergraduate *adviser?*" Whoever thought that term up must have had an odd sense of humor. As far as I could tell, "advising" undergrads in Berkeley's sociology department meant that some nameless professor sat at a desk and blindly signed the study lists that students put before him as they shuffled wearily by.

The undergrad adviser that year was Kenneth Bock, one of the more humane members of the department. When my turn came, he looked up at me questioningly, wondering, no doubt, about this unlikely undergraduate with graying hair. He invited me to sit down, asked what my goals were, questioned me about how I was doing. "Don't you get bored taking undergraduate classes?" he asked. Surprised at the question, I hesitated, wondering how to respond. Finally a halting "Not really" fell from my lips. "Not a very convincing answer, is it?" he countered, smiling. And before I could say another word, he suggested that I might want to take some graduate classes. I was stunned into total silence. Surely, I thought, this is some kind of a joke, or, if not that, a silly mistake. But he went on to instruct me on how it could be done.

I didn't know then that this brief exchange, this moment of civility, this acknowledgment of my anomalous situation would soon change the direction of my life. But it was an offer I couldn't refuse, not because I thought I had doctoral potential; I still wasn't sure just what a Ph.D.

was. We knew about doctors and lawyers in the world I grew up in, but had never heard of a Ph.D. In fact, long after I got my degree, my mother still couldn't figure out what I do, nor could she see any reason why I had earned the title "Doctor." "You can't give me a prescription, so what kind of doctor are you?" she'd sniff dismissively. So why did I act on Ken Bock's suggestion? I don't know. Perhaps simply because I sensed an opportunity from which I ought not turn away; perhaps because it was a challenge, from which it's never easy for me to retreat.

My first graduate course was Reinhard Bendix's comparative sociology—a lecture class in which he read from the manuscript of his soon-to-be published book. I lost the fight to listen most of the time. Later I knew him to be a dear man and even a good teacher in face-to-face situations. But at the time I was bored, disappointed, and distinctly unimpressed with graduate education. Fortunately, I didn't have to pay attention to the lectures, since the only requirement for the class was a term paper, which by then I had learned how to write. I wrote on a subject dear to my heart—the Aid to Families with Dependent Children program, comparing it with family welfare programs in several European countries.

Emboldened by the A I got for that paper, I went on to Phil Selznick's sociology of law, where I spent the semester in a panic because I barely understood a word he and his coterie of graduate students spoke. I reminded myself that Ken Bock had warned me not to be scared off by what I have since come to think of as "graduate-student-speak." But the problem wasn't only the students; the professor, too, spoke in an alien tongue. So more than once I went home in tears, as I struggled unsuccessfully to make sense of the words my ears took in but my mind couldn't translate.

Fortunately, we had the option of taking a blue-book exam or writing a paper. For me, the latter was the only way to go. The War on Poverty had recently been declared and the enabling legislation included a phrase that called for "maximum feasible participation." That phrase soon started its own war as the various vested interests—intellectuals, bureaucrats, politicians and the poor—sought to interpret its meaning and to specify who should participate maximally, which meant, of course, who would define and control the programs. I decided to investigate the origins of the phrase, to look at the debates in the *Congressional Record,* and to write to the framers and ask about their intent.

A week or so after I turned that paper in, Phil's secretary called to say he wanted to see me. We set an appointment for eight days hence, which left me with plenty of time to let my fantasies run wild. He wasn't just any professor; he was the department chair. What could he possibly want of me, an undergraduate who happened to have taken his class? I thought I had made some real progress in overcoming my anxieties about my adequacy by then. I had, after all, demonstrated that I was a worthy college student. But as is so often true in psychological life, the lived experience gave way to the archaic fears. The inner refrain was unmoved by reason and logic: *You've been found out! You're about to be driven out of the tribe.*

A sleepless week later, I presented myself in his office. He pointed to a seat opposite his rocker, but my legs would hardly move as I recognized my paper in his hand. Mutely, I crossed the room and sat, struggling to contain both fears and tears. After another moment or two of interminable silence, he said, "This is an interesting paper. How did you get the idea for it?" I looked at him blankly for what seemed like an age. How do you know how you got an idea? I don't remember how I answered, or even if I did. But I'll never forget his next words. "Have you thought about publishing it?" he asked as casually as one might mention the time of day. *Thought about publishing it?* my mind shrieked. *I thought you were going to tell me I can't come to your school, and you want to know if I thought about publishing a term paper!*

Some months later, the paper was accepted for publication in *Poverty and Human Resources Abstracts,* a journal published at the University of Michigan. It was an accomplishment beyond my dreams, as so much of my career has been. I was hooked. Law school would wait; I was on my way to a Ph.D. But would they take me? I had a husband in business, a daughter who would soon finish high school. The Bay Area was my home; my only chance for a graduate education was at Berkeley. But this was before the women's movement had sensitized universities to the problems and potential of middle-aged women, before there were reentry programs to give such women a chance. I would be forty-three years old when I finished my B.A.—far too old, from the standpoint of institutional priorities, to waste valuable training resources on.

I had by then come to know Hal Wilensky, who liked my work in his undergraduate class on the sociology of work and who asked me to be his research assistant during my senior year. My best shot at overcoming the hurdles to graduate admission, he advised, was to keep taking graduate courses throughout my last undergraduate year. By the time I earned my B.A., therefore, I had finished the graduate methods requirement, had satisfactorily completed four other graduate courses, and had worked as an RA for a year. Reinhard Bendix, Phil Selznick, and Hal Wilensky championed my application to the doctoral program.

In 1967, when I entered the graduate program, the number of women in it was small. We hadn't yet reached the critical mass necessary to create the kind of anxiety and hostility that would come later. Nor had we found our collective voice. It was still a year or so before the women's liberation movement would shake the Berkeley campus. Sociology was distinctly male turf. I doubt that anyone seriously entertained the idea that we would one day change the language of the discipline, threatening not only men's hegemony but many of their most cherished theories.

While there were people who helped and taught me along the way, no one filled the role of mentor. Michael Rogin, then a young associate professor in political science, was the outside person on my dissertation committee. His was the voice that supported my work, that offered the constructive criticism I needed, and that has remained a vital part of my professional and personal life ever since. Troy Duster, who was relatively new to the sociology department at the time, became a friend who helped me find my way around some of the obstacles every graduate student encounters. Gertrude Jaeger Selznick's Freud seminar was the most enlightening and intellectually stimulating classroom experience of my graduate years. But she was only a lecturer then, relegated by the university's nepotism rules to an insignificant and peripheral role. So while we formed a warm bond, she wasn't in a position to mentor a fledgling graduate student.

I worked as Hal Wilensky's RA for two years and profited greatly from the experience. His focus on social structures and institutions had obvious appeal to someone with my Marxist background, and I was happy to concentrate my intellectual energies in that direction for a while. With time, however, the inability of the structuralist perspective to take adequate account of human behavior and motivation became increasingly frustrating for me.

At the same time, I had come to look skeptically at the quantitative methods that dominate the mainstream of sociological research. It seemed to me that in the disciplinary quest for legitimacy, in its hunger to claim scientific validity, sociology achieved methodological rigor and trivialized its research. We gained reliability and lost relevance. Whatever else these methods might serve, they were of little use in understanding the kind of complex sociological and psychological phenomena—and the interaction between the two—that engaged me most deeply. Yet it was these very concerns for which Hal Wilensky had so little tolerance. In the end, therefore, I refused his request to chair my dissertation committee—a decision that left scars for both of us.

In writing this, I don't mean to lay the blame for the rupture of our relationship on him alone. We each played our part. Certainly I wasn't easily led, either methodologically or theoretically. And equally certainly, he wanted his students to be demonstrably his—a wish I couldn't accommodate.

I asked Bill Kornhauser to supervise my dissertation, not because I knew much about him or his work. But I was studying a political conflict—a Northern California community that had been torn apart over a court-ordered school integration plan—and political sociology was his domain. No sooner did those last words find their way to this page than a voice inside nudged: *Ah, c'mon—that wasn't the only reason.* Indeed it wasn't. Bill Kornhauser's was the one undergraduate sociology class in which I hadn't done so well, and I wanted to show him, to prove him wrong. It didn't work out that way. He didn't love my dissertation, which turned out to be a confrontation with his theory of mass society.

I'm not terribly respectful of authority, it's true, but I didn't plan to challenge the life's work of my dissertation chair. When you do the kind of research that has marked my career—call it symbolic interactionist, call it grounded theory, call it ethnography, or just call it qualitative research—you don't start out to test a theory. You hope instead that your data will help you to formulate one. In this case, they dictated a re-examination of those aspects of pluralist theory on which my adviser's work rested. To his credit, he signed off on my dissertation despite his obvious distaste for it.

The most significant intellectual figure of my graduate student days was Herbert Blumer, with whom I never studied. From the time I encountered his symbolic interactionist perspective, its ideas beckoned to me like a beacon of light in the midnight sky. Yet I didn't discover it until very late in my graduate career, having gotten sidetracked early on into the structural-functionalist side of the department. In that quarter, symbolic interaction theory and method was dismissed as unscientific, and Herb Blumer was seen as a relic of a past long dead. Nevertheless, he was a presence in the department that could not be denied—a presence that gave legitimacy to the kind of work I wanted to do. For the students who were privileged to know him, however, he was more than a presence that enabled their work; he was a revered teacher and as humane a man as the theory that is his signature.

If my recounting of life in the classroom is fragmentary, it's because when I recall those years, it's not the classes I took that come first to mind. It's the whirlwind of political events and the friends with whom I shared both politics and intellectual life that occupy center stage. The Free Speech Movement, the antiwar movement, the women's liberation movement, the Third World strike, People's Park, the bombing of Cambodia, Kent State, the rise of the counterculture—these were the defining events of my graduate school career, not just in political terms but in the intellectual discourse as well. For the two are not as easily separable as most academics would have us believe. It was my involvement and participation in each of these events that forced me to rethink old thoughts and to think new ones, to test the classroom's theories, to see what they looked like when they bumped up against events that were rapidly changing the face of the social world.

The most personal of these experiences, a three-week stint in jail, was shared with my nineteen-year-old daughter, a Berkeley undergraduate at the time. It was the fall of 1967. A student demonstration was planned at the Oakland Induction Center during the Christmas break. It was time, it seemed to me, for respectable, middle-class adults to join the fray. At about 5 A.M. on December 16, 1967, my daughter and I, along with sixty-eight other women and about one hundred men, sat down in front of the buses that were carrying the young men who had been drafted to the induction center. As the buses approached each line of protesters, the police swept us away into wagons that carried us off to the Oakland city jail.

No matter how long I live, I shall never forget the moment I was locked into a cell. The finality of the barred door clanging shut, the welling up of panic, the menacing look on my cellmate's face, her disgust as she spat out the words, "One of those goddamn commie protesters, huh? Jesus, what did I do to deserve you in here?"

We pleaded no contest in court the next morning, were sentenced to three weeks by one of Governor Ronald Reagan's first judicial appointees, and transported to the county jail at Santa Rita. Compared with most state and federal prisons, Santa Rita probably is not a very malignant institution. But as a test of Erving Goffman's theory of total institutions, it's as good as any. I found his work intriguing before going to jail. Afterward I became a real fan, partly because it helped me to take the role of sociological observer, giving form to those endless days and allowing me to distance myself from the immediate pain and anxiety of the experience.

Since Berkeley was on the quarter system then, classes had already been underway for two weeks when I returned to school in January

1968. But being in jail had been a whole new kind of learning, one that haunted me and left me wondering why I was still a student. I had already shared with Bob Blauner, whose class in race relations I was taking, some of my observations about the subtle forms of racism among the political demonstrators with whom I spent time in jail. When I told him a week or so later that I was thinking about leaving school, he responded in true academic style. "Why don't you write a paper about your jail experience, then decide what you want to do?" That paper, which was published in *Trans-Action,* was another knot that tied me to the academic world.

I had become a sociology student because I wanted a better understanding of the institutional structure of our society, in the hope of changing it. But even before I took my first class in college, my political experience had taught me one thing with certainty. One could change institutions overnight if necessary, but the minds and hearts of the people who live in them would not necessarily follow. At the same time, as feminists have learned to their sorrow, a changed consciousness may be a precondition for social change, but is no guarantor of it. So I was frustrated when, at the end of my training, I had learned a great deal about social structure, about institutions and organizations, about roles and norms. But I knew little more than I had known when I started college about the women and men who peopled the organizations and occupied the roles, which meant also that I still didn't understand the process by which social change could occur.

As I cast around for a way to gain the understanding I sought, I decided that training in clinical psychology would be useful. So as I was finishing my dissertation, I entered a clinical training program. I never expected to practice psychology. I only wanted a deeper understanding of internal dynamic processes, which, I thought, would not only help me to a clearer understanding of the subjects of my research but would serve to fine-tune my interviewing skills as well. But en route to those goals, I got caught up in unexpected ways, and before long I was seriously training for clinical work.

As I look back now, I think the decision to become a psychotherapist as well as a sociologist was the single most important one of my entire career. I was awarded my Ph.D. in 1971, when I was forty-seven years old. Even at a much younger age, I would have made an unruly assistant professor; by that advanced age, it would have been impossible for me to fill that role gracefully. I have always been too much a rebel to have bent easily to the authority of the discipline and the treadmill of a tenure-track job. The need to publish in the right journals, to cultivate the right people, to study the right things in the right way, would surely have pushed every contrary button in my psyche. In becoming a licensed clinician, I was freed to stay out of the university system and still find satisfying professional work and economic independence. Moreover, the practice of psychotherapy being what it is, I was able to limit the number of hours I gave to it each week so that I had time for research and writing, which by then had become the core of my professional identity.

No recounting of my graduate student years is complete without a long, low bow to the women's movement, which emerged as a force on the Berkeley campus around 1968. Yet in some ways this is the most difficult of all for me to write about, perhaps because of the enormous impact it has had on all aspects of life. What can I say in a few sentences about a movement that shattered the paradigms that until then had dominated our personal, social, and intellectual worlds? How can I enumerate briefly the ways in which the movement transformed women's relationships to each other, to themselves and, not least, to the way they understood and gave meaning to their own experience? I said earlier, for example, that as a child it was my poverty not my gender that felt oppressive and defined me as outsider—feelings I carried with me into adulthood. The movement taught me how much gender, not poverty, actually determined the direction of my life.

The bonds I forged in the early years of feminist activity were the beginnings of lifelong relations of colleagueship and friendship, without which my intellectual life would have been infinitely more difficult and my personal life immeasurably impoverished. And the new feminist scholarship, which has stirred such ferment, has not only directed much of my work but continues to be among the most exciting intellectual developments of our time.

Finally, I have no doubt that whatever successes I've had would not have been possible without the women's movement. It's another example of the incredible power of collective action. The women who came before us were no less thoughtful, no less wise, no less capable than we who came later. Yet even those few who had the requisite credentials were largely ignored because each spoke alone, as an isolated individual. It wasn't until we found our collective voice that we were able to open the door, not just to the academy, but to a worldwide publishing market. It was my good fortune to come of age professionally at the very moment when it was both "in" and profitable to listen to what women had to say.

Retrospectively I could present the work I've done as if it all happened in some planned and ordered way, as if each project evolved naturally from the previous one or, at the very least, had some close relationship to it. But it wouldn't be true. Chance, luck, timing, the politics of the moment, the issues in my own life that cried out for understanding—all these played a part in the choice of a project and how it developed. The research proposal funded by the National Institute of Mental Health that started me on the road to *Worlds of Pain* (1976) was entitled "Women's Liberation: Is the Definition Class-Bound?"—not a study intended to examine life in the working-class family.

I didn't plan to shift gears; the process of research dictated that I do so. When I went into the field to interview working-class women about the women's movement, I found that what interested me so intensely was largely irrelevant to them. And it's one of the great advantages of doing ethnographic research in a symbolic interactionist framework—research that doesn't force you into any preconceived postures, that allows unanticipated data to emerge, that is, in fact a true learning experience—that I could allow myself to follow where my respondents would lead. In this case, they took me into the lives of their working-class families and taught me about their hopes and dreams, their pleasures and pains, their successes and failures.

In emphasizing chance, I don't mean to dismiss the various elements I brought to the project. The fact that I accompanied my respondents so eagerly undoubtedly was related to my own working-class background, to my wish to understand that past better once I had gained some distance from it, to the Marxist understandings about class and to the feminist sensitivity to the issues of gender that I brought with me to the research field.

Women of a Certain Age (1979) was a natural. By the mid-1970s, the feminist movement was in full flower, but it was still devoted largely to the concerns of the young—to women who were at the beginning of adult life, not to those in the middle of it. Having spent my early adult years in the traditional housewife-mother role, I felt a particular empathy with the midlife women who were watching their children leave home and wondering what they would do with the rest of their lives. A study of how midlife women were faring in the face of changing gender rules seemed like a perfect project to me. In telling the story of my generation of women, I hoped to work through some of my survivor guilt, to figure out why my own life was so different from theirs, and most important of all, to give something back to those I'd left behind.

Like *Worlds of Pain*, *Intimate Strangers* (1983) came to life through the back door. I had received an NIMH grant to study friendship and its connection to family life. But once again, I wasn't in the field very long before it became obvious that although friendship was my primary concern, it was a secondary one for most of the people I was interviewing. It was their love relationships that preoccupied and troubled them, the difficulty of finding a way to live together that they wanted to talk about. So I began to include their concerns in the interviews. It wasn't long before friendship became the subordinate theme, the problems of men and women living together in intimate relations the dominant one.

But I hadn't given up my interest in friendship. It seemed to me then, as it does now, that our well-developed ideology about marriage and family, our insistence that these are the relationships that count for the long haul, have blinded us to the meaning and importance of friendships in our lives. Indeed, my experience in the field, the fact that most people—even those with rich friendship networks—were more interested in talking about their love relationships than their friendships reinforced my conviction that friendship is the neglected relationship of our time. Once I finished writing about marriage, therefore, I turned eagerly to the analysis of the data on friendship. Finally, then, *Just Friends* (1985) saw the light of day.

Quiet Rage (1986) was born out of conversations with a friend. I hadn't done anything in the field of race since my dissertation, which was published under the title *Busing & Backlash* (1972). But despite a series of books about women, men, and interpersonal relationships, race and class remained the issues closest to my heart. So I was startled and angered when Bernhard Goetz, a white man who shot four black youths on a New York City subway, evoked a sympathetic response from some of my liberal friends and colleagues in Berkeley. I shared my observations with an old friend in the publishing world who happened to be visiting a few days after the shootings. A week or so after he went back to New York, he telephoned to say he'd been thinking about our conversations and asked me to write a book about the case.

I was fascinated by the idea, but thought it an impossible one. I lived on the West Coast; this was a quintessential New York story. It should be told by someone who lived there, I thought, someone who understood the city and its problems in ways that I could not. He argued that it was my very distance from the scene that made it my book, that would give it the objectivity it needed. A few days and many long telephone conversations later, he convinced me to give it a try.

For the next year, I spent three days a week in the Bay Area fulfilling my clinical obligations, then flew to New York to do the research for the book. Once in a while I skipped a week; every now and then, I canceled my patients' appointments and had the luxury of ten straight days for research in the East. It sounds like a hard year, I know. But I remember only the excitement and exhilaration of the project and the pleasure in writing the book.

Finally, there is *Erotic Wars* (1990), my most recently published work. During the last half of the eighties, the media were filled with stories about how Americans were returning to the sexual conservatism of the past—stories that didn't match my clinical or research experience. Instead, they seemed to me to be part of the feminist backlash, a gleeful telling of tales about the cost to women of their sexual freedom. But I couldn't be sure. The AIDS crisis had sparked a great deal of debate and discussion about sexual behavior. Some feminists were, indeed, counting the cost of the sexual revolution. Everywhere people were talking about our changing sexual norms, but no one knew much about what heterosexual people were doing, let alone what they were thinking and feeling. It was time, I decided to take to the field once again, this time to find out what happened to the sexual revolution. Fortunately, my publisher agreed.

One major unifying theme in my work has been the effort to build a bridge between sociology and psychology. Each has much to teach us; standing alone, neither is complete. Therefore, my whole professional life has been engaged in the attempt to bring together the social and psychological in both my intellectual and clinical work. Sociology, the discipline that remains closest to my intellectual side, provides the broad vision, a way of seeing the world that's indispensable to understanding it. But people get lost in the process. What they think or feel, how they respond to the social forces that seek to mold them, how they interpret their behavior and attitudes—in essence, what subjective meanings they give to their own experiences and how those affect their relationships to both self and society—these are of small concern to sociology.

My adopted discipline, clinical psychology, is equally myopic, but in the opposite direction—so concerned with the particular and the individual that it loses sight of the social context within which human life takes place. It fails, therefore, to comprehend the ways in which society and personality live in a continuing reciprocal relationship with each other.

Neither discipline has been a comfortable resting place for me, since both have little tolerance for the kind of synthesis that has concerned me through the years. Nor am I a comfort to them. About my earlier

work, psychologists have complained that I've given too much attention to the social forces that frame people's lives and not enough to the internal dynamic ones that may lock people in. But I'm not, after all, one of their own, so what I do and how I do it doesn't make a great deal of difference to them.

Among the sociologists, the complaints go the other way. My earlier work is the more acceptable; in the later period, they say, I've given too much power to the psychological explanations, not enough to the sociological ones. There, however, where I'm counted as one of them, the reaction is different—more akin to the feelings in a family when a child strays from the accepted path. There's a kind of bewilderment, a wondering how I got that way, hoping I can be made to see the light, and finally, when it becomes clear that isn't going to happen, the sort of grudging acceptance families give to a deviant member.

In truth, neither set of complaints is wholly off the mark. Human life is so extraordinarily complex that any analysis must take some issues as matters of central concern and leave others on the periphery. Therefore, when the task was to understand the issues of race or class, as it has been in some of my work, the analysis fell more heavily on the sociological side; when the drama of interpersonal relations was the issue to be explained, the work leaned much more toward the psychological. For while I may have found some success in integrating these two modes of thought, balancing them—that is, giving each, with all its complexity, equal time—is another matter.

An autobiographical essay is of necessity a selective rendering of a life. Among other things, this one leaves out the role my family and friends have played—how we have lived and loved together, how we have angered each other and made peace, how we have molded each other and found ways to resist as well, and most of all, how they affected the work I have done. It leaves out a husband who has been unswervingly supportive at every step of the way and the reality that, without such acceptance, a woman who wants both marriage and career may have to choose between them. It leaves out the good fortune of having a healthy, intelligent, independent child who could make her way without her mother's constant ministrations. And finally, it leaves out the cost of upward mobility—the discontinuities that sunder my life, that rend me in two and leave past and present with nowhere to meet.

People ask me often whether the path I've chosen has been a lonely one. It's not an easy question to answer. My early life so accustomed me to loneliness and marginality, marked me so deeply as an outsider, that I doubt I'd feel very comfortable being on the inside anywhere. That, however, doesn't wholly erase the pain or loneliness; it simply makes it more tolerable. But marginality has its advantages, too. Being an outsider means there's little to lose by not playing by the rules of the insider. No tenure or promotion anxieties dictated what subjects I would study; no irrelevant methodological rules obstructed my work; no narrow disciplinary strictures circumscribed the analysis. I was free to do the work I wanted to do in the way I wanted to do it—work that has brought me psychological, social, and economic rewards well beyond even my wildest childhood fantasies.

I'm frequently asked also if I regret not having started sooner. My answer is an unequivocal no. I was a product of my time and place. As a woman who became a mother in 1948, I found that restlessness with the narrowness of my role was a constant theme. When it got too hard, I went to work at some small job, then struggled with guilt because I wasn't at home where I thought I belonged. Eventually guilt won out, and the cycle started over again. Those surely weren't the best of times. But when I look at the struggle of working women with children today—the enormous pressures with which they live, the desperation for time with the family, the difficulty of what Arlie Hochschild has called "the second shift"—these times don't seem very much better. Different, yes, but with their own problems for women who want to be mothers and wives, and also live in the adult world of work.

And there's something else as well. At sixty-seven, I have been a professional person for a scant twenty years. While my male age peers feel that they're at the end of their creative careers, having been at it for perhaps forty years, my internal experience is that I am now where they must have been twenty years ago—somewhere in midstream. At sixty-seven, that's a marvelous place to be.

Lillian B. Rubin

Chapter 18

Epilogue

KATHRYN P. MEADOW ORLANS
and RUTH A. WALLACE

The proportion of women graduate students, Ph.D. recipients, and faculty has increased markedly in most disciplines in the past twenty years. The trend is striking in all social sciences, particularly sociology, where a revolution has occurred. Women's increased participation is rooted in socioeconomic changes, government funding for higher education, affirmative action, legislation—and in the contemporary women's movement.

While the changes have influenced their career opportunities, women continue to receive much of their education from male professors and to teach or do research in male-dominated institutions. They still have primary responsibility for their children, and most do home chores as a second shift.[1] We read about a backlash against women as well as minorities; the glass ceiling has been scratched but not broken.

Academic jobs, promotions, and tenure appointments for women have not kept pace with the increased number receiving Ph.D.s. In 1974, women comprised 16 percent of full-time social science faculty. By 1985, the proportion had increased only to 21 percent.[2] In 1987, three-quarters of female members of the American Sociological Association held academic positions, compared with 81 percent of male members, but only 79 percent of women were employed full-time, compared with 91 percent of men.[3] Thus, women remain disproportionately "outside the sacred groves"[4] and in "the outer circle"[5] of academia. Nevertheless, at Berkeley from 1969 to 1974, three of nine regular sociology appointments went to women, bringing the proportion of women faculty to 11 percent of the twenty-eight member department.[6] By 1991, seven of twenty-nine active teaching faculty members (24 percent) were women;[7] of the five tenured, three were full professors.

In some respects, the Berkeley climate today differs from that twenty years ago; in some, it is relatively unchanged.[8] Women graduate students say, "Men almost totally dominate class discussions" and, "Men certainly get more air time." Professors voice different, not necessarily opposing, views. One agreed that "the big blustering male will yak on about his opinions even though he hasn't done the reading, and the quiet woman student won't say a word, even though she's read everything twice." Another felt that "the women who are coming now are more assertive, more self-confident, more fully participants in the program than twenty years ago."

These professors spoke of the high caliber of recent women students: "seriousness of purpose and commitment"; "earnest, low-key, modest . . . even self-effacing"; "a whole cluster of outstanding women." A striking change has occurred. During 1952–72, a third of entering graduate students in sociology at Berkeley were women; in the fall of 1991, 70 percent (16 of 23). Formerly, minority students were rare; in 1991, 11 of 23 new grad students at Berkeley were minorities: two black, four Hispanic, five Asian.[9]

With the women's movement came increased interest in the sociology of gender. Courses and research on gender and feminist theory proliferated. Gender, a professor said, is "one of the hottest topics in sociology," and Berkeley has a reputation as "the place to be." "Virtually every woman registered in the last three or four years has gender or feminist studies as their prime focus." A student remarked that most women specialize in gender; many men, in theory. The trend creates problems for both faculty and students. Professors who teach gender are overburdened; those in other areas lack students.

Women students sympathize with female professors who balance career and family responsibilities. They would like to postpone children until they finish graduate school, but fear that further postponement may then be necessary when they strive for tenure. They hope, but seldom expect, academic jobs to become more flexible and humane.

Our work on this book has sharpened our view of the forces fostering change for women. We gained a new understanding of friends and colleagues who revealed previously unknown struggles, illustrating the interplay of personal and political events.

As C. Wright Mills would say, some of those personal struggles have now become public issues, like the provision of child care, which has become a major policy concern. While the two-career family is more common and attitudes toward working or student mothers are less negative, many issues of gender equity are still unresolved. The barriers overcome by women pioneers of the fifties and sixties are different from those facing women today, but the central task remains: resolution of the tension between individual and societal needs. Perhaps the experiences chronicled in this book can give younger women a new and different perspective on their own struggles.

Notes

1. Arlie Hochschild with Anne Machung, *The Second Shift: Working Parents and the Revolution at Home* (New York: Viking, 1989).

2. Mariam K. Chamberlain, ed., *Women in Academe: Progress and Prospects* (New York: Russell Sage Foundation, 1988), pp. 228–29.

3. Bettina J. Huber, *The Status of Minorities and Women within* ASA: *Second Biennial Update,* mimeographed (Washington, D.C.: American Sociological Association, 1987), p. 3a.

4. Nadya Aisenberg, and Mona Harrington, *Women of Academe: Outsiders in the Sacred Grove* (Amherst: University of Massachusetts Press, 1988).

5. Harriet Zuckerman, Jonathan R. Cole, and John T. Bruer, eds., *The Outer Circle: Women in the Scientific Community* (New York: Norton, 1991).

6. In the summer of 1975, search committees were appointed to fill three positions; 285 applications were received, one-fourth from women. Two men and one woman were hired; a second woman received a joint appointment in sociology and political science. See Neil J. Smelser, and Robin Content, *The Changing Academic Market, General Trends and a Berkeley Case Study* (Berkeley: University of California Press, 1980), pp. 69, 100, 149.

7. They were Victoria Bonnell, Nancy J. Chodorow, Laura Enriquez, Arlie Hochschild, Kristin Luker, Ann Swidler, and Kim Voss.

8. In September 1991, Orlans interviewed three women graduate students in sociology at Berkeley, assuring them of anonymity. The following December, Wallace spoke with four of the Berkeley sociology department's former chairs. We are grateful to students and faculty members for their frank and perceptive comments, and to Neil Smelser and Elsa Tranter for facilitating the interviews.

9. Six of these minority admissions (or a quarter of the total number) were women.

Kathryn P. Meadow Orlans and Ruth A. Wallace

The Contributors

Sherri Cavan, professor of sociology at San Francisco State University, received B.A. and M.A. degrees from the University of California, Los Angeles, and a Berkeley Ph.D. in 1965. Major publications are *Liquor License: An Ethnography of Bar Behavior* (1966); *Hippies of the Haight* (1972); and *20th Century Gothic: America's Nixon* (1979). Her primary teaching area is deviance and conformity. Forever restoring her Victorian home in San Francisco's Haight Ashbury district, she is also a talented figurative sculptor.

Arlene Kaplan Daniels is director of the Women's Studies Program and professor of sociology at Northwestern University. A founder of Sociologists for Women in Society, she has served as secretary and council member for the American Sociological Association, president of the Society for the Study of Social Problems, and editor of the journal *Social Problems*. Her 1960 Berkeley Ph.D. was the fourth awarded to a woman. Among books she has written or coedited are *Women and Trade Unions in Eleven Industrialized Countries* (1984); *Invisible Careers: Women Civic Leaders in the Volunteer World* (1988); *Women and Work* (1982); and *Hearth and Home: Images of Women in the Mass Media* (1978).

Ruth Dixon-Mueller moved from assistant to full professor (and chair) of sociology at the University of California, Davis, after receiving a Berkeley Ph.D. in 1970. She resigned that position in 1988 to devote full time to consulting and writing. Her research on women in economic development, fertility, and family planning resulted in many publications, including *Rural Women at Work: Strategies for Development in South Asia* (1978). A former member of the Committee on Population, National Research Council (National Academy of Sciences), she has consulted for the United Nations, Ford Foundation, and International Women's Health Coalition. She now lives in Costa Rica.

Dorris W. Goodrich was one of the first group of sociology graduate students at Berkeley and the first woman among them to receive a Ph.D. (1952). The original four-member faculty included her mentor, Robert Nisbet. She taught in the department for two years, resigning to devote full time to her husband and four children. Currently she is combining sociological and Jungian perspectives to explore the polarization of attitudes about women.

Shirley Foster Hartley is professor and former chair of sociology at California State University, Hayward. A demographer, she worked under Kingsley Davis at Berkeley, receiving a Ph.D. in 1969. Her books include *Population: Quantity vs. Quality* (1972); *Illegitimacy* (1975); and *Comparing Populations* (1982). A manuscript on friendship nears completion. She was elected to the board of the Population Association of America, served on the Population Research Study Section of the National Institutes of Health and as associate editor of *Contemporary Sociology*. Her volunteer service benefited retarded children, foreign students, and migrant farm workers.

Arlie Russell Hochschild is founder of a subfield, the sociology of emotions. A Swarthmore graduate, she received her 1969 Ph.D. from UC Berkeley, where she is now professor of sociology. Her books are *The Unexpected Community* (1973); *The Managed Heart: The Commercialization of Human Feeling* (1983) (Charles Cooley Award), translated into German and Chinese; and *The Second Shift: Working Parents and the Revolution at Home* (1989), translated into German, Dutch, and Japanese. She received a UC Berkeley Outstanding Teacher Award, and fellowships from the Guggenheim Foundation, the Ford Foundation, the National Institute of Mental Health, and an honorary degree from Swarthmore College.

Mary Haywood Metz is professor and chair, Department of Educational Policy Studies, University of Wisconsin, Madison. She received the A.B. degree from Radcliffe College (magna cum laude), and a Berkeley Ph.D. (1971). She held Woodrow Wilson, Kent (Danforth Foundation), and German Academic Exchange Fellowships, and filled faculty positions at Earlham College, Marquette University, and Mount Mary College while following her sociologist husband's career and caring for their two children. Her books are *Classrooms and Corridors: The Crisis of Authority in Desegregated Schools* (1978) and *Different by Design: The Context and Character of Three Magnet Schools* (1986).

Kathryn P. Meadow Orlans is senior research scientist and professor, Department of Educational Foundations and Research, at Gallaudet University (the only liberal arts college for deaf people) in Washington, D.C. After completing her Berkeley Ph.D. (1967), she helped pioneer a program of research and mental health services for deaf people in the Department of Psychiatry, University of California, San Francisco. She wrote *Deafness and Child Development* (1980), coauthored *Sound and Sign: Childhood Deafness and Mental Health* (1972), coedited *Educational and Developmental Aspects of Deafness* (1990), and is credited with furthering the use of sign language with deaf children. Denison University conferred an honorary degree in 1986.

Harriet B. Presser is director of the Center on Population, Gender and Social Inequality and professor of sociology at the University of Maryland, College Park. Her research has broken new ground, beginning with her dissertation on female sterilization in Puerto Rico (1969), followed by studies of the determinants and consequences of the timing of motherhood, child care constraints for women, and the diversity of work schedules among parents. Elected president of the Population Association of America for 1989, she also served on the American Sociological Association Council and was twice a fellow at the Center for Advanced Study in the Behavioral Sciences.

Lillian B. Rubin is a research sociologist at the Institute for the Study of Social Change, University of California, Berkeley. Until resigning in 1993, she spent half her time at Queens College, where she was Alumni Professor of Interpretive Sociology. In 1967, she received a Berkeley B.A. (magna cum laude) at age forty-three, and a Ph.D. four years later. A licensed psychotherapist and prolific writer, her books include *Worlds of Pain: Life in the Working-Class Family* (1976); *Women of a Certain Age: The Midlife Search for Self* (1979); *Intimate Strangers: Men and Women Together* (1983); *Just Friends: The Role of Friendship in Our Lives* (1985); and *Erotic Wars: What Happened to the Sexual Revolution* (1990).

Dorothy E. Smith is professor of sociology in education at the Ontario Institute for Studies in Education (Toronto). Previous faculty appointments were at the University of British Columbia, the University of

Essex (England), and the University of California, Berkeley (Ph.D. in 1963). She received the John Porter Award for *The Everyday World as Problematic: A Feminist Sociology* (1987). Other books are *Texts, Facts, and Femininity: Exploring the Relations of Ruling* (1990) and *The Conceptual Practices of Power: A Feminist Sociology of Knowledge* (1990). In 1992, her contributions to feminist theory were recognized by the American Sociological Association's theory section.

Metta Spencer (Berkeley Ph.D., 1969) was associate chair of the department of sociology at the Erindale Campus of the University of Toronto during 1989–91. She was founding president and director of the Canadian Disarmament Information Service; director and secretary of Corporate Nuclear Concern, Inc.; secretary of Canadian Pugwash 1988–90; and has been editor in chief of *Peace Magazine* since 1985. Her text, *Foundations of Modern Sociology* (1976), is widely used, with four editions in the United States and four in Canada. She is general editor for volume 13 of *Research in Social Movements, Conflict, and Change* (in press).

Mely G. Tan returned to her home in Jakarta after receiving the M.A. from Cornell (1961) and a Berkeley Ph.D. (1968). Currently, she is senior researcher in the Center for Social and Cultural Studies, Indonesian Institute of Sciences. She served on the steering committee of the Task Force for Social Science Research on Reproductive Health of the World Health Organization in Geneva from 1977 to 1981, and was reappointed in 1990. She has conducted research on the ethnic Chinese in Indonesia, on social change, and on women's health issues. An edited book, *Indonesian Women, The Future Leaders?* (in Indonesian) appeared in 1991.

Ruth A. Wallace is professor of sociology at George Washington University, where she has taught since 1970, after two years at Immaculate Heart College. Her latest book, *They Call Her Pastor: A New Role for Catholic Women* (1992), continues the research on religion that began with her Berkeley dissertation under Neil Smelser. She will serve as president of the Society for the Scientific Study of Religion in 1994. Other co-authored or edited books are *Contemporary Sociological Theory* (1980); *Gender in America: Social Control and Social Change* (1985); *American Catholic Laity in a Changing Church* (1989); and *Feminism and Sociological Theory* (1989).

Audrey Wipper, born and educated in Canada (B.A. and M.A., McGill University), returned to teach at the University of Waterloo, where she is now professor of sociology. Research in Kenya for her dissertation (Ph.D., 1969, UC Berkeley) launched a pioneering career in studies of African women and development. In 1972, she edited a pathbreaking issue of the *Canadian Journal of African Studies: The Roles of African Women: Past, Present and Future.* Other publications include *Rural Rebels: A Study of Two Protest Movements in Kenya* (1974) and *The Sociology of Work* (1984). Currently she is shifting her research focus to a long-time interest, an ethnographic study of the community of people involved with horses, particularly jumpers.

Jacqueline P. Wiseman, professor of sociology at the University of California, San Diego, has been visiting professor at Yale, Dartmouth, and Helsinki University. Publications include *Stations of the Lost: The Treatment of Skid Row Alcoholics* (1970; C. Wright Mills Award) and *The Other Half: The Social Psychological Situation of Wives of Alcoholics* (1991). She received the George Herbert Mead Award for a scholarly career from the Society for the Study of Symbolic Interaction. Professional service includes president, Society for the Study of Social Problems; council member, American Sociological Association; and Alcohol Policy Panel, National Academy of Sciences. Interpersonal relationships and interior design are current sociological interests.

Index

Index

266